BLOODHOUSE

DARCY DUGAN
with **MICHAEL TATLOW**

HarperCollins*Publishers*

HarperCollinsPublishers

First published in Australia in 2012
by HarperCollins*Publishers* Australia Pty Limited
ABN 36 009 913 517
harpercollins.com.au

Copyright © Michael Tatlow 2012

The right of Michael Tatlow to be identified as the author
of this work has been asserted by him in accordance
with the *Copyright Amendment (Moral Rights) Act 2000*.

This work is copyright. Apart from any use as permitted under the
Copyright Act 1968, no part may be reproduced, copied, scanned,
stored in a retrieval system, recorded, or transmitted, in any form
or by any means, without the prior written permission of the publisher.

HarperCollins*Publishers*
Level 3, 201 Elizabeth Street, Sydney NSW 2000, Australia
31 View Road, Glenfield, Auckland 0627, New Zealand
A 53, Sector 57, Noida, UP, India
77–85 Fulham Palace Road, London W6 8JB, United Kingdom
2 Bloor Street East, 20th floor, Toronto, Ontario M4W 1A8, Canada
10 East 53rd Street, New York NY 10022, USA

Dugan, Darcy, 1920–1991.
  Bloodhouse / Darcy Dugan with Michael Tatlow.
  ISBN: 978 0 7322 9552 3 (pbk.)
  Dugan, Darcy, 1920-1991.
  Criminals – New South Wales – Biography.
  Prisons – New South Wales.
  Escapes – New South Wales.
  Other Authors/Contributors:
  Tatlow, Michael.
364.37309944

Cover design by Darren Holt, HarperCollins Design Studio
Cover images courtesy State Library of New South Wales
Typeset in 12/16pt Minion Pro by Kirby Jones

'Mike, a lot, sometimes rot, has been written about me. If you stay around, please hold this, my *real* story, to edit and present to a new generation, with your own chapters, after I and the crooks we've exposed have turned to dust.'

Darcy Dugan

ACKNOWLEDGMENTS

Many astonishing events related in this book were revealed to me by the brilliant Noel F. Bracks, of Sydney, who was Darcy's brave solicitor in the 1960s and '70s. Noel thereafter investigated the corrupt events that sent his client back to jail. I am indebted to Noel for his frank revelations. This is a better read thanks to HarperCollins's freelance editor Vanessa Mickan. I also thank my excellent literary agent, Keelane Lake, of Freestyle, Launceston. And I appreciate help given by Sydney *Daily Telegraph* history editor Troy Lennon and News Limited librarian Peter Gatehouse.

Michael Tatlow

AUTHORS' NOTES

For decades after the British took possession of Australia in 1788, the land at the southern end of the earth was little more than a dump for criminals and hungry and poor men, women and children from Britain and conquered Ireland, Canada and New Zealand. Also deported were political malcontents, plus 92 heroes of the American Patriot Army.

This book shows that the brutal penal system of colonial Australia was not dead when I was incarcerated. Of course, many of my jail keepers were fine and fair-minded. Others were no better, probably worse, than their sadistic forebears.

Men and women who break the law should, of course, be punished. But not systematically tortured. My guts churn at memories of Grafton jail — that hell on earth.

You can judge me here for yourself. If you know a young Alec who reckons it's smart to flaunt the good laws of society, you can scare the hell out of him or her by recounting what happened to this Alec.

Darcy Dugan

In his late 40s, when he wrote this book with my help, safe-cracker, robber and cat burglar Darcy Dugan had spent most of his life in reformatories and jails. He spent 11 harrowing years — longer than any other prisoner — in Grafton jail, the Bloodhouse, Australia's most horrid institution.

Darcy very nearly pulled off at Grafton what would have been the bloodiest mass break-out in Australia's penal history. He escaped from custody six times and narrowly missed breaking out five times. For daring and brilliance in execution, his jailbreaks are unparalleled. On his way to a court appearance, under heavy guard, he managed to saw a hole through the top of a moving prison tram (which is now a star attraction at the Sydney Tramway Museum at Loftus) and escaped onto the streets of Sydney. He once spent only 25 minutes in Sydney's Long Bay jail before bursting through a ceiling and a roof and leaping over the wall, in daylight, only 30 yards from an armed guard.

He deserved most of his jail sentences. Not, though, the months of black and solitary confinement and flogging that, day by day, turned him and other prisoners into blood-lusting animals.

Yet this tale is told with surprising humour, insight, objectivity and eloquence — plus a burning passion to curb corruption in the police force and politics. After relating his life story to me, Darcy was set up by the Mr Big of Australian crime and the police and was imprisoned again to stop his public — and accurate — accusations of corruption by police and politicians.

Fearing what Mr Big and the police on his payroll would do if revelations in this book became public, the Houdini of crime urged me to suppress it until he and his enemies were dead. One threatening former policeman still lives, but rather than wait for his demise, his name has been deleted.

Michael Tatlow

PROLOGUE

'I sentence you, Darcy Ezekiel Dugan, and you, William Cecil Mears, to be taken to the place from which you have come and, at a date to be set, to be hanged by the neck until you are dead.'

The sonorous words from Mr Justice Herron two days earlier in the hushed Supreme Court, in Sydney, pounded in my mind. *You bastard, Herron. You judicial bastard. And you, you screws and cops here. Gloating over us! You'll get pissed celebrating this tonight.*

From the Catholic convent a mile away, the sombre ringing of a solitary bell wafted over the grey walls of the state penitentiary at Long Bay, an awful hour's trip from inner Sydney. I was in the jail's Observation Section, the maximum-security wing — Sydney's death row.

Is it me for whom that bell tolls? Nah, it's calling them to evening Mass.

The cell's naked globe in the ceiling glared down on me. Would they ever turn that damn light off?

'Darcy. Hey, Darcy!' It was Billy Mears again, calling from his cell three doors along the row.

God, is this happening to me? That long, grey beam was waiting in the next building. They hanged men from that beam. I had seen it a hundred times in the past few years. Now I was waiting for its rope to wrench my head from my shoulders when the trap door snapped open.

Waiting. All of us who were condemned; those callous screws outside the cell; the priest; the police; Dick, my pop; my mother and brother, Tom. The hangman.

I pondered on the condition of Leslie Nalder. The bank manager was fighting for his life in some hospital bed, a .38 slug from Mears's Webley revolver embedded beside his heart. It was his legacy from our abortive bank hold-up.

And June was waiting — maybe fretting about me. What was she doing now?

'Darcy! You awake, Darcy?'

Mears. He was advertising his terror before those screws, his hoarse, high-pitched voice pleading.

I put my feet on the housing to the left of the steel-plated door and levered myself up so my head was against the thick ventilation grille leading to the corridor.

'Of course I'm awake. What do you want this time?'

'Ah, how are you?' He sounded relieved. The poor wretch just wanted someone to talk to.

'I'm all right.'

He asked, 'Have you heard anything?'

'No, of course not. I don't know any more than you.'

'Do you think we'll die?'

I did not reply. If Nalder died, the chance of a reprieve was a lot slimmer. I didn't want to think about it.

'Hey, Darcy. Are you there?'

Heck, where else would I be? 'Look, mate, how the hell do I know? If he dies, these bastards here will tell us soon enough.'

The two screws sniggered. 'Hah. The pair of yous are gunna swing, anyway,' said one of them, a big and balding brute. 'You're all over the front of the papers. And we've got ya this time. You 'specially, fucken Dugan.

'People are betting on whether you hang. And *my* dough's on them gallows. I'll sure be in there to see you take the drop.'

My neck jerked as I leapt from the housing. I could not see my harasser through the slits of thick glass embedded in the door.

'You bastards!' I yelled.

They sniggered again.

The other screw shouted, 'You shuddup, Dugan, or we'll go in there and kick your bloody face in.' His boots would be itching for action.

I paced the cell — twelve feet by seven. The church bell donged on. *Control that ego, boy.*

Billy had taken fright during the bank hold-up and had shot the scared bank manager. But the laws of this land said that, even though I didn't shoot, as his accomplice I was equally guilty of attempted murder. Which might soon become murder.

'Hey, Darcy!' Billy was back at his grille. 'What if the Liberals get in?'

I empathised with his panic but did not want to hear his voice again that night. I jumped back on the housing. 'Then we'll bloody well hang!'

A screw kicked the door. 'One more noise from you and we'll be in there, swinging, Dugan.'

I lay on the coir mat that was my bed. The New South Wales general election the previous day — Saturday, 17 June 1950 — would determine who governed the state for the next three years.

The Australian Labor Party had governed for the last term. And ALP policy was to commute death sentences to life imprisonment. The screws had cheerfully told me, however, that early vote counting showed a big swing to the Liberal Party, which carried out executions.

If the Liberals governed, we would surely swing, regardless of whether Nalder died.

If not hanged, I would go up the coast to the Grafton jail, Australia's hell. The Bloodhouse. Many considered it the most brutal penal establishment in the civilised world. Strong words? Later, you will find out why it had that reputation.

The Bloodhouse, that thick grey beam — everything, everyone was waiting.

Really, I was secretly positive that night of one thing: they would not hang me. If it developed that we were to hang, I would make my most desperate escape bid of all. It would make my other escapes look like strolls in the park.

The chances of me making a successful break were 100/1. But there was a chance. For my plan to come off, I would probably have to flatten at least four screws. I would not kill them, though. I had never killed anyone and loathed the thought of doing that to get out of this place, even though *they* wanted to kill *me*. I knew the jail and its routine well. And the flaws in its security. If I was going to hang in any case, what was there to lose?

The cold from the winter night crept up through the coir mat into my bones. God, were these my last days? I dearly hoped, in any case, that Leslie Nalder would survive. And the ALP would win the election.

1

Leaching envy, I watched the boy on his bike. It was just after Christmas, 1929, in the Sydney slum suburb of Newtown, where I was born on 29 August 1920.

The nation's economic depression had gripped us. There had been no cash at home for my parents to buy Christmas presents for me or my brother, Tom, three years my junior. I sat propped against a fence, watching the kid ride his Christmas bike up and down the lane. He was a couple of years older than me but I knew him pretty well.

'How about a ride?' I called. 'Just for a while.'

I wanted nothing more in this world than a bike like that. Mum and Pop had explained that they couldn't afford to buy me a bike. But just riding that gleaming new machine would erase my childish depression.

The bike rider flatly refused my request. I went home in tears. His refusal, however, must have stirred up a determination deep in my gut. Somehow, I was going to ride that bike.

A few days later, I spotted the machine propped against the kid's back fence. With no hesitation, I shot a short leg under the crossbar and rode off, grinning with delight. I felt no guilt. No fear. I had an hour of childish paradise.

When I returned on the bike, two uniformed police constables were there. The kid's father had reported it stolen.

The towering constables were gentle in their reprimands, apparently appreciating my motive. They took me home and told my pop, Richard, what I had done. It was my first brush with the law. It terrified me.

Pop flayed my bare buttocks with his belt. But I did not cry out. Screaming demonstrated submission. Somehow, etched on my mind was a determination never to show weakness. Never to submit.

The sight of me standing there immobile, just taking it, frustrated Pop terribly. But it was probably tough Pop who made me that way.

He, I must admit, had his faults. The product of Irish ancestors, he did not drink much, but he gambled. With him it was a disease. Many times he would slip away from home on the evening of Friday, pay day. He did not return until early Monday morning, just in time to change to go to work as an ornamental tiler.

By then nearly all his pay usually had gone on horse racing and cards. Later, although I did not understand it at the time, a great deal of his cash was frittered away on other women.

These things caused regular and bitter arguments between Pop and my mother, Nonie, a beautiful and kindly person plagued by illnesses. She was proud of her tiny feet and long, auburn hair. My earliest childhood memories are of Pop and Mum arguing. It was not a happy home, although our parents loved Tom and me.

There was the general conviction in our family that we were entitled to more of the material goodies of this world.

Most people in our district were poor. But I often wandered around other Sydney districts that oozed wealth. Some day, I privately vowed, some day I, too, would have wealth. Still, I suppose most poor kids have that sort of daydream.

Perhaps my Irish-Catholic heritage implanted my fiery temper, a spirit of rebellion against authority in general. Implanted, too, was flamboyance and a more-than-average thirst for the things in life only money could provide. Starting from the back of the pack, I would have to fight for money.

And, my warped mind figured, respect. In my part of Sydney, we revered a person with money, regardless of how he got it.

'Never let anyone beat you, son,' Pop used to say. I was proud of the fact that he had been a champion in the illegal bare-knuckle fight rings.

If I came home with a bloodied face, he would ask, 'Did you beat him, Darce?' If the answer was yes, he smiled and patted my head. If I admitted defeat, he scowled.

'Well, tomorrow,' he would command, 'you show him who's boss. If he beats you again, keep at him. Wear him down. You're my son and don't you ever give in! Keep at him until you thrash him.'

Although not big for my age, I was agile and liked fighting. And winning! I would tenaciously stick at some adversary who lived nearby or went to the Christian Brothers school I attended, until I beat him. I was not a bully but I certainly had plenty of scraps, usually with older, bigger kids who were bullies to other kids of about my age.

Sometimes my Irish maternal grandfather, Patrick O'Connor, who lived with us, would quietly call me aside. 'Darcy, me lad,' he would say, smiling, 'would you like to be earning yourself a shilling, lad?'

Then the dear old gent would tell me about some kid who had been cheeky to him in the street. 'Go teach him a lesson, lad,' Grandad urged, pressing a shilling into my hand. 'Go and thump him real hard in the eye.'

The offender would be thumped, all right. Not that I always won the contest. Regardless of the outcome, my adversary and I usually would cut out the shilling on ice cream and lollies at a local store.

I must have been the despair of the Christian Brothers. At least once a week, I was made to lean over the school vaulting box, buttocks bared, to receive six cuts with a cane. The charge, nearly always, was brawling in the school grounds.

Incidentally, I was never a good Catholic. But I have always admired those dedicated teachers, especially those running schools in tough neighbourhoods. They really tried with me. It would be unfair to measure their success by my later exploits.

I was a regular truant from school but I usually topped my class in subjects that interested me: history, geography, English. I was regularly near the bottom of the class in mathematics and science. Perhaps the brothers tried so hard because they thought I had potential.

Mum and Pop often said the brothers had told them that on the rare times I tried at school, I was brilliant. What an ass I've been! My brother, Tom, grew up under the same conditions as me but he never committed a criminal act.

When I was 12, we moved to Annandale, another tough district, where, at my new school, I became pals with a kid called Jimmy. He was the envy of our classroom. Jimmy always had chocolates and lollies, new toys and plenty of marbles. His parents were not rich. How, I wanted to know, did he get these things?

'Easy,' he grinned. 'I pinch 'em. Just pick 'em up in shops.'

After school that day he took me, like a mother hen leading a chick, into a large department store on Parramatta Road, Leichhardt. I think it was Coles. Tensely, fearing being caught, I watched Jimmy adroitly slip two toy cars off a counter and into his pockets. Once he had them, I wanted to bolt from the premises.

Any moment, firm hands of authority would land on our shoulders. But, taking my cue from Jimmy, I acted casually as we strolled back out to the footpath and away.

It was ridiculously easy, I thought, as Jimmy handed me a toy car in a vacant block off Parramatta Road. My apprenticeship in shoplifting had begun.

In the following few months, Jimmy and I raided shops three or four afternoons a week. Not once did we look like being caught. I, too, was now a school hero with plenty of marbles, lollies and toys. I liked that.

The spree temporarily ended one afternoon when three of us young toughs, with dirty faces and grubby clothes, had just stuffed our pockets with marbles in Grace Bros.

Despite our impeccable record, I was ever on the alert against being collared — certainly more so than Jimmy and our new young confederate, chubby Lennie McPherson. Farther along the store, I noticed that two men were watching us closely. Store detectives! The immense two began walking towards us.

I turned to Jimmy. 'Here,' I said, 'have mine, too. I've got stacks of marbles at home. I'll empty my pockets and get something else.'

My two companions eagerly stuffed the extra loot into their pockets. They turned around, into the arms of the store detectives. A detective grabbed me by the shoulder.

'Look,' I cried, turning out my pockets. 'I'm clean! I haven't taken anything.'

My bewildered partners in crime were led to a room to get a severe lecture. It was some time before Jimmy or Len saw any humour in the episode.

The only source of conflict between Jimmy and me was a pretty, blue-eyed girl at our school named Mary. She had long, golden hair. Mary liked both of us but did not seem to favour one more than the other. Jimmy and I continually vied for her attention. Often the two of us walked Mary home after school — one on either side, each eyeing the other. We showered her with gifts — shoplifted, of course.

One day we decided that Mary should have a grown-up present. A handbag. So that night, each armed with a brick wrapped in cloth, we arrived in front of a leather goods store near where George Street becomes Broadway. We waited on the darkened footpath, under an awning, until a tram went by.

The grinding of the tram smothered the noise of shattering glass as our bricks crashed through the window. I had to kick away more glass around the holes before I could put my head and shoulders through and grab everything in reach.

Jimmy and I got off with 12 expensive handbags. Six each! We hid our booty overnight in a hole in the ground in a vacant block near Jimmy's place. Each of us would give Mary six handbags at her home before school in the morning.

Even in those days, I must have felt that all was fair in love and war. So I did a pretty awful thing. I wanted Mary all for myself, and I saw here my golden opportunity.

The sun was just showing over the rooftops the next morning as I went to our cache alone and took all the handbags. I lugged them several blocks to Mary's place and called out to her from behind the back fence. In case one of her parents came instead, I had hidden the bags in long grass nearby.

Mary arrived and I presented her with the bags. The poor girl was overwhelmed. Yes, she promised gravely, she certainly would be my, and only my, girlfriend from now on.

I was tempted to then return to the vacant block and meet Jimmy as planned, feigning shock at the hiding place being empty. But I knew Jimmy would know the truth after seeing Mary at school. I didn't care, really, what Jimmy thought. He could not squeal on me and I had won our last little fight.

Jimmy arrived at school late that morning. As the teacher reprimanded him in front of the class, he shot furious glances at me. I grinned at him — then at Mary. She smiled prettily. She was mine!

A couple of hours later, however, the headmaster summoned me to his office, where two policemen were waiting.

Yes, Mary's mother had told them about a pile of handbags her captivated daughter had brought in to the breakfast table, and of my visit to the back fence. My love affair with Mary was over.

I found myself in the Children's Court. It was my first experience before the bench.

Normally, I would have been sent to a home for delinquents. But the court's consulting doctor pleaded valiantly on my behalf.

Sitting there, amazed, I heard him say I was a mild epileptic. I had a weak heart, too, he declared. Putting this basically good 12-year-old boy in a reformatory, he continued, amid the strains and tensions of living with young delinquents and away from his loving parents, could prove fatal. I was let off.

When he had taken me home from the court, Pop quite rightly expended a great deal of energy giving me a hiding. Again I did not cry or protest. Just stubbornness, I suppose.

Of course, I had no heart trouble and there was no suggestion of epilepsy. Months later, Pop told me he had bribed the doctor £10 to lie. It was a lot of money in those days. And it kept me out of a reformatory.

By now, Mary was giving all her attention to Jimmy. But I would not be beaten. After school, I used to stick to the pair of them like a bear to a beehive. They repeatedly told me to go away, but

I doggedly followed on. Sometimes Jimmy rushed at me and we fought. He was slightly bigger than me, but I usually won. Even when I lost, I still followed them. What a little pest.

After such an event one afternoon, I was sitting atop a fence around the grounds of Sydney University, about a mile from home, watching Jimmy and Mary playing in the grass. Jimmy obviously wanted to explore her body. He put one hand under her dress.

That made me indignant. 'I want to do it, *too*,' I yelled. 'Can I do it, too, Mary?'

Jimmy swung his head around. 'No, clear out!'

'No, you can't,' my old flame called to me.

'Aw, come on,' I pleaded. 'I'll go second!'

Jimmy now had both hands up her dress. 'Well, all right, Darce,' Mary finally replied.

'No!' Jimmy burst out. 'No, you can't. She's *my* girl.'

This seemed to decide it. 'No,' she echoed. 'No, Darce, you can't.'

Jimmy had her pants down to her ankles. I was furious. If I could not do it with her, Jimmy was not going to either.

About 20 yards along the road, some half a dozen workmen were digging a hole in the footpath. At the top of my lungs, I yelled, 'Jimmy's fucking Mary over there!'

I chanted it several times, pointing at the couple now in a flurry in the grass. The men charged towards me. I jumped off the fence and ran off. Jimmy and Mary were tearing through the grass in the other direction. Trying to pull up her pants as she ran, Mary was left well behind. So much for male chivalry.

The workmen thought it was a great joke. Not that they would have had much of an opinion of the jealous young urchin who gave the lovers' game away.

I hoped it had nothing to do with her lawless companions but, soon after that, Mary's parents moved to another neighbourhood. We never saw her again.

Jimmy and I soon patched up our differences. Through my twelfth and thirteenth years, we had our wicked ways with quite an assortment of local girls. Often we had the girls together.

A boy in my school class regularly experimented with his sister, who was in her final year at school. For several weeks I accompanied my new chum to his home after school. His sister was big for her age, and fat. She used to meet us in an old shed at the back of the house.

I told Jimmy about it. On the second occasion, Jimmy and I, the girl and her brother were dallying together in the shed when the girl's mother walked in. Jimmy and I fled, never to return there.

About this time, Jimmy and I saw a blind man begging for money at Wynyard railway station, in the city. In his outstretched hat were several shillings. What a great lurk it would be, we thought, if we could just stand like that and collect money.

Jimmy volunteered to give it a go. On a piece of cardboard we scrawled: 'I am blind. Money for Food please.' Jimmy slung the board around his neck.

He did well, standing near the station in a grubby T-shirt and shorts, feet bare on the cold pavement, looking forlorn. He kept both eyes tightly clamped shut.

Every 15 minutes or so, I strolled by and took a few shillings from his outstretched cap, then resumed watching from my position 20 yards away. I must have looked like a robber.

I don't know how the ruse could have fooled anyone. Perhaps it didn't. People probably gave him money to reward his initiative.

I was about to make my fifth or sixth collection call, my pockets bulging with coins worth about £2, when I saw a uniformed police constable coming from the other direction. He was in front of Jimmy before I could do a thing. I froze.

'What's this, son?' he asked sternly. 'Nice little caper you've got here.'

Jimmy, his eyes still clenched, held his cap towards the voice. 'I am blind, sir, and I'm hungry.'

'Who do you think you're kidding?'

Startled, Jimmy popped one eye open. At the sight of the uniform, he jerked back his head, his two eyes now very wide open and all seeing. He whipped the cap to his side, spilling a few shillings onto the footpath. He looked at me as I turned and looked into a shop window.

I turned back as the grinning constable, our placard under one arm, led Jimmy past me towards Central police station.

I waited outside the station for half an hour before my accomplice was let out after receiving a severe talking to. There would be no more lurks like that for him, he announced grimly.

A few days later, however, I tried a variation of the caper. In upper George Street, near Central railway station, a man stood for hours every day playing a mouth organ. He played it pretty awfully, too. But I had seen his pockets bulging with coins dropped into the hat he kept at his feet.

Now, I had been led to believe I had a reasonably good singing voice. To my enormous embarrassment, my parents regularly got me to render songs to friends who visited us. So why not exploit my talent for cash?

With Pop's old felt hat at my bare feet, I took up a position in George Street, about 50 yards from the old mouth organist, and gave forth. My first item was 'Silent Night, Holy Night'. Unseasonal, it being midyear, but the money flowed in. I must have been a pretty sorry spectacle.

I didn't last long, though. After putting up with my bellowing for about half an hour, the mouth organist moved in. He was not going to have a young screecher queering his pitch. He was a surprisingly agile old man. He chased me a good 200 yards along the street before I gave him the slip.

Despite this setback, I was convinced there was money for me in the charity game. All I needed was to hit on the correct formula to tear at the passing public's heart, and consequently purse strings.

The following week, I arrived at the main pedestrian ramp at Central railway station, several hundred yards from, and well out of sight of, the mouth organist, with a new approach.

My feet were again bare, my hair ruffled and face dirtied. I wore the oldest and grubbiest singlet and shorts I could find at home.

Slung around my neck was a placard that read: 'MY MOTHER HAS NO MONEY AND MY BROTHERS AND SISTERS ARE HUNGRY.'

The ramp was busy and the cash flowed in. Dear old ladies, smiling compassionately, pressed 2-shilling pieces into my hands. In one hour I received £4. In those days, a labourer would work for several days to earn that much. I kept it up for a couple of hours every day for about a month, instead of going to school.

I sometimes took the ferry across Sydney Harbour to Manly for the day at twopence for the return trip. For lunch, I bought ice creams, lollies, chocolates. I made a big fellow of myself at the shark-proof swimming pool near the ferry wharf, buying girls rides on little hired canoes.

Truant officers sometimes reported to my parents that I was not attending school and I was duly thrashed. It made little difference. I had a ready income. Life was good.

While on duty at Central station with the poor boy routine late one afternoon, retribution descended in the form of Pop. He was passing through the station when he spotted me. He walked up behind me and grabbed me by the neck.

As soon as we got home, he pounded my bare bottom with his belt until much of the skin had lifted. It was my greatest childhood hiding of all. Again I did not cry out. Pop sometimes hated thrashing me, and it often made Mum cry.

But I deserved every belting I got. Mum slipped the 25 shillings I had in my pockets into the Catholic Church's poor box. But, this young cynic wondered, did the poor really get it?

I must have been a constant source of exasperation to Pop, of painful anxiety to my mother. She lived in fear of what I would do next. A longtime tummy disorder gave her a great deal of pain. Sometimes she pleaded with me to knuckle down, to behave like young Tom did.

Her appeals got better results than did Pop's violence. I could not bear the sight of dear Mum crying. It caused me to behave and regularly attend school for a week or two. Then I succumbed to temptation and went on a juvenile rampage.

One afternoon during school holidays, two pairs of brothers and I stole 60 empty hessian potato sacks that had been stacked in a railway goods yard at Alexandria, near Newtown.

Planning to sell the bags to a dealer for 4 pence each, we had gone 100 yards with the haul, stacked on two carts made from packing cases, when a big man aged about 40 and wearing an overcoat came up behind us.

'Righto, you kids,' he boomed. 'I saw you pinch those bags.'

A railway detective! Or a policeman! My first impulse was to abandon the sacks and run. Bill and Harry, the eldest of us, seemed to recognise him. I caught Bill giving Harry a sly grin.

'It's no good running,' the man continued. 'I know where you live, Billy, and you, David.' He turned to Harry and his brother, Tim, the baby among us. David's and Tim's reactions confirmed that the man knew them all right.

'And I know where *you* live, too,' he snarled at me. 'So none of you get any smart ideas.'

I felt sure he was an official of some sort. I knew also, however, that he could not possibly know me. I lived farther away from this spot than the others. I seldom knocked about with them.

'No, you don't,' I challenged. 'You don't know where I live. I didn't do anything.'

The big man gave a covetous smile. 'I could take you all back to the railway and report you,' he said. 'Or bundle you off to the police station.'

He waited, smirking, gauging our reactions as we looked at one another. We were in a fix. I knew that even if I ran away, my companions would tell him my name and address.

'Or I could tell your parents.'

More fear registered on the faces of my accomplices at this than at his mention of the police. Who the blazes was this man?

'If you're sensible,' our antagonist continued, 'I'll let you off this time.'

He gazed on Harry, a handsome youngster with fair curly hair, blue eyes and an olive complexion.

'One of you has to come over there with me for a little while,' the man murmured, nodding towards a narrow strip of land between two storage sheds. Timber was stacked here and there, surrounded by long grass.

Now his motive was clear. A few times beforehand I had been propositioned by homosexuals offering lollies, free tickets to accompany them to the pictures, rides in their cars. But boys who had been seduced had told me about them. I never accepted.

'What about you, Harry?' the man said, smiling sweetly. 'Only for a little while, and I'll let you all off.'

This was our only way of avoiding retribution. All of us looked hopefully at Harry.

'No!' Harry burst out fearfully. 'No, I won't.'

'If one of you doesn't,' the queer continued quietly, 'all of you are in big trouble.'

He dug into a pocket and turned to me with a 2-shilling piece in his hand. 'You come with me then, and I'll give you this as well. I won't hurt you.'

Impulsively, I spat at his feet. The man tensed, about to lunge at me, then checked himself. He regained his cool and smilingly repeated the offer to Billy and David, without success. Then he confronted little nine-year-old Tim, a blond with smooth, dark skin.

'This money will be yours and you won't get into any trouble at all if you come with me for a while,' he said.

Tim also knew about homos. He wordlessly backed towards the fence by the footpath. The big man followed him, holding out a hand. 'Come on. It'll be good fun.'

'I don't want to,' Tim said, his voice trembling. His blue eyes looked up at the rest of us, pleading.

We other four kids exchanged glances. Obviously one of us would have to go with this man if we were to avoid punishment for stealing the bags. So why not Timmy? He had nothing to lose. He would not be hurt. And there was the two bob.

'Go on, Tim,' his brother Harry urged. 'You'll be all right. And you can keep the dough.'

Tim remained there, his back hard against the fence. The rest of us tried to coax him into it. Better him than one of us. And if Tim went with the man, we would keep the bags.

'If you don't go,' Harry said after a while, 'I'll belt ya!'

Tim let the man, grinning eagerly, take him by the hand into the gap between the sheds. Tim was sobbing. The pair went out of sight behind a stack of timber. Twice we heard the youngster cry out. The sound, on each occasion, was muffled. We did not dare interfere.

Some 15 minutes after he had been led away, Tim returned, looking violated. The sight of him rubbing his bottom with both hands made us laugh.

'Jeez, it hurts,' he cried. Tim tearfully told us what the man had done to him. Of course, most children have a streak of sadism. We could only laugh at Tim's harrowing tale.

'Now you'll have a bum baby!' Bill exclaimed.

'No,' the little boy cried as we continued towards his home, pushing our carts of stolen sacks. 'I don't want a baby. Will I really have a bum baby?'

'Yes!' we yelled, delighted. We let him keep the 2 shillings, which he told his parents he had found.

We told Tim and Harry's parents we found the sacks on a small rubbish dump and left them on the carts in their backyard. The next morning we would sell them to the local bag merchant. Sixty bags at 4 pence each meant exactly £1. Four shillings per thief. I felt sure, however, that it would not work out that way.

The others owned the carts and had discovered the bags. And the two elder boys were considerably bigger than me. I would be lucky to get 2 shillings out of it. So, it was time to take precautionary action.

When it was dark after dinner, I crept from home to Harry and Tim's backyard and stole 20 bags from one of the carts. I hurried home with them slung over my shoulders. It was as many as I could carry, and every 100 yards or so I had to put them down and rest.

My parents believed my story about finding the bags dumped in the street.

The next morning, I arrived at Harry and Tim's place to witness a tense scene. Bill had accused Harry of secreting 20 bags to sell all on his own, and Harry was indignantly denying it.

Bill saw me coming through the gate. 'Bastard Harry's knocked off 20 bags,' he called out. I hurried over as Harry threw himself at Bill.

'I didn't bloody take them,' Harry cried as they rolled in the dirt. 'You took 'em yourself.'

'It was *you*, all right, Harry,' I contributed. 'They were in your place.'

No one accused Darcy Dugan.

Eventually an uneasy truce was declared and the five of us sold the bags to the dealer for 13/4 (13 shillings and 4 pence). Bill, being the eldest, handled the sale. And my earlier suspicions were justified. My fifth share of the proceeds should have come to 2/8, but Bill gave me only 1/6.

When I protested, Bill and Harry pointed out that they had found the bags and we had used their carts. I could like it or lump it.

I made a swing at Bill. He and Harry grappled with me and threw me to the ground.

They took 5 shillings each; David got 1/4; and they gave Tim, still with a sore rectum, only 6 pence. 'You've already got two bob,' Bill said, and laughed.

That afternoon, I arrived alone at the bag dealer's with my 20 sacks, for which I received 6/8. My young friends never found out.

The episode embedded in me a sound lesson about selfishness and rewards for sneakiness. Crime, it seemed, paid.

I see now that I should have instead been upset, planned vengeance for raped little Tim. It never occurred to us kids in those days to report such a crime to the police. We were somehow sure that the cops — the 'demons' — were the enemy. When we confronted them in the street, they usually called us dirty little rats. And perhaps we were.

2

I was nearly 15 when, one afternoon, an usherette admitted me free to see a movie because I gave her a make-up case I had stolen from a store. The following week, a new film showing, I was back with a bottle of perfume for her. Again I went in free.

She told me she would buy, for half the retail price, any quality cosmetics I could nick. And perhaps, she added, she could sell to other usherettes any items she could not use herself. She was aged about 19, fairly small, with long, black hair and blue eyes.

The word spread around the usherettes. Soon about 30 girls from several city cinemas were getting all their cosmetics from me. As I did my rounds, delivering goods about twice weekly, they placed orders for particular products. Usually I delivered them within a few days.

I had a great business going. I kept the money in a screw-top jar planted in a vacant block of land near our Annandale home. It was in a small hole, the top flush with the ground and covered by an inch of dirt. On that was a block of wood. I stored my stolen compacts, lipsticks, nail polishes and the likes in a big tin similarly hidden nearby.

No other person knew of my new business, clientele or cache. Not even Jimmy. He would have wanted to join in and share the proceeds. Or set up a rival caper.

I stole the goods from a total of about 15 stores, mostly in the city. A youth did not look out of place sauntering around in them, as they also sold toys, confectionery and school stationery.

I must have become a pretty nifty operator, seeing that I kept it up for nearly a year without being caught. Once I ran out of a store with a shop assistant at my heels and escaped in the crowd.

One time I was virtually forced to *buy* a stick of lipstick! I had picked it up off the counter and was about to pocket it when I felt the presence of a man standing behind me. He smelled of authority. A shop detective, for sure.

I already had a couple of stolen items in my trouser pockets and could not afford arousing his suspicions sufficiently to search me. With him breathing down my back, running away was not on.

'Getting it for your girlfriend, sonny?' he asked, smiling thinly as I turned around. He was suspicious. I hoped he had not been watching me for long.

'N–no,' I stammered. 'For Mum. Her birthday.' That seemed to win him over.

'Well, the assistant can fix you up,' he said, motioning to a sales girl behind the counter.

Ruefully, I paid 4/6 and left the premises. As I walked out, the store detective was still grinning. He knew what I was up to, all right, but at least I had not been searched. I never graced that store again.

The usherette who commissioned me to get the lipstick, that exact shade and brand, gave me only 3 shillings for it. Vanity prevented me from admitting I had actually bought it legitimately.

I could now gain free admittance to most of the cinemas in urban Sydney. Sometimes I made a big man of myself by taking girlfriends to the pictures, flaunting my influence with the usherettes by walking in without buying a ticket.

'Oh, they're friends of mine,' I casually explained.

After I had been in the business a few months, I regularly called on usherettes in their communal dressing rooms. As they sat changing stockings and dresses, many of them seemed indifferent to the presence of a small 15-year-old boy. I lingered in those dressing rooms longer than necessary. A few girls flaunted their nakedness in front of me.

One buxom bird named Lily got a kick out of doing this. She would sit, grinning, in varying stages of undress while I stood with my little box of booty, ogling.

One day when I arrived, Lily was in the dressing room alone, wearing only a dressing gown. Once I was inside, she locked the door, threw off her robe and stood before me, voluptuously naked. I felt weak at the knees, excited between the thighs. She was aged about 25 and extremely inviting.

Lily sat back on a sofa and opened her arms. 'Come on, Darcy,' she said, smiling. 'This is what you want, isn't it?'

I fearfully moved forwards. She took my hands and pulled me to her.

I had been fumbling on the sofa with her for only a minute when I heard giggling. Four other usherettes, all clients of mine, were peering around a curtain from an adjoining annexe. They were all dressed.

I leapt from the sofa, frantically adjusting my trousers as they walked in. The girls were laughing their heads off. Lily was doubled up on the sofa, chortling.

She had set up the whole thing so they could get a laugh at my expense. I rushed to the door and left, my box of goods still on the floor. I could still hear their infuriating laughter as I hurried down the theatre stairs into George Street.

I have pleasant memories of those usherettes, however. Every week, one theatre girl, smaller and younger than most of them, favoured me with the use of her body for a supply of about £1 worth of cosmetics. She was a fine tutor in the ways of women.

When I was nearly 16, I got into more strife with police when they correctly accused me of being involved in petty thievery and smash-and-grab raids.

Mum grew worried about my naughty ways and what they might lead to. She took me for an appraisal by Sydney University psychologist Professor Dawson.

They were interesting sessions. Mum later revealed that Dawson believed I had an exceptionally high IQ but was hyperactive, with a resistance to authority that was probably ingrained, perhaps inherited.

There was the potential, however, for my spirited nature to be redirected to commendable achievements as an adult. A good first step, the professor recommended, was to get me away from depraved and lawless associations.

Pop and Mum were happy for me to leave school, a place of naughtiness, from which I was still a regular truant anyway. They sent me to stay with relatives on a farm near the mining town of Mackay, in Queensland.

They hoped that a break from the city and my 'young crook' associates would straighten me out, but to no avail. When I returned home seven months later, I was soon in more strife with the coppers. But I received only abusive reprimands from them.

I was sent to stay with relatives in the Bathurst area, out west beyond the Blue Mountains. Again, several months there did no good, and I returned to the city and my wicked ways.

I can't recall getting into trouble at Bathurst or Mackay, but I had the feeling that those relatives were relieved when I returned home.

About that time, I developed an intense interest in things mechanical. I spent hours blissfully pulling apart old car engines and clocks, then reassembling them. I had a definite flair for it. My parents were delighted; Tom was impressed. Had naughty Darce at last found a vocation?

Portentously, my interest turned to locks. The new hobby did not, I swear, stem from any criminal motive. However, I soon realised the possibilities of the new-found ability.

I picked open and pulled apart every lock I could get my hands on. It became fairly easy for me to make keys to open locks after getting just a brief look at the proper key. I even paid several visits to the Sydney public library and read all about locking devices. Almost any type of lock could soon be recognised at a glance, its composition of metals known.

When I went out in the evenings, often to see a girlfriend, I told Mum and Pop I did not want a key and not to bother leaving a door or window unlatched for me to get back in. I would get in somehow, I added confidently.

Many times Pop was baffled to find me in bed the next morning. At first he accused me of cheating, saying I must have a spare key. I certainly could make one, I boasted. Getting in that way, though, would not give me a feeling of accomplishment. No, I told him honestly, I had used another method of entry.

Pop made a game of it. After I went out of an evening, he carefully went right around the house, bolting shut every window and door from the inside. He once spread sugar on the floor near a window he felt I was prising open.

He lay awake upstairs waiting to hear the crunch, crunch, crunch of sugar. But he never did. Sometimes, after noiselessly sneaking in, I heard him moving about in his bedroom, waiting to catch me getting in.

'Locks,' I pointed out, 'are made only to keep honest people out.'

Pop proudly agreed.

By now he was teaching me his trade: laying ornamental tiles. Pop was a master at it, and he wanted me to be a perfectionist like him. Unfortunately, I was either too self-centred or immature to appreciate his noble aspirations for me. I quite liked the work, and employment was not easy to get then. I think I would have made a pretty good tile layer.

Pop, nonetheless, continually criticised my work loudly in front of the other apprentices. He praised *their* work, which I knew was often inferior to mine. I felt I was being baited, victimised, and I finally stormed off the job, never to return.

I sustained myself for quite a while on the proceeds of shoplifting. I renewed dealings with some of the old theatre usherettes.

But yours truly became overconfident and too greedy.

Shop staff twice caught me lifting goods from counters. Even in the stores where I had not been caught, I became a familiar figure. As I foolishly never bought anything, I was viewed with suspicion.

But that ambition for wealth surged on. Forged in my mind was the notion that society was really of two parts: them, and us villains. It could be further divided into four groups:

1. The stinking rich, which I aspired to become. 2. Simpleton do-gooders, who laboured, struggled, did not break laws and remained poor. 3. The mean enforcers of those laws, who punished their prisoners and were always coldly abrupt with, sometimes swore at, kids in the streets. 4. We clever crooks, young and old.

Compared with other sorts of crime, shoplifting had virtues from a crook's point of view. Even if you accepted that sooner or later you would be caught red-handed, the penalty would be minimal. They could convict you of stealing only what they caught you with. You risked a stiff penalty only after running up a decent string of convictions. If the collared urchin spun a sufficiently heart-rending tale of contrition and woe, shop managers were just as likely to let him off with merely a warning.

But, I decided, it was time to broaden the net. Go for bigger fish.

An ideal new market was Sydney's big ring of prostitutes. They had plenty of money and would not mind cheaply buying quality goods they knew were nicked. After all, *their* profession was illegal, too.

I walked up to a kindly looking woman standing in front of one of the many two-storey terrace-house brothels in Palmer Street, in the inner-city waterfront slum of Woolloomooloo. She looked old to this teenager. I learned later that she was 37.

After realising the kid was not offering her a bottle of perfume for a session in her boudoir, she presented a sisterly smile and took the bottle from my hand.

'So you've got a real business deal, have you, kid? Where'd you get this?'

'Oh, I just picked it up. But I can get a lot more good new things, too. At half price!'

'Real little sharpie, aren't you, kid?' she teased.

Masking annoyance at being called 'kid', I grinned awkwardly. 'I can get enough of that and other stuff to supply you and your friends.'

The madam said I could call her Tilly — Tilly Devine. Heck, I had heard of her. She was Sydney's queen of vice. This was one of about 20 of her brothels. What a lucky stroke it was, me walking up to the madam of madams!

Tilly put an arm around my shoulder and took me into the brothel.

A small knot of men standing across the street looked over, chuckling. They must have thought I was about to buy some female tuition.

The premises had gaudy wallpaper and furnishings. The carpet in the reception lounge was red, punctuated with big bright-green floral patterns. It smelled of stale cigarettes and human sweat. Three heavily made-up women in flimsy, frilly dresses lounged on an enormous settee, smoking.

'Got a kid here with a business proposition,' my new ally announced.

The women were friendly, if at first a little condescending. Yes, they agreed after a while, they would buy stuff from me if I could fill their specific orders. Mostly, they wanted lipstick and black and sexy stockings.

In three weeks, 20 prostitutes from half a dozen Woolloomooloo brothels were regular customers. 'Clients', I liked to call them — what an upstart I was. Often they gave me bonus payments, so I received almost the products' retail prices.

The brothels fascinated me. The prostitutes, with some exceptions, were a friendly lot once I got to know them and they trusted me. To some, I was a sort of mascot.

Pop and Mum, meantime, must have known their unemployed son's money was ill-gotten. But the strugglers, who enjoyed food and cash and other things I took home for them, did not ask about it. Anyway, what could they do?

Some afternoons and evenings, I sat in brothel reception lounges for hours yarning with the friendly sex machines. And, after they had placed their shopping orders, I quietly listened to their frank shoptalk.

Their male customers looked startled sometimes when they walked in to see a 16-year-old boy sitting on the settee with the women, looking entirely at home. A boy pro, they must have assumed. A girl would be selected and lead her customer off to a room.

Usually within 15 minutes, the customer quickly walked back out through the reception room, his eyes lowered in apparent embarrassment. Soon afterwards, the girl returned to the settee, looking no different, taking up the conversation where she had left off.

Sometimes she first made a remark such as, 'He was a busy little bastard' or 'He didn't get much value. Blew in a minute.' It was quite an education.

I was now and then treated to the favours of one of the girls, on the house. The muscle-man bouncers, always about the brothels in case a customer got rough, treated me as a bit of a joke.

One afternoon as I sat on the settee with the women, a man walked in and fixed his eyes on me. He walked over to me and asked flatly, 'How much for you?'

He was not joking. Dear Tilly Devine happened to be there that day. Before I could explain to the man, she screamed at him, 'You filthy bastard. *Out!* Get out of this house before I have you thrown out.'

The perplexed man looked at her, then at the other women, who were scowling menacingly, and left. For me it was a sobering moment. The girls were genuinely outraged. Had that man insisted on remaining, they would have not waited for the bouncer to arrive. The homo would have been clawed, kicked and bitten to pieces.

I had seen prostitutes fight men. A sane man who has been around does not lightly pick a fight with a seasoned Sydney prostitute.

I was now, though, regularly accused in the Children's Court of stealing. Time and again, the court's consulting doctor, after receiving £10 from Pop or from my stash, repeated that because of my delicate health, it would be too risky to send me to a reformatory. Of course, I was still as healthy as the proverbial bull.

The knowledge that a court verdict in my favour could be bought lessened my respect for authority — the law.

While awaiting a hearing in court, I sometimes had to spend a few days in the Albion Street Children's Shelter, in the inner-city suburb of Surry Hills. Scores of problem boys were housed there under fairly rigorous conditions while officialdom decided what should be done with them.

I suppose I was a reasonably handsome youth; I was proud of my brown, wavy hair. I usually found it easy to pick up girls. The same features, however, evidently made me appealing to predatory poofters.

Even at the Children's Shelter, two different officers of the court quite blatantly undertook to ensure I would receive light treatment from the court if I succumbed to their advances. I refused. Life in the shelter became tougher.

One night, an officer forced a boy to stand naked under a cold shower for more than an hour, his body turning blue from the winter cold, while the sadistic beast stood watching. The boy's crime? Refusing his advances.

Boys who spent a long period at the shelter knew which men there were queers. And once a boy began receiving special treatment from them, we kids knew the boy had given in. In such cases, it was common for the officer to stand up in court and announce that he had been watching over the nice lad.

'There is a lot of good in this boy,' he would swear. 'I have had a long talk with him. If the court is agreeable, I am prepared to take this lad into my charge and see what I can do for him.'

Rightly not wanting to expose a basically decent kid to the harsh realities and associations of a juvenile penal establishment, magistrates invariably agreed. The boy's parents would gratefully applaud the officer of the court, this selfless humanitarian, for keeping little Johnny out of a reformatory. For steering him away from the path to real crime.

Blimey, if those parents, if the court, had only known. Boys selected for special attention by those men became the officers' regular lays and were irreparably corrupted, ruined for life.

Meanwhile, I kept up my interest in lock smithing. For a while, I even imagined myself one day becoming a professional magician specialising in escape tricks. What irony.

I sometimes used my knowledge to break into houses and steal any small item of value I could find. I regularly had to climb to upper-storey windows, cat-burglar style.

For many months now, relations at home had been sorely strained. Pop, I'm afraid, took out many other women and did not seem to hide the fact from sickly Mum. Pop was still also a pretty hopeless gambler.

My parents had not slept together for years. I knew my mother had decided that once Tom and I were old enough, she would leave my father. Tom was now 13. The time had come.

Mum dispassionately discussed it with Pop. They agreed that they should take a son each. Now, my leaning towards Mum was stronger than it was towards Pop. Also, I felt Mum was closer to me than to Tom, who was closer to Pop.

However, Tom was younger and my parents determined that he should go with Mum. I was upset by the whole business. I loved both of them. Cheeky Tom, too!

Pop, despite some deserved thrashings he gave me and many unforgivable things he did with Mum's knowledge, was a kind and usually generous father. So I stayed on with him. Mum and Tom moved into a house with relatives in the suburb of Marrickville.

The break-up of his marriage and family hit Pop pretty hard. And son No. 1 continued his lawless ways.

After a while, Pop persuaded Jim Geraghty, an uncle of mine who owned the Crows Nest Hotel — in the suburb of Crows Nest, north of the harbour — to give me a job. I went there, living in, as assistant cellar hand.

'Make good here, Darce,' Uncle Jim said, 'and your future's assured.'

He told me that if I proved suitable, he would later put me in charge of the cellar. Then, when I was old enough, I could work in the bar. Perhaps one day become bar manager. Then ... who knows? He had no children.

Things went well at the hotel for several months. My aunt and uncle were delighted with my application to the job, which I liked. They were particularly pleased that I neither smoked nor drank liquor. For a while, I saw my future all neatly before me. The world was my yo-yo.

Pop and Mum, whom I often visited, were overjoyed.

I lost contact with the prostitutes and usherettes and no longer stole goods from shops. The pay of 15 shillings weekly at the hotel was enough for my immediate needs.

I still wanted a push-bike, though. That desire, which first brought me at odds with the law, had never left me. I realise now, of course, that a period of only saving cash instead of splurging it would have got it for me.

After cleaning out the barroom one night, I spotted the key to the money safe hanging on a nail. It was often kept there, but suddenly it had a particular significance. I knew that safe contained several bundles of paper money. A thousand pounds, at least.

My mind raced. Here was my chance to get a bike. And more. I opened the safe and took a small bundle of notes. It might not be missed, I thought. Anyway, I would not be a suspect. Anyone could have walked in and taken the bundle.

I returned the key to the nail and went to my room upstairs. After locking the door behind me, I feverishly counted the takings — £106! I pulled up a section of linoleum under my bed and placed the flattened notes, no more than three deep, under the newspaper that lay beneath the lino.

Later, lying awake in bed, I felt positive I had pulled off a perfect crime.

For several days, nothing was mentioned about the missing money. They had not even noticed that it was missing, I felt. The key was still left on the nail at nights.

About ten days after opening the safe, I paid cash for a shiny new bike and spent hours riding around the North Shore. It was my undoing. Where, Uncle Jim wanted to know, did I get the money for it? All the time, he had been convinced one of the staff had taken the money. He was simply waiting for a sign of lavish spending.

He searched my room as I voiced innocence. He found the remainder of the money under the lino.

Uncle Jim was done with me. Quite rightly, he showed no compassion. The police were summoned. Relations with him ended. He went on to be a state member of parliament.

It was my tenth appearance in the Children's Court. This time, with 97 convictions, mostly for stealing, I had no escape from justice. Actually, I had committed fewer than half of those crimes. When the police were confident of a conviction, it was convenient for them to charge you with similar offences committed recently in the same district. That way, their books were cleared. Ironically, though, I found out too late that a few young men were convicted of crimes I was guilty of.

The court's consulting doctor, again bribed with a hard-earned £10 from a devastated Pop, half-heartedly claimed that I was still in delicate health. But the magistrate, my criminal record before him, was in no mood for mercy.

Pop looked on brokenheartedly, and I heard my mother sob, as I was sentenced to nine months at the Mount Penang Training School for Boys at Gosford, a rural district near the coast, two hours' train ride north of Sydney.

The Gosford training school, I had been told by many boys who had been there, was a tough place.

'Step out of line there,' a boy told me at the Albion Street shelter, 'and they'll kick you senseless.'

Well, they can kick me if they like. But the bastards will never break me. I'm tough. If they kick me, I'll kick back, harder.

Pop was at Central railway station to watch a Child Welfare Department officer take me aboard the train for the trip.

In retrospect, I think I was so furious because it registered that I had been a greedy fool. Had I not stolen that money for the bike, I might one day have been manager, perhaps even the owner, of the whole hotel.

3

In 1937, the Mount Penang Training School for Boys housed and, officialdom hoped, reformed the state's most lawless youths. It was largely self-sufficient, being virtually a farm staffed by 200 boys. A few were as old as 21, but most were aged from 13 to 18.

Most of them lived in Sydney. Young hoods from concrete canyons, they were, ruefully and regimentally harvesting the earth.

Some of the inmates at Gosford, however, had broken no law. They were orphans who had run away from orphanages. I know a few orphans who, because of undesirable associations formed at Gosford, became criminals for life.

In charge were officers of the Child Welfare Department, some of whom were 'butch' sexual predators. The officers were assisted by some 60 senior boys, termed JOs, junior officers.

The inmates were split into groups, termed sections, of about 10 to 15 boys. The sections were then grouped into three companies, each of which slept in one of the school's three dormitories. There were a few JOs in charge of each section. Ordinary inmates called them bully boys. To become a bully boy, a youth had to prove he was tougher and rougher than most. He had to be reasonably loyal to the officers and able to force his will on others.

The bullies continually competed with one another on a points system. The one with the most disciplined section on the day got the most points. Good points earned rations of tobacco and other perks, such as visits to the cinema at Gosford.

These were pretty strong incentives, utter luxuries the rest of us could only dream of. Also, bully boys did less labouring.

Hoping to become bully boys, inmates regularly spied on their fellow prisoners. Sometimes aspirants invented tales of other boys' wrongdoing then bashed them to show how tough they were. And once they became bully boys, they were much harsher on their charges than the average adult officer. The system encouraged brutality. If a boy was a sadist, this was the place to develop his trait.

Arriving at Mount Penang with a sense of wariness, I was issued with two thick shirts, two pairs of shorts, two pairs of long socks of thick wool and a peaked cap. All of them were of army khaki — the Gosford uniform.

A junior officer escorted me to the boot shop. Inside, three boys, who were repairing boots, stole quick glances at me. Their faces were grim. Obviously they were fearful of the adult officer in charge in there, whom I shall call King.

He took a slow, menacing look at me and drawled to the JO, 'Who's this little bastard?'

The JO told him my name, and King looked me up and down as I stood there sullenly. He said, 'This'll be a cheeky bastard, I bet.' Pointing to a stack of black boots, he snapped, 'What size do you take?'

'Fours,' I answered.

King leaned across the bench between us and crashed a stinging backhander across my mouth.

'When you speak to an officer,' he shouted, 'say "sir".' He grinned at the JO who had brought me in there, as if recalling a private joke.

'We've got no fours,' said King. He threw me a pair of sixes. 'Wear these.'

I protested that they were too big. 'Sir, can't I wear my own shoes until you've got the right size, sir?' I began to dislike this man intensely. He was not one to be nettled. But I was not going to cower. Not to him. Not to anyone.

King walked around the bench to my side and smashed a fist into my face. I went sprawling across the room. I lay there for a moment, dazed and shocked. The officer walked over and nudged me none too gently with his boot.

'Get up, Dugan!' he commanded. 'Don't argue with your officers. Just do as you're told. Understand?'

I was still groggy, but on my feet. Hate for this man, who was more then twice my size, burned inside me. I looked at him and did not answer.

Next thing I knew, King was belting punches into my body, then my face. I was knocked against the wall. King moved in and kept pounding me against the wall.

When he stopped, I slumped to the floor. The other boys pretended they were not looking and continued working. The junior officer was gazing out a window as I got to my feet.

'Stand to attention,' King barked. I stood to attention. A stream of blood poured from my nose over my lips and chin. My ribs ached. My jaw was swelling. I looked up at him.

'Now,' he said, still glaring, 'do you understand?'

I was too shaken to speak. I nodded. Another punch to the face sent me flying back on the floor.

My eyes became glazed by fury. This time I sprang to my feet, crying with rage, and ran at him, wildly throwing punches. My head came up to the big man's shoulders.

King battered me. I doubt if I landed one proper blow. It was over quickly and I was back on the floor, sobbing.

Both my eyes were turning black. My mouth was bleeding, as well as my nose. The senior boy dragged me to my feet and told me to stand to attention.

I heard King again. 'When you are addressed by an officer,' he said, 'you don't nod your head. You reply, "Yes, sir." Understood?'

I was only a boy but was not without spirit. I still wanted to hit that animal, who was enjoying himself. I murmured, 'Yes, sir.'

King walked back to his side of the bench. 'Get him out of here,' he told the JO.

It was my first lesson at Gosford: learning to hate authority. The world was dividing in two. There were *us*, on the receiving end. And there were *them*, who dished it out. Authority.

I got another dose from one of *them* when bundled to one of the dormitories for the night. The room's bully boy in charge walked up and glared down at me, the pitiful, bleeding newcomer.

'I'm the boss here, kid,' he announced, as the others sitting on beds in the dormitory quietly looked on. 'Step out of line just once and I'll plaster ya to the wall.'

I merely nodded and he strutted away. There would be plenty of time to sort out him and the other beasts here, I thought. Maybe he was really a decent bloke. If not, he might be sorry later on if he tangled with me.

Being still 16 and small at that, I had been placed in a section of 15- and 16-year-olds. Our head bully boy was 17 and considerably bigger than me.

A reformatory for young hoodlums had to be run firmly or there would be chaos. But I felt at the time, still feel, that the system at Gosford was downright sadistic. How the hell would that turn wayward youths into useful members of the community? Rehabilitation! It was a school of thuggery.

Most Gosford inmates were thieves, like me. A few were convicted rapists and murderers too young to go to adult prisons. They would populate them later.

Statistics at the time showed that 83 percent of the boys from Gosford later committed more crimes and went to jail. Other graduate crooks, no doubt, avoided jail. I figured that nearly every kid dispatched to Gosford became a repeat offender.

The sun had just arisen into a clear sky; two roosters were crowing somewhere, competing for rights to the still, cool air as I marched out with the others for my first full day at Gosford.

I was curious to know what the place looked like. I had kept to myself during the night, wanting to have nothing to do with anyone until I found out what was what at this place.

My blackened eyes surveyed the surroundings. The country air smelled clean and alien to citified yours truly. I had taken ten paces when something crashed into my right ear. I swung around, and a fist glanced across my right cheek.

'Eyes front, Dugan!' my assailant yelled.

Automatically, I lashed out at him, the head bully boy who had fronted me in the dormitory after my battering in the boot shop.

I swung a left fist, striking the right side of his head. My right hit his belly. He doubled over. With both hands, I grabbed the top of his head and, as I jerked it down, brought up a knee.

I felt his nose flatten on my kneecap. He sagged to the ground. But others were running up. An adult officer standing nearby yelled, but did not move.

This was it. They would know of my run-in with King. They were testing me out. Well, I was not going to disappoint the bastards. A swollen face, sore ribs, two black eyes and all, I could still have a go.

I lunged at the first big bully boy rushing in. My head butted his chest, knocking him off balance. I kicked him in the leg and, as he bent down, put all I had into an uppercut to his jaw.

Something hit the back of my neck. Another bully boy. As I turned to face him, a third one grabbed my shoulders and kneed my back. While he held me, the bully who had hit my neck threw three punches into my belly. My legs weakened as he clouted me on the temple. I lost consciousness.

Boys later told me that, while I lay there senseless, four boys continued kicking my head and body, until the adult officer told them to ease up.

When I regained consciousness, the officer stood over me. My mouth tasted of blood. As it had the night before.

'On your feet, Dugan,' he ordered.

I moved to get up. A sharp pain shot through my side. My head was ringing.

'Get up!' he screamed. 'Or they'll give you more of it.'

I then saw the big four were standing behind me. Three were grinning. My initial assailant, however, held a hand to his nose, which was bleeding.

Well, it had taken four of them to get me down. The test had been passed. Painfully, I got to my feet.

'You're on jump,' the officer announced. He grinned at his bullies.

'What's that?' I asked.

The back of his hand smacked across my face, knocking me backwards a few steps. By now the bully boys had formed a circle around me. From behind, I received a jab in the kidneys. I lurched forwards.

'Don't you speak unless I tell you to,' the officer said. 'And then say "sir".'

Two of the bullies were moving in front of me. Hands raised to ward off the expected blows, I copped another crack on the back of my head and collapsed again.

An hour later, most of my body sprouting fresh bruises, I was 'on jump', a punishment designed by some men of sorely limited charity who apparently wanted to create human springs.

That's what the jump made you. A tense, brittle spring. You had to stand and touch the ground in front of your toes, without bending your knees. Then straighten up, arms held erect above your head. Then jump! Jump at least six inches clear of the ground. Touch the ground again, straighten. Jump! 'Faster, you bastard. Six inches off the ground!'

That first term on jump lasted seven days — from seven in the morning to nine at night, minus two meal breaks of an hour each. The pain became excruciating. The muscles along my bruised and cut legs, back, shoulders and neck were knotted like rope.

On average, there were half a dozen of us on jump at any time, being punished for a variety of offences. Gazing around in front of a guard could earn you an extra day on jump. Answering back to the guard could lengthen your sentence by a week or more.

One of the toughest bully boys was always on close guard over us jumpers, firing off insults. And an officer was never far away. If a jumper's feet did not rise six inches from the dust, the bully clouted him. If they still did not rise high enough, the kid was knocked to the ground.

Boys on jump often fainted from exhaustion. Then the senior officer would come over, prod him with a boot to make sure he was not malingering, and order that a dipper of water be thrown over him. When he regained consciousness, the boy would be given 15 to 30 minutes' rest before resuming the jumps.

At night my legs twitched, wanting to thrust me six inches off the bed, even as I slept.

We prisoners were like robots, living lives of pain and disciplined monotony. With a little pre-planning, I knew I could easily escape, but I was determined to see out my nine months. Otherwise, I would always be on the run.

Most things at Gosford were done by numbers. You got up at six in the morning, dressed, made your bed. Then you stood at attention by the bed. When everyone was at attention, we were marched out of the dormitory in a column, four abreast, to the washbowls. We stripped to the waist and washed our faces and hands.

In winter, these ablutions with cold water, which took place out in the open, often in frost or mist or rain, had everyone's teeth chattering. Everyone, that is, except the officers, who were in overcoats and wore scarves. And the senior boys, who washed under shelter. With hot water!

After washing, we were marched to the mess hall for a breakfast of porridge, a slice of bread with butter, a mug of tea. After breakfast, we marched for a brief time on the playing fields. There were three fields, one for each company.

Company No. 1 was for small boys, No. 2 for big boys. In No. 3 were the boys considered unstable — kids who were obviously moronic, neurotic or known homosexuals. And any boy caught masturbating. I was in No. 1 company.

On the sporting fields, we either played cricket or kicked a football, depending on the season. Everyone played, except those on jump.

At about 8.30 a.m., the boys were ordered to fall into ranks, and, to the beat of kettledrums, we marched to the long verandah in front of the administration block. Here, the three companies stood at rigid attention while our names were read out. When your name was called, you answered, 'Yes, sir.'

The verandah at Gosford was called the quarterdeck, a term from the days when the New South Wales Government used the *Sobraon*, a big sailing ship, as a corrective institution for delinquent boys.

Sobraon sailed up and down the coast, laden with boys. She was apparently as unhappy as any ship that graced the Pacific. The officers in charge were tough men. They generally forced the boys to keep the ship sailing continuously. Up the coast, then down. Up and down. In all weather. They called at Sydney only to drop off and take on more prisoners and provisions.

From what I have been told about that ship, the life of the boys at Gosford was, by comparison, a piece of cake. Almost daily, boys on *Sobraon* were flogged while tied to the ship's triangle, a structure made of three timber beams in the shape of a pyramid.

A couple of years previously, I had seen a young man with a mass of scars over his entire back. My mother saw the scars, too. 'The lash on the *Sobraon*,' Pop had explained to her.

Some boys on *Sobraon* were driven to try to escape by jumping into the water with the sharks. In 1911, *Sobraon* was renamed *Tingira* and became a naval training ship.

A couple of the guards at Gosford when I was there had been keepers on *Sobraon*. Both of them were ruffians.

It was on the quarterdeck that I first saw and heard the Gosford training farm's officer in charge, whom we called the Duke. He was a rigid disciplinarian, a former army officer. He believed that anyone who really bucked the system should be drilled and flogged into submission. When the Duke was upset, he raved and frothed at the mouth like a madman. Even his adult officers feared and hated him. Many years after my time at Gosford, the Duke went to a lunatic asylum.

After morning muster on the quarterdeck, we boys were marched off in our work sections. One section worked in a dairy, another in the carpentry shop and so on. Most sections, though, were gardeners.

Even gardening was done by numbers. Each of us was given a spade and we moved together. God help any boy who fell behind.

The bully boys stood about, ready to attack lads whose work suffered because of fatigue.

We could say a few words to one another only while working in the fields. But if a youth was caught speaking in an unauthorised way, punishment was inevitable.

Initially a bully boy's fist smashed him to the ground. If he cowered there, kept quiet, and the bully did not have a particular set on him, things might be left at that. He would have only a bruise or minor cut to show for it. If he protested, he might be kicked unconscious.

At noon we marched, again to the beat of kettledrums, to the mess hall for lunch. This was meat and vegetables, with a dessert of boiled rice or sago. Sometimes with a small helping of stewed fruit. Then, a slice of bread and a mug of tea.

The food at Gosford was plain but clean. We seldom had cause for dissatisfaction on that score. But there was never enough food — except for the JOs, who ate and drank all they wanted.

Another brief period of football or cricket, strictly controlled, followed lunch. Then off we went again to the quarterdeck, to the infernal beat of those kettledrums. I can still hear the damn things.

The Duke named the company winning the most points for the previous 24 hours. Then he delivered any haranguing that came to his warped mind.

Any slackening of discipline on the part of a boy cost his company marks. Bully boys in charge of sections getting low marks knew whom to blame. They recalled, for instance, a boy being slow making his bed, another who had coughed while standing at attention …

The JOs, with the tacit approval of the adults, bashed the culprits. Some boys were belted every week. For naturally slow movers, it was hell. Every night it was a race to undress and get into bed. And, as in every race, someone had to be last — and was bashed.

It was not uncommon during the noon assembly on the quarterdeck for us to be kept standing at attention for an hour while we were lectured by the Duke. There was no roof and, on hot days, boys fainted. It was agonising standing there, sweat often pouring off you, wanting to move your feet or arms, knowing that any move would bring an attack. Sometimes a boy next to me, perhaps a mate, fell on his face in a faint but I dared not move to help him. All the time, the Duke bellowed and snarled about some boy who had committed some 'crime' against his rule.

We worked until about 5 p.m. More marching back with the kettledrums. The evening meal, like lunch; a little more cricket or footy; then to the dormitory. Lights out at 9 p.m.

Some four times daily, 40 or 50 boys at a time were marched to the lavatories. These consisted of six pedestals and a urinal long enough to accommodate seven or eight. The company stood at attention some 20 feet from the lavatory. A senior boy in charge would bellow, 'Six sit-downs, *in*! Seven stand-ups, *in*!'

Thirteen boys marched inside in single file. Those standing up, urinating, were allowed 30 seconds to relieve themselves. The senior boy then bellowed, 'Stand-ups, *out*!' Any kid who had not finished urinating copped a belt on an ear. The sit-downs were granted two minutes. Then the senior boy called, 'Sit-downs, *out*!' Any boy who did not get up immediately was knocked off his seat, finished or not. This happened a lot and was, of course, a messy affair.

All this was carried out under the observation and approval of officers of the New South Wales Child Welfare Department. *Welfare?*

Nearly every night at Gosford, a couple of boys wet their beds. This was often brought about, or at least aggravated, by the fact that a simple function like going to the toilet was made an ordeal to be avoided. Naturally, a boy who wet his bed got a blow or two from the JO on duty.

One small boy, aged 14 or 15 and new to the place, was deformed in the legs and one arm. He was also slightly paralysed on one side. The poor kid had almost no control over his bowels. Now I come to think of it, I don't know how the hell the authorities could ever have arranged for someone so profoundly disabled to be sent to a place like Gosford. I don't recall what crime he committed. Every night he urinated, sometimes defecated, in his bed. To begin with, the JOs and officers did not knock him about, because of his pitiful condition. But when the kid continued soiling his bed, their attitude hardened.

The bully boys began knocking him about. Week by week, they terrorised him, with the officers' approval. The kid was not actually bashed. He was slapped repeatedly across the face and booted on the backside.

Crippled as he was, with the use of only one arm, this kid was made to wash his bedclothes every day. He was abused and sneered at for costing our company daily points. He lived in constant fear and pain.

None of us boys at Gosford was an angel. But quite a few of us in the dormitory wanted to help this disabled kid, whom I'll call Nigel. I was hit for insubordination when I stepped forward and volunteered to an officer to help Nigel hang his bedclothes on the washing line.

Nigel's state of continuous terror finally did him good, in a way. There came nights when he did not soil his bed. I remember only too well that kid's look of ecstasy and pride when he got out of bed after realising it was dry.

Dry beds for him became more frequent. And the time came when one-armed little Nigel had control of his bowels. The officers, proud of the result, did not consider the lifelong mental damage Nigel's constant anxiety caused him.

A few adult officers at Gosford were homosexuals. They preyed on the weakest of the younger boys in their charge. Most of the other officers knew; we inmates knew. But everyone seemed to consider it a bit of a joke. We saw officers wink and snigger at one another as a known poofter selected a boy to go and 'work' in his quarters. Nearly all the officers lived near the training school in houses the government provided. Each was allowed a boy to work in and around his residence.

One of the officers was married to an attractive brunette. They had a young child. This officer also seduced his houseboys. Any boy who refused his advances was sacked and another replaced him. When he got a sufficiently compliant type, the officer kept him for a few months, until he tired of him. The cast-off boy was warped for life.

We at least got laughs at the expense of the above-mentioned officer. Some of the older boys, senior JOs with comparative freedom to move about, used to lay his wife. No doubt her husband neglected her sexually. I recall one instance when three bully boys visited her at one time — while her husband dallied with his houseboy nearby. And she must have known about that.

Surely, I reckoned, the magistrates who sent kids here thought we would receive only firm discipline and learn the virtues of peace and abiding by the law. They and most Australians would be disgusted, demand reforms, if they knew of the homo officers' regular buggery of boys.

But there would not be any raping of me.

Of course, some of the officers at Gosford were not brutal. But only one of them tried to prevent brutality. Once I overheard him telling an officer who had just backhanded a boy for a minor indiscretion that the officer ought not to do that sort of thing. This man with the guts to stand up to the brutes had little success, however. He was transferred to another institution.

It was the custom to test the mettle of new boys. This was done on Saturday nights — fight night. Several boys fought bouts in a makeshift ring, and the rest were allowed to watch. The combatants wore gloves and an officer refereed.

If a new boy showed fighting ability, the officers usually invited him to be a JO. It was important that the JOs were the best fighters. And mean.

I was fast and handy with my fists. Over several years, gutter fighting, which knows no rules, had become my specialty. But I could handle myself pretty well in the ring, with rules. When sometimes I fought a boy who was a good fighter, my determination not to be beaten won the contest for me.

I was victorious the first Saturday I graced the ring, and on successive fight nights I fought seven different senior boys in my No. 1 company. I beat them all except one, the ward captain. He was older and bigger than the rest of us. And he could fight. He thrashed me on four consecutive Saturday nights, but I lasted longer every time. None of the other bullies in our company would fight me any more.

The adult in charge of our company, despite my comparative lack of discipline, offered to make me a JO. I refused the job. Being my brothers' keeper did not appeal. This polite rejection attracted the ire of the officer. And I was a thorn in the side of my section leader, whose nose I had bloodied. He now did not dare impose his will on me.

I deliberately did not march properly. I did not hurry when making my bed or dressing. A glare from me was usually enough to stop him from bashing one of my mates. The now-sulky leader was in trouble all the time for getting poor marks.

Then, when he spotted me breaking discipline, the adult in charge called over the ward captain, the one who had out-boxed me. Nearly all the time, I scored a black eye or puffed lip.

In the name of sport, they got that big bloke and me to fight every Saturday. After six weeks of it, I was scared and knew the officer was trying to make me cower. He wanted me to refuse to fight. To show weakness in front of the company, but nonetheless become a JO.

I knew I could not beat the senior boy but made up my mind to give him at least half a thrashing. When I managed to land a punch, it hurt him. I concentrated on his face. A few times he wore a cut or puffed lip for a few days, advertising the fact that I was not defenceless.

Finally, the officer must have tired of trying to break me. My example not being favourable for the discipline of the others in No. 1 company, I was moved to No. 2 company, among bigger and older boys. I was out of my depth there. Every No. 2 bully was keen to prove he was my master. There was no end to the fighting. I was bashed, in varying degrees, many times over many weeks.

Finally, in bed nursing a sore head, I decided that I would take it no longer. The next day, section leader and chief bully boy Spike Kavanagh came towards me, grinning. His fists were clenched, ready to pound me.

'You lay a hand on me again,' I told him, 'and I'll put you in hospital.'

Kavanagh was outraged. 'You little bastard!' he yelled. He laid into me, knocking me to the ground. He dug his boots into my ribs for good measure.

The following morning, I awaited my turn to bat, then walked up to him on the cricket field. Without saying a word, I cleaved Spike Kavanagh's head with a mighty blow with the bat. He collapsed on the ground. I belted his big body, smashing down the bat with all my might. I did not intend killing him. I wanted to make an example of him to the other bullies, to let them know they could not belt up little D.D. with impunity.

Around the field, there was an outcry. My fellow prisoners on the field stood dumbfounded. But the other bullies and a couple of officers came running. By the time they reached us, chief bully boy Kavanagh no longer moved. His eyes were shut. Blood spurted from a gash on top of his head.

As bully boys surrounded me, I screamed, 'I told him I'd do that! There's more of what that rat got for the first one who lays a hand on me!'

The bullies in the circle dived together and wrenched the bat off me. They held me, but not one struck me. They must have thought I was a madman to be wary of.

Kavanagh was carried to the reformatory's hospital, where he spent two weeks. I was bundled, under heavy guard, to the administration block. There, two officers took me into an office — where the Duke sat glaring behind his desk.

'Mutiny!' the former serviceman screamed. 'That's what it is, you little runt. Mutiny, you bastard!' He was obviously using restraint in not leaping out and hammering me.

'I'll have you flogged,' he continued. 'Nobody gets away with that.

You think your junior officer's been hurt? It's nothing compared to what you're going to get, Dugan! You'll be flogged to within an inch of your useless life!'

Saliva visible in the corners of his mouth, he continued to rave as I stood across the desk from him, between the two officers. I was promised solitary confinement, a diet of stale bread and water. I was a gutter-bred animal, he said, and would be treated as such.

After a while, the Duke settled. 'These officers will take you to the cells, Dugan, where you'll get something you'll never forget.'

The night before, I had realised this would happen. Lying in bed, I had quietly rehearsed my lines.

'Just a minute, sir,' I said. 'I bashed that bully boy of yours because he was ill-treating me. I warned him what I would do.' I paused to let the words sink in. 'If you lay a hand on me, I swear, one day, one day, I'll kill you.'

My guts churned. The Duke sat there, speechless.

I added, 'Have me flogged, and one day, I'll kill you.'

I meant it. My time at Gosford had put me in such a state that I felt I had little to lose. If he had me bashed again, perhaps years hence I would terminate the mad tyrant.

Stilled behind the desk, the Duke stared at me. Dumb. Collecting his thoughts, I supposed.

'You'll kill *me*? I'll kill *you*, you little rat,' he bellowed.

For a few minutes, the Duke called me every name he could lay his tongue to. He ordered his officers, both looking startled, to lock me in the cells. I knew that they, too, hated their boss. 'I'll fix you, Dugan,' the Duke menaced as I went out the door.

I was locked in a cell twelve feet by seven. All my clothes, barring my shirt and trousers, were taken away. I lay awake all night, barefoot, waiting for perhaps even the Duke himself to give me the first of a long series of batterings. I had heard boys screaming from these cells. I had seen them afterwards, after time in hospital, patched up and eyes still black, teeth missing, bruises all over.

In the morning, the cell door was opened and a metal jug of water was placed on the floor near the door. Beside it they put a few slices of bread. All through that day, I waited for a flogging. I hoped they would use rubber hoses, not steel rods and batons. Or would it be fists and boots?

But they did not come that day, nor that night. Next morning, an officer again silently passed in bread and water and collected the stinking tin dish that was my toilet.

I spent seven days in this confinement and there was no physical punishment. I only lost a little weight through lack of food. When taken from the cell, an officer told me I would be 'unprivileged' for the remainder of my sentence. That meant that most of the time I would be on jump. When not jumping, I would cop the hardest work, including cleaning out the lavatory pits.

I saw nothing of the Duke except for his lectures on the quarterdeck. He must have decided I was a psychopath better left alone.

I jumped for six weeks. Every morning, every afternoon and then for four hours every evening, while the others relaxed in the dormitory until the lights went out at nine. Seldom was I away from the supervision of two or three bully boys.

Down, hands on the ground. Straighten. Hands high. Jump. Six inches off the ground. *'Six inches, I said!'*

I became a physical wreck and collapsed several times. I was threatened every time I got back on my feet. Prepared to take that, I snarled back.

I was cuffed, but not bashed. The bully boys evidently remembered well my threat on the cricket ground to kill the next person to batter me.

I became worried when they kept telling me the boy whose head my bat had split open was dying. In fact, he was rapidly recovering.

I developed amazing endurance. The killing drill on jump was not killing *me*. I could jump all day, every night. Thousands of jumps a day, despite being on a meagre ration of food.

The officers were clearly amazed, and disappointed, at the endurance, the physical condition, of this human spring.

* * *

Without any warning, the Duke left Gosford and a new superintendent took his place. My period of punishment was immediately terminated.

The new man was appalled by the brutality at Gosford. In an impassioned speech from the quarterdeck, he told us all — officers, JOs included — that things were going to be different. Bashings were to be cut out. Justice was to prevail. Honour and trust would be the order of the day. He was going to trust us, he said, and he knew we would not betray his trust.

But this good man, a real revelation to us boys, went too far, too soon. We nearly destroyed him, thanks to the poisoning of our minds by the Duke and his system. So many of us had become vicious, hate-ridden animals.

We despised all screws. We were not going to let Mr Simms, the new superintendent, put anything over on us. He was a screw, wasn't he?

After a few months, Mr Simms was in a sorry, disillusioned state. We abused every gesture of trust, every privilege, he extended to us. He trusted us and lightened the guard, so dozens absconded, only to be tracked down and returned within hours.

I appreciated Simms more than any other boy at Gosford because he had taken me off the jump. I could talk to other boys again, play games, read. I made no attempt to run away. I had only six more months to go.

I watched this humanitarian give way to despair and finally reintroduce the old system of violence and spying. And fear. No kidding, I felt sorry for Simms.

4

The highlight for me of this period was when, one evening in the dormitory, a boy called Billy, in a bed near mine, mentioned that he needed a haircut. But he was not satisfied with the standard of the kids who usually cut his hair. Billy was proud of his dark, curly mop.

'Who else can I get to cut it?' he asked quietly. I decided right there to have a crack at it. Why not? Cutting hair looked simple enough.

I drew Bill aside. 'Now, look,' I said, 'I don't want this to get around, or else they'll all want me to cut their bloody hair, but I used to be an apprentice barber. I'll do it if you like.'

Billy delightedly jumped at my offer.

I began cutting at the back, in poor light, but after a while saw his hair was higher on one side than the other. So I lopped hair off the low side. Then I realised I had taken off too much there. So back to the other side … Of course, the back section had to be brought up level with the shortened sides. But I took off too much at the back. To the sides again …

Billy nonchalantly sat there talking to me. I was glad there was no mirror for him to see the lopsided mess in. As I took off more and more black curls with the basic scissors and clippers, I began to worry. A few of the other boys came over and sat on nearby beds. All of them were watching behind Bill's back, smirking and nudging one another.

As I tried to level the back and side ridges of his hair, the scissors went higher and higher. Billy was shorn clean up to the crown of his head. Suddenly he stopped talking. His hands flew to the back of his head.

'Christ!' he cried. He lurched from the chair, frantically rubbing his baldness. The others were falling about in convulsions.

Billy swung around, his jaw sagging in dismay. 'Dugan,' he yelled, 'Dugan, you bastard! You told me you were an apprentice barb—'

His voice was drowned out by the others' laughter. Blimey, he looked a sight! Bald as an egg from the back of his neck to the top of his skull, like Yul Brynner. From there forward, a forest of black curls that I was about to lop. And poor Billy's face! A portrait of horror, it was.

I stood before him, fighting to keep my face straight. The kids thrived on the black comedy. It was rare refuge from general depression.

'You've ruined it!' Billy whined, not daring to find a mirror. 'Some bloody apprentice barber.'

'Don't worry,' I cut in soothingly. 'It'll be a real neat job. Now, I just want to take a bit off the front and —'

'You'll never get near my hair again!' Billy vowed.

At this, I lost my self-control. I turned to the others. They were pointing at Billy, still rolling on the beds with mirth. Their funniest time, it was, since they came to Gosford. Tears streamed down some faces. Laughter began deep in my belly. I could not control it. Struth, the sight of him. I dropped the scissors and clippers and flung myself on my bed. My body shook with hysterics.

The commotion attracted the attention of the dormitory's adult officer, who had been reading at the other end of the big room. He strode down, took one look at Billy's head and demanded, 'Who did that?'

'It was *him*,' cried Billy, pointing at me. 'Dugan did it, sir!'

The officer called me over. 'Did you do that?'

'Yes, sir. I meant well.'

Next thing I was flat on my back on the floor. The officer had planted one on my giggling chin. He abused me and announced that I was on jump. Right away. There on the floor, I suddenly didn't think things were so funny.

But as soon as I began jumping, looking across at Billy sitting on his bed, glaring at me and rubbing at the bald back of his head, my hysterics returned. I was jumping and laughing. I could not help it.

The officer came over and threatened to flatten me again. But it was no use. The laughter would not stop. Most of the other boys in the big room now also laughed again. The officer, I saw, was battling to keep his face straight. Finally he, too, let forth with hysterics. All of us were having a ball, except luckless Billy.

'All right, Dugan,' the officer declared. 'You can stop jumping. Get back to bed. But God help you if you ever touch the barbering tools.'

No one at Gosford ever asked me to cut his hair again.

The time was nigh, I figured, for my release. There were only a few days left, surely, before the nine months had passed. I had myself paraded before Mr Simms and asked when I would go.

'Darcy,' he said, smiling awkwardly, 'I can't really say.' It was the first time an officer had called me by my given name.

'But, sir,' I blurted, 'I was sentenced to nine months, and I've been here —'

Simms cut in. 'Yes, I know. But you have misunderstood the magistrate who sentenced you. Any term mentioned was not really binding.'

He went on to say that I probably would be kept at Gosford until I was 18.

'But, sir,' I countered, 'that's another *year!*'

I must record in his defence that Mr Simms went to great pains to explain to me how I must have misinterpreted the magistrate's remarks. How my conduct at Gosford determined how long I stayed there.

After nine months, the spectre of another year at this place appalled me. For all those months, I had so looked forward to my day of liberty. Of rejoining Mum and Pop and brother Tom, who had travelled to Gosford a few times to visit me.

'All right, sir,' I said to the superintendent. 'You know that while I've been here I haven't once tried to escape.'

Simms nodded, watching me closely.

'Well,' I continued, 'now I'm going to.'

The superintendent seemed sympathetic, but rightly warned me of the penalties for attempting to break out. In any case, he said, escape was impossible. Surely I knew that every attempt at it had failed. My mind, however, was made up.

My old schooldays mate Jimmy was now an inmate of Gosford, serving time for repeated thievery. Inevitably, a lot of kids of our ilk and environment turned up at Gosford. Later, in jail.

Jimmy and I were still good mates. As good as possible under the stringent rules at Gosford. But Jimmy did not want to shoot through with me. He was serving a short sentence and was positive of his date of release. Trying to shoot through from Gosford, he said, was too risky.

To belittle any kid who ran away, the officers called him a dingo. And it did require courage and the cunning of the wild dog to 'dingo it'. If any boy ran, the nearest JOs blew whistles. The dingo had a pack of chasers on his heels.

When they caught him, they looped a leather belt around his neck and dragged him back like a dog on a leash, striking him with fists and belts. Fine sport! When the would-be absconder was handed over to an officer, he was usually a bloody mess. Officers took him to the cells and beat him up. After a week or two there, and possibly a stay in the reformatory hospital being repaired, the boy went on jump.

I was a fair runner. Most of the bigger boys could beat me in a sprint, but I was a stayer. I could run all day, particularly since my conditioning on jump. To be able to stay ahead of any boy at the reformatory for a couple of hundred yards, I would have to get at least 20 yards start. If they did not catch me in the first few hundred yards, they would never run me down. I planned accordingly.

On the football ground a few days after my confrontation with the superintendent, senior boys, as usual, ringed it as a safeguard against escape. They stood about 30 yards from one another. I knew the superintendent had put out an alert that Dugan might try to dingo it.

I kicked the ball out of the field, close to a JO I knew was a slow runner.

'Damn it,' I yelled. 'I'll get it!'

The bully stood there as I ran past him towards the ball. Before he realised what I was up to, I had my 20 yards start, sprinting for liberty. I heard whistles blowing. Excited voices screamed, 'Dingo! Dingo!'

I put my head down and ran for all I was worth. I heard them running behind me like a pack of hounds after a hare, and yelling. It seemed only seconds had passed before I heard the thudding feet, gasping breath of several senior boys right behind me. I dared not look back. One or two were closing in. I strained, putting all I had into getting extra speed. For several hundred yards, it seemed they were only a few feet behind. Gasping for air, I thought my lungs would burst. I was not sure if fear was making me run faster or slower. Were they just playing with me? Could they pounce whenever they liked?

Gradually I drew away. At last I could not hear footfalls, only distant calling. 'Dugan! You come back here, you bastard.' I saw only one boy in pursuit. I continued well into bushland. The reformatory was miles north. Somewhere ahead of me was Sydney!

But I was not yet in the clear. There were only two highways from Gosford to Sydney and one railway line. They gave the only crossings of the wide, shark-spawning Hawkesbury River, which lay ahead. Whenever a boy eluded immediate capture, as I now had, I knew it was customary for officers and senior boys to stand guard on the crossings and along the two roads and the rail line for days. I could not wait that long, without food or shelter, in the rough country that separated me from the river. I decided to make my way, avoiding roads, to the rail line several miles north of the rail bridge. Somehow, I would jump aboard a goods train, perhaps as it slowed on a hill. Of course, the police would have been alerted, too. Plus the people on local farms, wary of dangerous young crooks on the run.

Sitting on a log in the bush, regaining my breath, I decided the best way to avoid being spotted was to cut across the mountain spurs that covered the miles between me and the Hawkesbury rail bridge. It would not be any more than 12 miles, but it seemed 100. No human inhabitants. All the way, it was up-and-down mountain country, studded with rocks, heavily timbered and with unending underbrush, thick as the wool on a sheep's back. I enjoyed creeping up on kangaroos, rabbits, kookaburras. I reckoned I could get through in a day and a night, with luck. If I fell over a cliff, broke a leg, too bad.

That mountain run took about 33 hours. I kept going all the time. Up steep slopes and down hills, tripping over tree limbs and loose rocks. There was no water. As I moved, I prayed to God my sense of direction would not fail.

It was winter, and at dawn a thin mantle of white frost covered the ground. I did not stop long enough to get cold, however. A couple of times I stopped to lick frost and dew from leaves to ease my thirst.

Late in the afternoon, I stumbled through a clump of bushes to the railway line. It was a wonderful sight. I lay panting on the ground for about an hour before thirst drove me on. I headed south along the line. I needed a hill where I could rest some more until a southbound train came along and, I hoped, slowed enough for me to jump on board.

I turned a bend. There at the track were about a dozen railway maintenance men. Tents were pitched by the line. They stopped and looked at me. Not having the energy to run away, I walked up to them, forcing a smile. My khaki clothing told them where I had come from, but there was no indication of them grabbing me, turning me in.

On the contrary, they gave me an old pair of trousers and a shirt, several cups of glorious tea, and an egg sandwich. Each man contributed a few shillings to help me on my way. One smilingly presented a small packet of sandwiches as he said, 'Good luck, young'un.' Those men flagged down a train so I could sneak aboard as it stopped. I completed my journey over the river and on to Sydney, the uninvited guest of the Minister for Transport.

Of course, once I was in the city I could not go home. The police would be keeping an eye out for me. And I knew that none of my other relations would want to have a thing to do with escapee Darcy. I did not blame them.

I spent the following six weeks in Sydney on the proceeds from my old caper, petty thievery. My only companions from time to time were a few prostitutes and some girls whom I sometimes spent a night with. Most nights I slept in a makeshift bed I assembled in an old excavation near Central railway station. The police caught me sleeping there, and back I went to Gosford.

You can imagine the welcoming committee awaiting me, perhaps rated the worst brat ever to reside at the Gosford juvenile reformatory. Few boys had escaped and stayed away from the place for more than a day or two. Understandably, the officers were anxious to make an example of this dingo who had. I spent a couple of weeks in the cells, was battered only twice. Thanks, probably, to new Superintendent Simms's restraining influence. Perhaps it was the memory that I appeared capable of killing my attackers.

After the confinement, I was taken out to the quarterdeck in front of the other boys.

'Look at him,' an officer bellowed, pointing at my bruised and bloodied self. 'This is what'll happen to anyone who tries to dingo it. This cowardly dingo, Dugan, ran away. He didn't have the guts to stay here and take the punishment at this school like a man. Well, he's being punished now like a dingo animal!'

The officer beckoned to a JO who held a pair of scissors and clippers. 'All right,' the officer said as the boy stepped forwards, grinning. The officer grabbed me by the hair and shook my head from one side to the other. 'Cut off the lot of it,' he commanded.

As I stood there in front of more than 200 boys, the JO went to work until I was nearly bald. A few kids sniggered.

The officer ordered me to take off my shirt. Another JO came up with an old football guernsey, striped green and gold. He ordered me to put it on. It was a humiliating experience.

The purpose of the haircut and donning of the guernsey was to make me a distinctive dingo. I was instructed to wear the jumper all the time, except in bed. I was going to stand out like an emblazoned country outhouse.

Two weeks on jump followed. This time, however, I was not preoccupied with counting how many times I thrust my body six inches off the ground. *Escape. Escape.* I thought of little else. I regarded the exercise as training for it. Another break would be even harder to pull off now, but it was justified. I had served my sentenced nine months and faced at least another year at Gosford. Perhaps longer, because I had escaped.

Every evening the boys mustered outside the dormitories and answered a roll call. Then we filed inside and were locked up until morning. A supervising officer remained in each dormitory until 9.30 p.m. A senior boy or two replaced him at a table near the dormitory entrance. The JO doing this was called the night records bully. He kept a written record of every happening through the night. If a boy wanted to go to the toilet at 1 a.m., he had to get permission from the records bully.

Each dormitory had its own small lavatory. The night records JO would write, for example, 'John Smith, toilet 1 a.m., sit-down, time taken 3 minutes, 35 seconds'.

I enlisted three accomplices for the break-out.

The dormitory windows opened only a few inches from top and bottom. They were covered by slats of wood a few inches apart. So a whole section of slats would have to be taken out and a big hole smashed in the glass.

Just on 11 o'clock, the four of us quietly sneaked out of the darkness and converged on the records JO, reading at his desk. I had a screwdriver, which one of my accomplices had smuggled from the carpentry shop. My partners had knives from the dinner table. One partner quietly grabbed the JO from behind and put an arm around his neck. The boy's other hand held a knife to the JO's throat.

'We're getting out,' I told the JO. 'Yell out just once and that knife goes right into you.'

I pressed the blade of my screwdriver against his chest for good measure, then looked up at my accomplice holding the JO by the neck. 'If he yells,' I said, 'kill him.'

The four of us had agreed most definitely that there would be no killing. But the JO was not to know that. My accomplice nodded.

By now most of the dormitory was awake. The other boys remained in their beds, watching silently in the filtered moonlight. Most of the lads, I was well aware, would be plugging for us. Some would be against us. Or at least they would raise an alarm for their own selfish ends, if they thought they could get away with it. I turned to the dormitory in general and said quietly but firmly, holding my screwdriver before me, 'The four of us are getting out. No one else move. The first one to yell out gets this in the throat.'

My three colleagues, each holding a knife at the records bully, followed me to a window at the back of the dormitory. They stood on guard while I worked at the window with the screwdriver.

I had to make a fair amount of noise, first tearing off the wooden slats, then smashing the glass with the handle of my weapon, wrapped in a sheet. I feared an officer might hear me and raise the alarm.

When the glass was smashed enough, one of my partners slipped through and sneaked to the front of the dormitory. He was soon back, carrying four pairs of boots taken from where all the boys had to line them up before going in at night. We slipped into boots, jumped out, and were off. By then, several in our dormitory were yelling their heads off. As we headed for the outer fields, I looked around and saw an officer at the dormitory window, where lights flashed on. But the outcry was too late. We were into the darkness.

We four knew we could not get far in the bush at night and did not even try. About 1 a.m. we emerged at the side of the highway to

Sydney, a couple of miles south of the reformatory. We planned to follow the road through the hills to near the Peats Ferry crossing of the Hawkesbury, where today there is a bridge. It was a lonely stretch of road. No houses. Just bush on both sides.

I knew the road would be patrolled within 30 minutes of our escape, but that did not concern us. It was a clear and still night. The lights and sound of a vehicle would announce its coming well in advance.

We hid in bushes beside the road as several cars went by. A utility from the reformatory stopped only a few hundred yards ahead of us, and a group of people got out and entered the bush. The utility went on. Obviously, the group was assigned to wait in the dark, pounce if we happened by.

We detoured well into the vegetation behind them, delaying our flight by about an hour. We arrived at the river just after dawn. It was wide and deep. A strong current was running. And besides, the Hawkesbury was infamous for its sharks. Sharks that could eat little boys, we had often been warned.

Days at Manly beach truanting from school had made me a reasonably strong swimmer. But two of the others were not.

'Darce, can we steal a dinghy?' a non-swimmer asked.

We turned a bend in the river, and there, anchored only 30 yards from the shore in a small inlet, was a motor launch about 18 feet long. We broke a long limb from a sapling and I swam to the launch, dragging the makeshift pole behind me. Aboard the craft, I let go the anchor rope and poled the craft to my mates.

As we half poled, half paddled with planks, the current took us nearly a mile downstream. For a while we feared we would come across the ferry that operated down there. But we made it across the wide stream, chuffed to be in comparative safety.

After an hour of hiking through the bush, we jumped a ride to Sydney by train. That night we broke into a store, got a change of clothes. I was glad to dump that football guernsey in a rubbish bin, put a cap over my still-short bristles.

More importantly, a till in the store contained about £200. The next day, a moll I knew fronted for us and rented a house in the inner eastern suburb of Paddington.

We four escapees ran wild, and raved over a newspaper report of our mass escape from Gosford and the wide search for us. We burglarised places nearly every night, smashing windows, grabbing what we could. We loaded up with furs and cosmetics, which prostitutes bought from us for half the retail prices. Tilly Devine was proud of us.

Our house became crammed with stolen stuff. Not believing in buying food, either, we stole a utility and raided a grocery store, leaving with the ute laden with enough food to last us for months.

My three pals, having plenty of money, soon had a girl each to live with us. We needed the girls. Before they moved in, the place was like a pigsty. I did not have a girl in the house. I had met a cute little number who attended to my sexual needs. But she lived with her family and would not leave them.

The three girls my pals shacked up with had run away from home. They knew where we were from. We gloating renegades were so proud that we were successful dingoes. Perhaps we secretly knew we would be caught if we kept up our high rate of crime and living. It was sure a change from Gosford.

One of the boys caught venereal disease from some stray moll he picked up in the street. He gave the infection to his girl at the house. The girl was secretly letting one of the other boys lay her as well. This was breaking one of the few laws of our establishment. In turn, the boy laying two girls gave VD to his regular girl. When the disease became evident, and it was realised that two of the boys and all three girls had VD, there was one hell of an argument and fight. The living room was wrecked.

A woman neighbour yelled through the window that she had called the police. The seven of us took off into the night, never to be all together again.

A few nights later, the police caught me burgling a store in the city. At the police station, I was identified as an escapee from Gosford. The next day, I appeared in the Children's Court.

By sheer chance, I copped the very same magistrate who had initially sent me north. He gave me a verbal dressing-down and told me I would be going back to Gosford. He had seen on my record sheet that I had previously escaped from the reformatory. But, more importantly, I felt I had a matter to clear up with this gentleman. And what did I have to lose now by speaking up?

'Your Worship,' I said, 'it is useless sending me back there, because I will not stay there. I must tell you that I will use whatever means necessary to get my liberty.'

I felt quite pleased with the terminology. I did not impress the magistrate, though. As he grew red in the face, about to thunder at me, I continued my little speech. 'You sentenced me to nine months up there and I served that time without trying to escape. I escaped only after appealing to the officer in charge and being told I had another year to serve. 'Your Honour, I think I have a right to be released.'

I knew that this last bit was asking too much, seeing that I had just been arrested under highly suspicious circumstances. But what the hell!

'You are a highly impudent youth,' the magistrate snorted. 'The department has ways of dealing with characters like you —'

'I won't stay up there,' I cut in. 'I should have been released after nine —'

The magistrate blew up. 'In that case,' he said, 'I'm sending you to a place where you will *stay*, young man. I'm sending you to *jail*! See if you can get out of *there*!'

If only he had known what the future held.

A policeman bustled me out of the courtroom and back to the Albion Street Children's Shelter. Despite a façade of bravado, I was scared stiff. *Jail!*

I had been in the shelter only about an hour when I was returned to the court. What the blazes was going on now? I wondered fearfully.

The magistrate, as it turned out, was a real trump. He addressed me in a mild manner. He even smiled. 'I have further examined your papers,' he announced. 'In no way can I condone your behaviour, young Dugan, but it does seem that there has been a degree of misunderstanding. I now have a better appreciation of your resentment. However, especially in view of the fact that you have broken the law since escaping from the reformatory for a second time, I cannot release you.'

He looked down at me closely, then leaned forward and asked, 'Would you be prepared to return to Gosford? If you return there, and behave, I am prepared to do what I can to secure your release within a reasonable period.'

I really warmed to the old fellow. He was being as lenient with me as his office would allow. Not accustomed to that sort of courtesy, I was close to tears. Embarrassed, I looked to the floor. However, regardless of this man's good intentions, I knew what awaited me at Gosford. I had no intention of willingly enduring further humiliation and pain there. I quietly, stumblingly, told the magistrate I appreciated his offer. But, I said, I could not promise not to try to break out of that reformatory again. It was a brutal place, I added.

The magistrate pondered over this for a little while. The Child Welfare Department officer standing near the front of the court looked strangely at me.

'Look, young man,' the magistrate said, 'say I sentence you to nine months' imprisonment and recommend that you spend it at an adult prison farm? Would you stay there?'

'Would I definitely be released after nine months?'

'Yes, providing you obey the rules. In fact, for good conduct you would get a couple of months off.'

This sounded too good to be true. What was the catch? 'What about when I'm released?' I asked. 'Will the Child Welfare Department have anything to do with me?'

'No,' the magistrate said adamantly. 'That would be it. You would be on your own. Free.' He looked down at my stern young face and grinned. 'But never engage again in robbery. Not in any crime, Mr Dugan.'

'Then it's a deal, Your Worship,' I announced. 'Thank you. Please send me to the adult prison camp.'

'You promise to stay there?'

'I do, sir.'

5

Before going to the camp, it was necessary to spend several weeks at the State Penitentiary, New South Wales's principal jail for men and women, in the suburb of Malabar, north of the entrance to Botany Bay. It struck me as a big, bleak complex, sorely overcrowded.

Australia's first white settlers, heavily outnumbered by soldier guards and convicts who arrived chained in the holds of ships, came initially to this bay from England. The penitentiary, near an inlet called Long Bay, is generally known as Long Bay jail.

Honestly, after a few days as probably the youngest prisoner at Long Bay, aged just 18, I wished I was back at Gosford. The food was putrid. Usually the meat was rotten, sometimes flyblown. I could not eat it. The men who did eat it suffered chronic diarrhoea. I subsisted daily on one large slice of bread and a dixie of cornmeal porridge each morning, a few unwashed boiled potatoes and cabbage for lunch. Another dixie of porridge at night. Like nearly everyone else, I was hungry all the time. When issued with my slice of bread, I ate it immediately. I had to. If you left a slice of bread in your cell, some hungry prisoner would steal it.

An older prisoner came up and confidentially told me he worked in the bakery. 'You seem a decent kid,' he said. 'It's not fair, you being stuck in here with all these bastards.'

The next day, the con came to me again. From under his blue prison shirt, he proudly produced half a loaf of fresh bread. I attacked it like a starving wolf eating a lamb. What a wonderful fellow he was! I knew that if he was caught smuggling bread out of the bakery he would be sent to the Black Peter, the dark and solitary confinement cell for prisoners getting special punishment. He would cop at least a week there on bread and water. He would also lose forever the privilege of working in the bakery.

I considered myself pretty lucky to have such a friend. Until one day he called me into a cell while the turnkey was absent. The con tried to put his arms around me and kiss me, as if I was a girl. I reeled back in shocked horror.

'Come on, young Darcy dear,' he whined. 'Be good to me and I'll be good to you.'

So this swine was a queer. He had thought he could buy my body for a few chunks of bread. 'No!' I cried. 'I'm not like that. No, get away!'

The man was much bigger than me. He lumbered towards me as I backed to the wall of the cell. I struggled to push him away, disgusted, afraid and ashamed. The con hung on to me. He undid my belt. He tore the buttons off the fly of my trousers. I lurched forwards, and fell to the floor. The con sprang on top of me. I wrestled with him all over the cell floor.

My pride would not let me cry for help. I felt so ashamed that anyone would think I could be used by a homosexual. We continued to wrestle on the floor, by now both covered in sweat. Panting heavily, the con pulled down my trousers a little, and I felt the hardness of his penis against me. I felt desperate. My strength waned. How much longer would I hold him off?

'Come on, dear Darcy,' he kept saying, 'I won't hurt you. Nobody will ever know. Haven't I looked after you?'

'Bastard!' I yelled. 'Let me go.'

The con began to curse me. 'You're just a cheeky little rat. Ungrateful. Even if I have to knock you out, I'm going to fuck you.'

I clawed at his face. My nails sank into one of his eye sockets. The con's hands went to his face and I broke free. But he was quickly on his feet. He stood, poised, between me and the cell door. I went to hitch up my trousers, and he lunged at me.

I dodged aside, grabbed the cell's wooden stool. Before my attacker turned around, I raised the stool above my head and swung it with all my might at the side of his head. He screamed like a stuck pig and sank to his knees.

I went for him again, the stool swinging. I crashed it down on him again and again. Blood spurted through his fingers, clasped over his head. I cried with rage at this filthy animal. At that moment, I wanted to seriously maim him.

'No, no, no!' he cried.

He was unconscious and I was kicking his head when two other prisoners, cell-block sweepers, rushed in and pulled me off him. One sweeper took me to the washbasin, where I tidied myself.

A turnkey arrived. He must have been told what had happened. After grimly looking at me without speaking, he went into the cell to examine the homosexual. The turnkey returned to the washroom a few minutes later. 'Are you all right?' he asked.

I nodded. He looked at my buttonless trouser fly, knowingly. 'I understand that con in the cell fell down the stairs. Is that right?'

I nodded again.

'You sure?'

I was still too ashamed and upset to speak coherently. I nodded again.

'All right,' he said. 'That's what you tell me. Stick to that. That bastard's been asking for this.'

The turnkey turned and walked out. It was the end of the matter. The screw did not want any trouble from his seniors for not being nearby to hear the altercation. My attacker was not charged but was laid up, 'sick in cell', for a week.

And I remained too ashamed to talk about it. Every other prisoner, and most of the turnkeys at the Bay, knew I had nearly been raped, though. The episode had one good result. The word went about that I was dangerous. 'Don't try anything on the young little brawler.'

I vowed that for the rest of my life — perhaps inside jails, perhaps outside — I would do all I could to protect kids from unwelcome advances from queers.

6

I was content to serve nine months at the prison farm at Emu Plains, then a pleasantly rural spot by the casual Nepean River, 90 minutes' drive west of Sydney. This centre was, still is, run by the state Department of Prisons. Never again would I be in the hands of the Child Welfare Department.

The inmates there were mostly young men who had committed minor misdemeanours. I was the youngest resident, but no one tried to exploit that fact by making things tough for me. The place did not have one poofter. Life was reasonably strict but it compared very favourably with Gosford. There was no officially organised, sponsored spy system, for example. No military-style marching and parading.

But there was no remission of my sentence. That was okay, though. On any day, I could have escaped, had I wanted to. I obeyed the rules and was released in mid-1939, as promised, aged 19. I had taken my punishment and owed nothing to society.

At Emu Plains, and especially at Long Bay, I had met many experienced crooks: smash-and-grab specialists, pickpockets, safe-blowers, gunmen. From each of them there was something to learn. Especially from the safe-blowers and lock specialists.

Now I would be a smarter crook, while staying with a happy Pop and regularly seeing Mum. I pulled off assorted robberies, mostly working alone, and began living pretty well on the proceeds.

There was a fair amount of dancing, too. I filled in a lot of time teaching at some dance studios. I had revelled in my aptitude for it since showing off at dances at primary school. And I had loved taking some of my usherette clients — and Tilly Devine twice — to dance studios.

With various partners, I won several prizes at dancing contests at suburban halls. I was banned from competing at some regular events after winning a few times.

There were plenty of clothes, plenty of women, plenty of money. Plenty of laughs, too, at the police, after I successfully completed a piece of thievery.

Until, inevitably, they caught me.

I had been out of Emu Plains less than a year when I was sent to Goulburn jail, 150 miles west of Sydney, for 12 months. Then out again, back to the robbery game, and into the long, waiting arms of the law.

Another 12-month term followed, this time at the prison farm at Oberon, a bleak little farming centre out west again, on the far side of the Blue Mountains.

By the time I was released, in December 1941, I was aged 21 and World War II raged in its third year. The Japanese had just attacked Pearl Harbor, and I wanted to help keep them and the Germans in their places. I must confess that my burst of nationalism was not associated with any moral reformation on my part. It was more that one who has been in prison usually has a greater sense of the value of freedom and prevention of oppression.

At a call-up centre at Woolloomooloo, I volunteered to join the Royal Australian Air Force. My mechanical ability would be useful there, I felt. And, like any youngster, I wanted to become a pilot. After they took my particulars, the RAAF men said they would advise me whether I was accepted.

Wanting to do my bit for the war, but wary that the RAAF would find out about my life of crime, I strolled a few blocks hoping to catch up with my favourite brothel madam, Tilly Devine. After my year locked up at Oberon, the buxom brunette from before and during the Gosford days was what I needed. I had never seen her go off with a customer at a brothel. The owner of 20 of them was probably above that. But she used to like me, had turned it on for me a couple of times for nothing, when I was supplying her pros with shoplifted merchandise and taking her to dance studios. I did not like her habit of calling me 'kid', however.

I reached Palmer Street mid-afternoon, too early for most of the girls to be flaunting themselves at the doorsteps. I stood in front of the old terrace house where I first talked to Tilly. Feeling awkward and hoping to hell that the old house of sex was still in business, I knocked on the door. The city smelled of dust, garbage and car fumes — nasty and foreign to me after Oberon.

A car cruised along the street. 'Getting in before the rush, cock?' one of several youths in it yelled. I ignored him. Maybe he was right.

Even if Tilly was not there any more, other prostitutes would be working. I ought to know some of them. In my trouser pocket was a roll of money I had hidden at Pop's place before being taken to Oberon. If necessary, I could pay for the best in the house.

The door opened an inch. And the head that cautiously peered through the crack belonged to Tilly. She recognised me in a flash. 'Kid!' She opened the door right back. 'Come in. Where you been, kid?' Her face showed real warmth. 'Darcy, isn't it? Come on in. Don't just stand there, luv.'

To a healthy young man just out of custody, Tilly's full figure, poured into a thin and low-cut black dress, conjured a hundred delightful visions. 'I've been away,' I blurted. 'In the bush.'

'Didn't get into trouble, did you, luv?'

My awkward look must have told her I did. Tilly closed the door behind me and led me into the familiar old lounge room. She introduced me to two young girls I did not know. They sat on the same old couch with cigarette burn marks.

Tilly was an understanding woman, generous to people she liked. Endowed with a direct nature. 'You must have been away a good year,' she opined after a little while. 'And not one woman?'

'I thought of you a lot, though,' I said, grinning eagerly.

'And you want to blow the cork off?'

I nodded. Tilly sat alongside me on the couch and put my hand on her lap.

'Well, you name it, luv. A couple of hours if you like. And don't you dare try to pay a penny. Me? Or one of these two young ones?' The other two prostitutes nonchalantly sat across the room, smoking.

'No, Tilly,' I said quietly. 'It's *you* I want.'

She sent me into her room to undress. She'd be in soon, she said. When Tilly came in, she stood still and let me undress her. We had just reached the bed — I felt as if I was burning all over, my pulse racing — when Tilly coughed.

The door burst open. I spun around. The other two girls, stripped bare as the morning sun, ran in towards us. Laughing, they jumped on the bed beside me. Tilly took one look at my bewildered face and laughed delightedly. A great organiser was Tilly.

The boys back at Oberon would never believe it.

Only a week later, while waiting for word from the RAAF, concerned at the depressing war news, I was drafted into the army. I went to its training centre at Cowra, the best part of a day's train ride west, way beyond the Blue Mountains.

I didn't mind. The RAAF would still be evaluating my aptitude test. If the RAAF accepted me, I thought, that's where I would go.

The town housed, behind high barbed wire, an enormous camp for more than 10,000 mostly Japanese and Italian prisoners of war. Their living conditions seemed to be okay. I had little to do with the camp but felt a bit sorry for a few English-speaking Italians I was able to yarn to, and deliver some war news to, through the wire. I automatically sympathised with any sort of prisoner.

I had been at Cowra seven days when Pop, now living in the industrial and then-slummy inner-city suburb of Ultimo, telegrammed the news that the RAAF had accepted me. I informed my CO. But, despite my protests, the army refused a transfer.

'You're going to stay in this service and like it, until the end of the war,' an officer told me.

'Will I see action overseas, sir?' I asked hopefully. I felt I could be good in combat.

'Maybe,' he said. 'Maybe not.'

From then onwards, relations between the Australian Army and D.E. Dugan were rather strained. Perhaps, if the army decided that I would be a useless soldier, they would let me go to the air force. But alas, I spent most of my time on boring fatigue duties, peeling thousands of spuds.

General morale among the soldiers at Cowra was not good. There was a great deal of strife between the officers and men. In three months, 100 men went AWOL.

I stuck it out for a while but saw finally that I would never be allowed to join the RAAF. Nor was I likely to join the combat against the Japanese or Germans. So I, too, shot through. Much as I wanted to fight my country's enemies, it was likely that I would have spent the rest of the war peeling spuds.

My flight from Cowra, by train, was well before the mass breakout by at least 545 prisoners on 5 August 1944.

Back in Sydney, I could not, of course, get a work permit. So no job.

I went to crime, specialising in solitary cat burglary. With the moonlight glimmering on wonderful Sydney Harbour, I sneaked up vines, onto balconies, through windows and into some of the most lavishly appointed homes in the fashionable eastern suburbs of Vaucluse, Rose Bay, Darling Point and upper-crust Bellevue Hill.

Generally I worked early, before midnight, when people were more likely to be out; my initial check of a garage indicated whether the residents were at home. There were a lot of sounds before midnight, too — radios, traffic — so noise from me then was not so likely to attract attention. And a man walking alone before midnight would not attract the interest from patrolling police as one would at, say, 2 a.m.

After a while, I seldom had to bother climbing to upstairs landings or bust windows. With some elementary equipment, I opened most homes' front and back door locks in less than a minute. To an inquisitive neighbour, I would appear to have the very right key.

I was at the front of a mansion in Vaucluse, the morning newspaper still on the front path, a couple of letters in the box by the gate. The curtains were drawn. I had just slid the bolt of the door lock back when a lady popped her head over the side fence.

'Mrs Donaldson is away for the weekend,' she called politely. 'Was she expecting you?'

'Not really,' I replied, honestly. 'There's something inside I want to collect, though.' The door opened.

'Oh, so you've got the key?' the woman continued.

'Actually, I'm breaking in,' I said with a laugh. The woman thought it was a lovely joke. 'Do tell Mrs Donaldson I called,' I added, and went inside.

As I walked out along the front path an hour later, both arms laden with merchandise, the lady neighbour waved goodbye. 'Can I give Mrs Donaldson your name?' she called.

'Sure, it's Rob Jolly.'

A few nights later, an accomplice and I burgled a house in the suburb of Woollahra. The place looked deserted and we turned on a couple of upstairs lights. We had pocketed a couple of diamond rings, a pearl necklace and £300 in cash. I had the light on in an upstairs bedroom, where the bed had not been made.

As I walked towards the dressing table, I saw a man's shoe sticking out from under the bed. Something was in it. A foot!

I stopped in my tracks. Was the wearer alive? I motioned to my accomplice and pointed at the shoe.

My first impulse was to run. The shoe moved. The fellow under the bed was probably more scared than me.

'Keep your gun handy,' I said loudly. 'We can blaze our way out of here if we have to.'

The poor bloke under the bed now must have been trembling. In true Hollywood fashion, I talked on like this for a couple of minutes as the pair of us packed our loot. Once in the hallway, we fled. I wondered how long the man remained under the bed that night.

Neither of us robbers ever carried a firearm. In moments of panic, guns can go off, as I was to bitterly learn. And if the police caught you with one, even though you might have no intention of using it, you faced a much stiffer penalty.

On another night in 1942, a chap called Roy and I were robbing a mansion in Rose Bay. We had ascended the stairs to the upper level when Roy bumped into a statue on a pedestal. It rocked precariously. Roy grabbed it so the whole set would not crash to the floor. Then, from a nearby room in darkness, came a woman's voice.
'Is that you, John?'
We froze. I cleared my throat and said in a loud whisper, 'Yes, it's me.'
Then, from another room, came a cry from a man. 'No!' he yelled, sounding hysterical. 'No, it's not me *at all*. It's not me. Oh, God!'
Roy and I hurried down the stairs and into the balmy night, laughing.

Soon after, again inevitably, I was arrested following a robbery and spent 30 months out west in Bathurst jail, a bleak and strictly run establishment near where I spent a holiday with relatives when I was a kid. It was the second toughest jail in the state.
Still, things were not too bad at Bathurst. I got to know some of the toughest criminals in the land. I learned more about beating the enforcers of the law. From, oddly, now I think of it, men who had failed.
After my release early in 1945, I wasted no time before returning to lawlessness. Thanks partly to my jail tutors, I was now considered one of the best tank men, or safe-breakers, in the trade. And tank cracking became my specialty.
I had spent hundreds of hours learning all I could about different locking mechanisms, the intricacies and limitations of a whole range of explosives, various types of metals and alloys used in tanks. Heavens, if only that knowledge and talent had been applied to legitimate pursuits! Even in surreptitious combat against the Germans or Japanese.

I sometimes showed friends how quickly I could unlatch locks, even got hold of a pair of police-type handcuffs and learned to slip open the catch. I mastered a few tricks I was sure no one else could perform.

In 1945, in a few months following my release from Bathurst, I busted at least twenty safes. I lost count. Sometimes my accomplices and I got only a few pounds. Sometimes thousands. Newspaper and radio reports told of a new, highly organised gang. Perhaps they were lock and explosives experts from the armed services, police reportedly theorised.

I hardly ever encountered a locking device I would not beat. My sole limitations were the availability of the correct equipment, information on how to get to a safe unobserved, and the time needed sometimes to work on a new lock. I will not go into what I learned. I don't want my autobiography to also be a guide for potential cracksmen. In any case, with the advance of technology, much of what I learned became outdated.

I was quite a lad around town. A lot of gambling. Snappy clothes. Plenty of girls. Dancing. Big spender Dugan. I was careful, however, not to be too flamboyant. That would invite the attention of the constabulary.

Nor did I mix with the group commonly called the underworld. My dealings with them, especially with fences, the people who bought and sold stolen goods, were brief and strictly business. That was safer, and the company of underworld types usually bored me. I still did not smoke or like strong liquor and, frankly, I found few things duller than standing around in pubs talking banalities or 'shop' with other crooks. A bit of a snob, I was, in the underworld.

And perhaps also Australia's best tank man, outside jails. Many crims knew how to contact me when there was a job they wanted help on. My square friends, including girlfriends, knew nothing about my criminal record or how I got money. Some thought I had an inheritance or rich parents.

But at times I earned legitimate money by teaching again at some of Sydney's dance studios. I was as light on my feet as ever and in 1945, as before, several lady companions and I were barred from dancing competitions after I notched up a win or two.

Most of my tanking resulted from information given to me by people who knew of particular safes that probably contained worthwhile hauls. The person usually detailed the layout of the premises, which was often his workplace, and knew if there was a burglar alarm. The informant would get an equal share of the take.

If the job needed three men, including myself, the informer would get a quarter of it. Of course, if the safe he promised would be bulging with cash was in fact empty, our informant instead got a bawling out. Sometimes a thick ear, too. But usually my accomplices and I had a pretty philosophical approach to that. Sometimes there was more loot than we expected.

A regular informant was Richard Gabriel Reilly. Dick later became one of the top tsars of Sydney's illegal baccarat and roulette casinos. He was a big, glib man, a snappy dresser, irresistible to many sheilas. Dick went to a lot of parties at the homes of the rich. If he noticed a safe or compartment likely to contain plenty of cash, he told me about it. He also knew the layout of the place.

A couple of times Dick put me onto safes in the homes of some of his wealthy lovers. He bragged about that, claiming that sometimes he squired a silvertail madam only until he found out where she hid her cash and jewellery, then telephoned a robber. I was his regular.

'Darcy, I've got ready that jewel box I promised you,' he said on the phone one evening. 'You know, with the old redhead who's married to a stockbroker?' Reilly's voice oozed satisfied vanity. We met so he could give me the details.

He gained thousands of pounds from my robberies.

I was still convinced that people who slugged away at dull jobs all week to clutch miserable packets of notes were dopes. I felt I had the knowledge, the ability and the guts to go out any time I liked and within an hour get more than most honest people earned in a month.

After celebrating victory over Japan and Germany, I considered warily that, with a formidable criminal record for a 25-year-old, no judge would go easy on me if I was convicted again. And more and more cops knew me by sight.

Late on Christmas Eve, 1945, an accomplice and I arrived in the surgery of a dentist in suburban Abbotsford. I was acting on information Dick Reilly passed along from Lennie McPherson, a long-ago mate from my childhood shoplifting days. Reilly had said the safe there held £6,000. It would be a big one. No burglar alarm to unhitch, and the safe was not new. Easy. We planned a quick job. Then, while the dentist sulked, we'd be off to celebrate Christmas. I had arranged to meet a girl at Manly at 11 that night.

My accomplice was Harry James Mitchell, whom I was destined to have a long association with. I had met Harry in Bathurst jail. He was a wiry little bloke and, at 21, was four years my junior.

I was about to tackle the tank, gloating over how easy this would be, when a voice thundered from outside. 'Righto, this place is surrounded! This is the police and we're armed. Don't try anything or you'll be shot. Come out with your hands up.'

It sounds like a third-rate Hollywood script now, but not so at the time. Flashlights went on all around. Harry and I surrendered peacefully.

As we rattled along nervously in the blackness of a police van, I wondered how long that girl would wait at our rendezvous at Manly, if she would then find another bloke. I wondered, too, if Dick Reilly or a confidant of his had dobbed us in to the cops. But if so, why?

Harry and I had no need to compose agreeing stories. It was understood that nothing was to be said to the cops without a solicitor present. Even caught in the act, I believed that statements relating to any charge against me should be reserved until I appeared in court. It was my code since childhood: tell the cops nothing. They would corrupt your statement anyway. I had suffered quite a few beatings, of course, but never had I undergone anything approaching what followed in the Burwood police station.

I was laid face-up on a table, my wrists handcuffed together in front of me. A detective grabbed each leg and two others grabbed me by the shoulders. In charge was a Detective Raymond Kelly, who had been in the force for four years. My criminal friends had told me that big and bespectacled Kelly was a dodgy brute. He leaned over me, his mouth split in a sinister grin.

'Right, Dugan. We mean business here, and you're going to write out a full confession to this robbery. You'll write it now.'

Foolishly, perhaps, I replied, 'Get stuffed.'

Kelly and the others laid into me. Handcuffed and pinned on that table by five big men, I experienced agony more excruciating than I thought a man could bear. My body was pummelled under a rain of blows, each one carefully aimed to cause pain but not to open the flesh. Bruises were more easily explained than cuts if the victim was silly enough to claim before a magistrate that the police had bashed him. Their favourite spot for pounding was on my breastbone. It knocked the wind out of me. I was continuously gasping. The detectives took turns at punching me. When one tired, he grabbed a leg or shoulder, and the cop he relieved there took over the assault.

Kelly grabbed my testicles. I yelped as he squeezed them hard. At the same time, an officer held me by the throat so my screaming was muffled. It would not do for the neighbours to hear that. I knew a criminal who was ruptured for life by this treatment from New South Wales police. My vision became blurred, awareness waned. I hoped like hell for the blessing of unconsciousness.

Every time the detectives seemed to know I was on the verge of fainting, the pressure on my throat and balls was eased. But the more torture I took, the more determined I became not to confess.

Tell the bastards nothing. Tell the bastards nothing!

Finally, Kelly must have realised I would not break. I was too weak to walk. They dragged me to a cell and hurled me to the floor.

Harry Mitchell later told me I had been away an hour and a half. It had seemed like days. The quiet and dark of the cold cell floor, after the glare of the light in my face, was heavenly bliss.

Then it was Harry's turn for the same sort of torture, which he took magnificently. He did not admit to a thing. About 3 a.m. on Christmas Day he was tossed like a sack of wet wheat, groaning, into the cell with me.

Through a small, barred slit high in the wall, we could hear the gaiety of Christmas Day parties in a couple of nearby houses. Maybe the police were particularly brutal that night because they were angry at having to be there at the station instead of being at such parties. Maybe. But they could have shortened the torture. Maybe they liked that recreation.

Later in the morning, Harry and I were charged with burglary and dispatched in a police van to Long Bay jail. That place and I were getting acquainted.

Escape. That word was uppermost in my mind as Mitchell and I arrived there. Somehow, I just had to get out. I had a long criminal record. The police had caught us cold. The sole way I could avoid my longest ever prison term was to make a break. I knew I had a talent for it, and talked it over with Harry. He, also with a reasonably long criminal record, felt similarly. Particularly as he was madly in love with a young girl.

'I'm with you, mate,' he said, much more readily than I expected. 'You'll come up with something to give us a decent chance.'

If he got away, Harry planned to take his girl to another state, marry her and live in obscurity under an alias. I, too, would leave Sydney for good. I had some money stashed away and would use it, once the heat was off, to go to Ireland to live. There was always the risk of being shot dead in a break-out attempt, however.

I had a few possible methods of exit in mind. There were, and still are, several security kinks at the Bay. I continually looked for the best flaw. The police used to take their prisoners to and from jails and court in vehicles called Black Marias. Prisoners were locked in four metal compartments on each side of a central corridor, which was patrolled by a guard or two. I had noticed during trips in Marias that the thick wire meshes covering small ventilators on each side were attached to flat frames of steel. All quite secure. But … the frames were secured to the vehicle's panel work by a dozen screws. Screws with slots in their heads.

We would soon face charges in Burwood Court. And we would go there in a Black Maria. Now, if I could get a screwdriver into the van with me … If I remembered the size of the slots … The air vents measured only fifteen inches by eight inches. A tight fit, certainly, but two little chaps like Harry and I should be able to wriggle through. Should.

Sitting in the cell at night, I pictured the attempt, looking for weaknesses in the plan, anticipating how the van attendants would react if they happened to look out the side and see one of us hurtling to the road. I calculated how long it would take to undo those screws. I assumed the van would be travelling at 30 or 40 miles an hour, which in today's terms is up to 65 kilometres an hour. And we would have to go through headfirst. There were no projections on the outside of the van to grip, so nifty acrobatics would be required for our heads not to hit the road first. With that, smashed-in skulls. What if one of us landed in front of a passing vehicle? Splat. Just before flipping in the air and dropping, we would have to hang from the vent by our toes. What if the vehicle braked then? Or another one passed close by? Was there an extra security lock on the outside? Hell, I didn't think so.

Harry and I talked it over further in the remand yard and decided it was worth a try. If we landed unharmed from the Black Maria, we stood a fair chance of getting clean away before being missed. If we fled from the jail itself, there was more likelihood of a bunch of warders using us for target practice.

I had quite a few convict friends in the jail. One of them got me a dining fork from another cell block. Once the utensil was missed, the block it went from would be searched. And a close eye would be kept on the prisoners in that block. The convict who stole the fork, incidentally, had no idea of what I had in mind for it. I had him paid in tobacco, the main currency in most jails, and he asked no questions. There are ways of doing such things in jails. Several privileged prisoners — trusties — on various assignments were allowed to move from one section of the jail to another. They were handy messengers. Also, it is surprising to new prisoners how helpful certain turnkeys can be — especially if you can arrange for them to receive financial consideration for their efforts from friends on the outside. Not that there is no money in jails. If he pulls enough weight in a jail, a prisoner can accumulate quite a cache of hidden money.

I busted off the fork's business end and hid the flat handle in a slit in my cell's stonework, packed over by dirt and dust. Every night, careful not to make enough noise to attract a turnkey's curiosity, I honed the end of the fork against the stone. I also spent hours in daytime leaning against the remand yard's sandstone wall, quietly grinding the fork handle against it when the turnkeys were not looking. Fortunately, the Department of Prisons' eating utensils were made of tougher metal than found in retail stores. So I was able to get a fine edge to my screwdriver and still be sure of its strength.

We were due to appear in court on 25 January 1946. By the 20th, the screwdriver was ready. Once we had cleared the Black Maria, Harry and I would be about a quarter of a mile apart. In any case, we would attract less attention by making our getaways independently. The police would be looking for two men. We arranged to meet at seven that evening in a quiet lane off Broadway, near where it becomes Parramatta Road. If one of us did not turn up and there was no report of him being caught, we would meet there at seven the following evening.

Harry's girlfriend tearfully visited him and he used great restraint in not hinting at what was about to take place.

7

Early on Friday, 25 January, the attempt began. It was a magnificently warm and clear summer's day. Harry and I had been in the remand section at Long Bay for 30 days. Just after dawn, turnkeys bundled a mob of us into the Department of Prisons' security tram in the jail yard. The tram took us to the Darlinghurst Distribution Centre at the Darlo police station. Then we cons, due to front suburban courts, were taken in the big Black Maria truck.

Being on remand, we were still in civilian clothes. These police vans transporting jailbirds to and from courts, from one jail to another, had been designed with care. No one had escaped from one. Foolproof, they called them. Such vehicles had been closely watched and made more secure since Joseph Schmidt (alias Fitzyackels) and John Edward Hilton brilliantly escaped from a Black Maria in 1930. The pair prised up the vehicle's floor and dropped to Parramatta Road, Annandale.

Harry and I positioned ourselves in a queue of 20 prisoners so we would go into a small compartment in the Black Maria's forward section for the trip to Burwood Court. There we were supposed to face charges of breaking and entering, and of attempted safe robbery.

Our lockup compartment was the farthest from the police guard, Constable Robert Dawson. It was also on the van's left side — out of the driver's view through his rear-vision mirror. We were the compartment's sole occupants.

As soon as the vehicle moved, I slipped the screwdriver from inside my pants and went to work. Harry remained by the door, where he would see Dawson if he came up the corridor. Looking at them then, I figured there should be enough time to work on those 12 countersunk screws. The thick wire grille should fall off.

The metal slats outside the wire were hinged at the top. One solid bash should push them back. Should!

'For God's sake, be quick,' muttered wiry Harry, his eyes fastened on the grille in the door.

Finally, all the screws were out. I ripped away the wire mesh and heaved on the bottom of the metal slat. It did not budge. I swore quietly and pressed my shoulder against it. Was there another set of screws?

I drove the screwdriver under it and wrenched hard. Suddenly, the panel of slats swung back on its hinges above. Outside in Cleveland Street, houses were flashing by. Freedom!

I heaved myself up to the opening headfirst. My shoulders only just squeezed through the hole. I had to wriggle like a snake as I pulled and pushed the rest of myself through. Harry gave my feet a push. He was smaller. At least, I reflected, he would find it a bit easier.

Below was a blur of bitumen. We were going a lot faster than the later police estimate of 35 to 40 miles per hour.

When planning this, I had feared having my head bashed to pulp by a passing car. Or landing headfirst on the road and in the path of a vehicle. Or merely breaking my neck. Now, in the tension and haste of the moment, such considerations had vanished. I swung headlong towards the road, hanging from the opening by my toes. *For Christ's sake, van, don't brake now!* With the leverage of my feet and my fingertips on the smooth panelling, I twisted and flung myself away, flipping in the wind.

I landed on my feet, crashed to the road and skidded a few yards. I sprang up and stood in the middle of the road. Momentarily dazed, I watched the van speeding on. And there, protruding from the side, was good old Harry's head.

Several cars sped by. One driver hooted his horn, waved me off the road. Two elderly women on the footpath looked on, dumbfounded. They had seen the whole show. Suddenly, the suit coat came away from my shoulders and fell in a mess at my feet. The strain of the fall had torn apart the seam running down the coat's spine. I left it there and walked off, nonchalantly. My ankles ached like hell.

Dozens of people silently stood along the footpath, apparently aghast at what they had witnessed. Some turned towards me after watching Harry's head and shoulders, as the van disappeared along the street. I ran on the footpath, turned into Bourke Street and went straight to the home of a man I knew I could trust. He was Richard Lloyd Day. We had been buddies since we were inmates together at Gosford.

I had not been able to let Lloydie know I was coming, but he gave me a change of clothes and £10, despite his shortage of cash. The police knew Lloydie and I were mates and they would probably not waste much time before searching his place.

A radio newsflash told of our escape. No one had been picked up, so I knew Harry had got away. Radio stations and newspapers during the day told how the Black Maria had travelled on, all the way to Burwood police station. The hinged metal slat had dropped back down on the opening. Prisoners from other compartments had been dropped at Campsie Court but the officers on duty had not checked the other compartments while there. It was not until the van reached Burwood that the police opened the section where we had sat. Red faces. They had no idea for a while just where on the long trip we had vacated the vehicle.

Public amusement!

These vans were not so escape proof after all, a commentator noted.

After meeting at Broadway that evening, Harry and I went to a house at Redfern. The police, we were sure, did not know of our friendship with the host. We learned on the radio of the police raiding scores of possible hide-outs. The homes of friends and relatives were repeatedly searched. Mascot airport and other transport points were watched.

After two weeks cooped up in the house, the police search had eased and we were ready to 'work'. We had assured the host and his wife that they would be handsomely repaid for their risk. We would blow a safe we had been told about, pay our debts and skip the state. Harry with his girlfriend.

Our informant, to get a quarter of the proceeds, was Lennie McPherson, my longtime crim mate. Lennie, via Dick Reilly, had put us onto the job at the dental surgery. He had assured Dick that there would be about £4,000 in the safe.

Early on the morning of 11 February, Harry Mitchell and I, with two assistants, arrived in front of the Mansions House Private Hotel, in Elizabeth Street in the inner city, in a stolen Chevrolet. The safe was in the hotel's office. Our accomplices were Lloydie and my dear old schooldays chum Jimmy, still living on the proceeds of crime. The hotel's watchman gave us a bit of trouble, but he was quickly quietened when I flashed a .45 Colt automatic at him. It was my first crime with a gun, but little did he know that the gun was empty. It was Lloydie's gun and a good frightener. Me having the weapon assured that no one fired a shot.

We lugged the safe into the boot of the Chev and drove to a deep stormwater channel in the suburb of Haberfield. To nearby residents, the noise of the safe being blown open would sound like a car backfiring. The canal was an ideal disposal place. In the past year or so, I had dumped dozens of safes in there. All of them had settled deep in mud. With gelignite I blew the tank open in a few minutes. But! Inside was a mere £241. We swore at informant Lennie's expense. We might have done just as well with a night's honest employment.

Harry and I moved into the home of a woman in Annandale, my schoolboy territory. The woman's husband was a criminal colleague, a professional tank man, in jail. I had known Jill from schooldays. She was a friendly girl, and generous.

The police, as reported by the papers, correctly suspected escapees Dugan and Mitchell of robbing the hotel and intimidating the watchman, who gave a graphic account of the episode. The search for us sharpened then eased.

By 17 February, we had decided it was safe enough to scarper to the relative safety of Melbourne. Harry and his girlfriend would get together there. Before leaving, though, he called at her home to say farewell. Visiting him in jail, she had had to give the prison authorities her address. But she had assured us that in the three weeks we had been on the loose, not a cop had been seen near her premises.

We knew they would watch the place for a while but the chance of them being there now, we reckoned, was pretty remote. She lived with her parents in a small apartment off a lane by Oxford Street, Paddington. You can see it coming, eh?

As Mitchell told me later, he left a taxi at his girl's front door, opened the unlocked door and stepped inside. There, sitting on the lounge talking to Harry's girl and her mother, were Detective Sergeant Jack Aldridge and Detective W. Linkenbagh. Harry recognised them.

'Oh, pardon me,' he said, stepping back. 'I'll see you later.'

He closed the door and raced back into the taxi as it was leaving. He ordered, 'Full ahead.'

'Who was that?' Linkenbagh asked the girl's mother, sitting there, thunderstruck. The police must have correctly interpreted the shock on the women's faces. They burst from the room in pursuit. Harry should have got away, but that lane happened to lead to a dead end. Harry, still in the taxi, was stuck there. The driver was not aware of what was going on. My trusty mate and his girl were arrested and quizzed at the CIB headquarters.

I was sitting at the table having an early lunch with Jill, about 11 a.m., when I heard a crash at the front door. It had to be the police. I dropped my spoon and fled down the back passage. To be confronted by three detectives, guns drawn. I surrendered quietly.

Jill was later charged with harbouring criminals. I am happy to add, though, that she was finally given a good behaviour bond.

Harry had not said a thing, and I could not blame his girlfriend for giving me up under pressure from the police, who threatened long incarceration for abetting escapees.

* * *

I was taken, handcuffed and under police guns, to a secluded room up several storeys at CIB headquarters. I knew what I was in for but was quietly determined, as usual, not to confess to a thing. No matter what they did.

The police had enough proof that we had done the hotel robbery. They had arrived at the hotel soon after we left it and also knew the safe was in the canal. Learning that confirmed my suspicion that someone was informing on us. We had not returned to the house at Redfern in case the informer knew where we were holed up. There is no honour among some thieves.

The police pretty bluntly implied that it was Harry Mitchell who told them where I was in Annandale.

'You're joking,' I said, and guffawed. 'It just wouldn't have been his girl, now, would it?'

Alarmingly, they knew about all our recent jobs, but I smiled my disbelief when they implied that Mitchell had confessed to those, too. Harry, meanwhile, was getting the treatment in another room.

We were 'questioned' for eight hours. Neither of us broke.

Later that night we were charged with taking the safe and, of course, escaping.

In Central Court of Petty Sessions the next day — Tuesday, 19 February 1946 — Harry and I demanded thorough examinations of our cuts and bruises by a doctor. We also wanted a medico to be able to testify in court that much of our hair had been torn out at the roots. A Dr English confirmed the injuries. But there was lively debate between Harry and me and the police over how, when and where the injuries were sustained.

We were remanded to face charges at Burwood Court. When there, we would also face the charges we were supposed to have pleaded to if we had not leapt from the Black Maria.

The arrests shattered my mate and recent helper, Lloydie Day. Years later, he died from a bullet in his head. It was fired by Detective Sergeant Ray Kelly during a car chase following a robbery. Kelly aimed his gun at driver Day and fired as the patrol car came alongside him.

* * *

Back at Long Bay, the warders were not pleased with us. But, I'm glad to report, there was no victimisation. After all, it was the police, not the warders, who had lost us.

I felt no remorse about bolting from the van. Cage an animal against its will, deprive it of its natural element and kin, and it will naturally try to escape — particularly if it can see a way out. The warders' job was to keep me in custody. My job was to get out. And I had already found another possible way.

It had come to me while going from the Bay to Darlinghurst in the prison tram. This, too, with its solid timber and steel sides, plus metal floor, was termed 'escape proof'. Nary a prisoner had been able to flit from it in all the many years of its service.

But what about the roof? Could a man get through it? My speculation, as I tried to remember the details of it, centred on whether the roof had a metal lining. I thought not. The outside was covered with painted canvas. The high, domed roof was lined on the inside with two-inch-wide slats of coachwood, about an inch thick.

Normally, a prisoner would never get through it. What about one with a saw? And how the hell could I get the right sort of saw? Even with one, it would be dicey.

The tram had six compartments. And right along one side was a corridor, which a couple of warders patrolled. Meshed windows gave them a good view of what was going on in the cells.

And how closely would they watch me in the tram on 4 March — only 38 days after escaping from a Black Maria — going to Darlinghurst before heading off again for Burwood? Still, what more did I have to lose? It might come off. If I got a saw I could hide on myself.

Perhaps it was possible to fashion a prison table knife into a saw. Those prison knives, like the forks, were of tough steel, and were much bigger than ordinary household dining knives.

As we paced up and down the remand yard, I sounded out Harry. 'Yes,' he agreed, 'you might pull it off, mate. But not with me.' He said he would go along with the pleas of his girl, who had visited him in jail the day before. He would see out his sentence. She would wait for him. And he at least could be confident of getting out some day a free man. By behaving himself, he would get remissions on his sentence. He might even be released inside six years.

In my view, six years was a long time. And the police prosecutors seemed to have a particular distaste for me. Also, my criminal record was far worse than Harry's. I could well cop ten years. An extra charge of escape or attempted escape should not add much to that.

A prisoner, again from another block, stole two knives for me by the same method that had been used to get the fork. He hid them in the jail yard. A big but fruitless search of the prison, including my cell, followed. They did not like prisoners having knives. When the pressure eased, I collected the knives and hid them in the flagstone floor of my cell.

At intervals, day and night, when warders were not in earshot, I clashed the cutting edges of the blades against each other. This made scores of serrations, which got deeper and deeper. Windy nights were best. I really went to town on the blades one night, when Mother Nature sent along a thunderstorm. I selected the blade with the deepest serrations, carried it under my clothes to the exercise yard at times, and rubbed it against the same sandstone wall on which the screwdriver was sharpened. The serrations acquired sharp points.

By court day, 4 March, a Monday, the tool was ready. Now, to smuggle it aboard the tram. The warders would be rather particular this time on the body search before I boarded it. Harry, who would go on the same tram, said he would help; we would use the same method we had employed to sneak out the screwdriver.

When prisoners left the Bay for court, we were filed into a hallway two abreast. We had to empty our pockets and take off our shoes. Warders examined every prisoner's possessions, piled in front of him. The turnkeys also frisked every con's clothing.

The sun was creeping up over the prison wall as Harry positioned himself in the queue directly to my left. I emptied my pockets, and the pair of us kneeled together by the edge of the mat to take off our shoes. The blade was up my sleeve. As Harry watched his right side to ensure that no warder was looking, I watched to my left. The coast was clear.

'Okay,' Harry muttered. I slipped the blade under the edge of the mat. It was a few inches in front of the shoe I was taking off. I placed my shoes over the blade and stood up. We were body-searched without incident.

Some other prisoners knew what was going on. In jail, every man with naughty intent must beware of informers, but in this case I needed to have a few in the know.

Harry and I again kneeled to put on our shoes. Using the same lookout system, as other prisoners in the know talked to the nearest screw, I grabbed the blade from under the mat and pushed it back up my sleeve. My neck muscles were taut with tension. If they caught me now, I had had it. I could see, too, that Harry was nervous. We all entered the tram at the jail gate.

I had positioned myself midway along the queue so I would be placed in a compartment amidships. That lessened the chance of guards stationed at the ends of the corridor hearing me at work. Of course, they could always start prowling.

A transport department driver and conductor were in the tram's driving cabin. Two warders, the jail recorder — who read prison records in court — and police constables W. Stop and Moylan were in the tram.

I scored the compartment smack in the middle, with four other cons. Harry had gone into the next section. Otherwise, he would be blamed for facilitating my break. As soon as the tram cleared the prison, Harry and two other prisoners, all in different compartments, followed our plan.

In his bullfrog voice, Harry began singing 'It's a Long Way to Tipperary'. Others joined in. Within a couple of minutes, the whole tram resounded to the raucous rendition. Two guards, going in opposite directions, passed my compartment. They were grinning. 'Merry lot today,' said one.

The tram's 25 prisoners, including a few women in a section at the back, began 'Waltzing Matilda' when I went to work. Few of the choristers knew of song leader Harry's motive. I blessed them all, the long and the short and the tall. No sawing could be heard above their cacophony.

The cons with me looked startled as I jumped onto the bench running the length of the pen and pulled the blade from my sleeve. 'The first one who squeals gets this in his guts,' I threatened. 'Tell me if a guard comes near.'

I thrust the sharp point of the saw into the coachwood roof, jabbing like a madman. Then sawing. The steel sank deeper and deeper into the timber. I feared it would strike metal. Suddenly, the blade burst through the roof. *Eureka!*

My four mates in the section now were caught up in the thing. They sang lustily, urging me on at the same time. Sweat oozed from my body. My knuckles repeatedly bashed against the roof as I frantically sawed away. Through one slab, then another. I had to cut a hole at least a foot square. The prisoners now yelled 'Roll out the Barrel'.

How long before we reached Darlinghurst? Where were we now? The cutting seemed to take an age. Actually, I cut a sufficiently big opening in 20 minutes. I dug my fingers into the cross-line I had cut. Bleeding now, they curled around the end of a slab. I pulled, and it snapped. Then another. Each broke where it met a supporting beam.

The biggest of the men in the pen pushed me through the hole. The tram was going along near Anzac Parade, passing Randwick Racecourse. Ahead was big Centennial Park. A grove of trees ran beside the tram tracks. Some 20 yards to the left was the roadway. I had timed it well. I crouched on the tram's roof to get my bearings. I was about to jump when I heard someone behind me.

It was Robert Porter Lewis, aged 18, out of the tram cell. He was headed for Central Court of Petty Sessions to face charges of housebreaking in Melbourne. 'Let me come with you, Darce,' he pleaded. 'I'm a fast runner. Won't get in the way.'

He was only five feet four inches tall. Slight build, like me. None of the others in there would have been able to get through the hole.

'You'll do better on your own, mate,' I said.

Lewis looked desperate. 'But I don't know where I am! I'm a stranger in Sydney. Can't you help me?'

I told him he could come along. The tram was doing about 15 miles per hour. At 7.45 a.m., we leapt from the roof and took off along Anzac Parade at a fast trot. Like a homing pigeon, I headed along traffic-free Robertson Road for Paddington, a couple of miles away. I had not been able to make any arrangements. But I had a friend who lived there. I needed a few quid. Quickly.

Meantime, an escorting constable inspected the cells when the singing suddenly stopped. And I had told the cons to keep singing all the way to Darlo! The constable took one look in my compartment and yelled to Harry Perry, the driver, 'Pull up. Two have gone!'

I later read how the guards searched the immediate area while police cars came in from all directions. They blocked off the area for a mile around. But young Lewis and I were already outside the net.

My fascinated friend at Paddington was able to give me a stake. Lewis and I went to the Empire Theatre, at the Haymarket in the city. Fortunately, none of my old usherette clients was there. We sat a couple of rows apart through two screenings of a shoddy western.

The period between screenings was spent in the lavatory. What better place to hide in a city when every cop is looking for you, every newspaper has pictures of you?

While Lewis and I were at the cinema, Harry Mitchell appeared in Burwood Court, was remanded on the old charges and returned to Long Bay. Prosecutor Sergeant Milne announced that Dugan had got away again. Harry was not implicated in the escape. 'But Dugan will not escape a second time,' Milne told the court. 'He will be given no chance again.'

He should have said a third time. Counting Gosford, fifth time.

Meanwhile, I later learned, the police were convinced the pair of us were holed up in Centennial Park, that big and, in places, heavily wooded public reserve. Policemen encircled it. Scores, some with dogs, combed the place. Launches searched the lagoons. I'm told the cops gave a couple of old deadbeats sleeping off the effects of metho a proper start when they sneaked up on them, guns drawn. The Centennial Park search continued until nightfall.

Lewis was as scared as a fowl in a fox den. But he seemed to be a pretty decent bloke. We slipped beyond Pop's place in the fading light and spent the night in the cabin of a truck parked in a quiet lane in Balmain, a couple of miles from the Haymarket. We did not dare visit any of my known friends — 'associates', as the police termed them.

The newspapers ribbed the searching police. The front page heading on the *Daily Mirror* called me Australia's Houdini. The *Daily Telegraph* said: 'The greatest manhunt in Sydney's history is the police search for Darcy Ezekiel Dugan, the India-rubber man, escapologist.' If the police grabbed me, that sort of publicity would not be in my interests.

An embarrassed Department of Prisons announced a coming inquiry into the escape.

8

It was too risky to spend the day sitting in a park or walking around the suburbs or hiding with associates. The best hide-out for the day, I decided, was in bushland near the Field of Mars Cemetery, Ryde, north of the harbour and northwest of the city. I knew the area pretty well, thanks to having played hide-and-seek there with a few mates when I was a kid.

Lewis and I were heading for the scrub after leaving a nearly vacant tram in Ryde when we saw a woman strolling along in the opposite direction reading the front page of a newspaper. Lewis was walking about 30 yards behind me. There was less chance of us being identified if we were not seen together. I was almost level with her when the woman looked up. Her eyes popped, then darted back to the front page. It featured pictures of Darcy Dugan and Robert Lewis. The woman looked at me again, with definite recognition. I walked on, then stopped in front of a shop window to see what she would do.

The next person she confronted was Lewis. She must have been in quite a state by then, but had the presence of mind to continue on as if she knew nothing. There was nought we could do about it.

I waited for Lewis. 'That woman,' I said. 'She knows who we are. She'll be on the phone to the demons any minute. We've got to get out of here. And fast.'

We walked off quickly to the next corner, into Gerrish Street, and sprinted. We had to put as much distance as possible, as soon as possible, between us and that woman. It was then that Senior Constable William McCracken roared up behind us on his motorbike. It screeched to a halt beside the footpath. McCracken, a fair lump of a fellow, leapt in front of us, gun drawn. He waved the barrel, aiming it from one to the other.

'Don't move,' he yelled. 'Not if you want to stay alive.'

Lewis and I exchanged quick glances and I nodded. We both ran, each in a different direction. Any second I expected to hear the crack of the pistol, the thud of lead hitting my back. Or head. I weaved slightly, kept my head low, and ran for all I was worth. But no shot came. Fortunately for me, McCracken took after my partner in crime.

Lewis was captured soon after by detectives who arrived in a radio car just after he had flattened McCracken by kneeing him in the groin.

The police, preoccupied with Lewis, did not get me. Already weary, I ran several blocks to Pittwater Road. I arrived there in time to board a bus heading towards the Field of Mars Cemetery. I don't think I could have continued any more than a hundred yards on my feet. My heart pounded like a drum from the run to the bus stop. Crouching low to lessen the chance of being recognised, I slipped into a seat. Could I get away?

My chances had at least picked up. The bus was carrying a fairly heavy complement of women shoppers. And, when I looked up, nearly every one of them was staring at me. The conductor whispered something to the driver. Recognised again. But what could I do? Just sit there and hope. I was in no condition for more running.

The conductor walked back down the aisle and, for a fearful moment, I thought he would grab me. I would have been a pretty easy mark. As he drew level with me, I held out a threepenny piece and said bluntly, 'One section, please.'

The conductor's stride faltered but he kept going, making out he didn't hear me. I stayed on the bus for two more stops. Every person who disembarked, I was sure, would head for a phone. By the third stop, I had regained my breath. The Field of Mars Cemetery bushland was about half a mile down to my right. I quickly got off the bus.

I was within 100 yards of my goal — that lovely-looking bush — when I saw a vehicle a half-mile away, racing towards me, parallel with the perimeter of the park. It was a police radio car. I could not let it get between me and the bush. Summoning all the energy I thought I had left in me, I sprinted for the scrub, raced into the bushes a bare 100 yards ahead of the car.

I heard policemen yell as they jumped out and began chasing me. They would be fresh. I had no chance of outdistancing them. So I tried a ruse. I veered to the right and continued in that direction for about 30 yards. Then, a sharp turn to the left.

The police, continuing in the direction in which they had last seen me going, crashed on through the undergrowth away to my right. The sound of their charge grew fainter. I knew, though, I would still be lucky to see out the day at large. A policeman would have remained in the car, alerting his headquarters. Within half an hour, the whole district would be surrounded.

I later read that my assumption was correct. Every policeman within five miles of the place rushed to the scene. A squad of searchers heavily armed and with Alsatians was dispatched from police headquarters. And, I found out later, every Sydney radio station issued warnings to residents at Ryde, as if I was a rampaging killer.

Experience had taught me that the police would be telling people I was probably armed and, if cornered, would shoot. That sort of talk was ridiculous, as I had never fired a gun in my life other than during many sessions of practising in the backyard at home with Pop's revolver and hunting rifle. Nor had I injured anyone other than brawling kids, attacker custodians and a Long Bay poofter. The inevitability of such warnings made me fearful. It was likely that some nervous policeman would shoot to kill as soon as he spotted me.

I ran on through the bush for at least a mile. Finally, I squatted like a rabbit, in thick scrub. I remained there an hour. The sound of the hunt, of Alsatians whining and barking, was all around. Sounds carried a long distance on that clear and windless day. The Alsatians did not worry me. Good watchdogs, I believed, but they were useless in a manhunt until the quarry was sighted. That belief has since been proven correct and beagles are now used as tracker dogs.

With every passing minute it became more likely that the hunters would find my hide-out. Somehow I had to get to a spot they had already searched, and at the same time give them the impression that I was miles off.

At about 2 p.m., I sneaked to the back of an isolated house facing Barons Crescent, Boronia Park. I approached a woman in the garden. Her startled look showed loud and clear that she knew who I was. Fine.

'Excuse me,' I said, 'could you tell me please how I can get to the Field of Mars Cemetery?'

Doing a good job in the presence of such a reputedly ruthless villain, she politely directed me to the cemetery, a couple of miles northwest. After thanking her, I walked northwestwards into the bush. Not a minute would pass before she was telephoning the cops. And the searchers would converge on the cemetery.

I knew where the cemetery was, of course. Out of sight of the house, I turned south, towards the city. Sure enough, a few minutes later, I heard men yelling in the distance, then the sounds of cars moving northwest. I also learned later that the police launches *Osiris* and *Horus* were directed to patrol Strangers Creek, which runs into the Lane Cove River from Buffalo Creek, passing through the Field of Mars Reserve.

Soon after this, two young girls playing on the grass spotted me. Their startled pointing said they, too, recognised the big-time escapee. They quietly followed me from a distance of about 100 yards. At least that gave me another opportunity to mislead the hunters, who would soon know I was not at the cemetery.

I headed into thick bush and ran down a gully until the girls were out of sight, then doubled back up a hill. From a crevice atop the hill, I watched about 100 police, tearing about like ants, searching every spot in the gully. But I had to get a more permanent hide-out than this.

The bush had ripped my clothes and flesh. I was hungry. My aching legs, I knew, would not see me through another run.

Nearby was a big rock, one end of which was raised above the ground, leaving a wedge-shaped little gap under it. Using a small, flat stone as a shovel, I enlarged the space. Flying dirt filled my ears and nostrils, stung my eyes. Once I had dug a hole about a foot deep and several feet long, I crawled in and pushed loose earth back behind me, sealing the entrance, save for a small breathing hole near my head. I felt fairly sure that when the police reached the rock and looked under it, there would be nothing showing to make them suspicious.

Late in the afternoon I heard policemen talking nearby. A searcher stood right beside the rock and apparently looked under it. Knees doubled up under my chin, I crouched in what might have become my tomb, until about an hour after nightfall. I stalked quietly through the bush for a mile and then suburban streets towards Augustine Street, Hunters Hill. All was quiet, but a squad car would be at every intersection. Pairs of policemen would be sitting quietly under trees, listening and looking for any movement. However, I was so weary and hungry that I had to try to break out of the ring.

I sneaked by a police car in the shadows off Augustine Street and, I hoped, was out of the cordon. Plastered in mud, I was probably hard to see in the dark. But a couple of minutes later, a chap exercising greyhounds passed me in the street. He ran to the squad car. The police were beside me in a flash and I submitted quietly. It was 8.45 p.m.

It seemed an age ago that I had run from the jail tram. In fact, I had been free only 37 hours and 15 minutes. *Fool, Dugan!* I should have collected water in the night, maybe some food, and remained in the hole under the rock for a further 48 hours.

One of the arresting police was Detective Sergeant (later Inspector) Ramus, who the underworld feared as one of the most dedicated and efficient policemen in the nation.

The news of my arrest was flashed over the police radio. I heard scores of horns tooting for miles around from police cars that had been quietly parked around those hundreds of acres of bush. They were telling the good news to their colleagues out on foot.

Heavily handcuffed, I was taken to the cells at Central police station for the night. Next day, hands still cuffed, I appeared in Central Police Court charged with escaping. Then, in turn, another pair of handcuffs attached me to my old accomplice and fellow escapee from the Black Maria, Harry Mitchell. Both of us were charged with that break. Eight armed wallopers surrounded the dock.

Solicitor Phil Roche represented me. Pressing for bail, he said, 'I don't know how Your Worship feels about bail for Dugan. It seems that he always comes back. There is no fear that he will not appear.'

Neither Police Prosecutor Condon nor the bench was amused. Harry and I, after being on remand again at a very watchful Long Bay jail, were found guilty of the charges at Sydney Quarter Sessions on 31 May 1946.

Three years of maximum security followed for me at Bathurst jail, with a few bludgeonings from screws and a few attempted assaults by gangs of prisoners, all of whom wanted to brag that they had mixed it with Dugan, their notorious inmate. The con assailants, however, got wounds to prove it. But by the time I left Bathurst, nearly all the prisoners there, even some warders, were friends.

Several times I saw likely ways to escape but did not try. I would see it out this time. Once released, I planned to take an honest job somewhere, join the mugs. Perhaps I could buy a truck and operate my own modest business.

The thought of being genuinely free was exhilarating.

9

After those three years' jail — my fifth term — I told myself it was the last term. Aged 28, I had wasted enough of my life. I would work, save enough cash to buy a truck. From Pop's spartan old home in Macarthur Street, Ultimo, I found employment with PDH, a large food processing and distributing company, packing and stacking canned butter. It was dull and monotonous but infinitely better than pacing the floor of a cell.

I was satisfied, slowly saving money. I did not go out much. Most evenings I listened to the radio at home with old Pop. I was young and healthy. I longed to get out and enjoy life, but I was resolute. I had my notorious name changed by deed poll to Darcy Clare.

I had visits from many underworld pals who were glad to see me back in circulation. Usually, they had a 'job' they could put me in on — a tanking or a stick-up. I was friendly with them all but told them it was no go. No more 'jobs' or jail for me.

Most of them wished me luck and left me alone. There were, however, two who kept telling me I was crazy to give the game away, nearly broke and wasting my safe-cracking skills. 'Why not do a couple of jobs and get a stake?' said a mate, whom I'll call Larry in order to protect him.

'You were caught on only one job in a hundred,' urged another mate, whom I'll call Johnny. 'How about doing a few, show me the way, then give the game away? Anyway, do you think the demons will give you a fair go? Even if you're working?'

I knew I might have unwelcome attention from the police but hoped they would leave me alone once they knew I was living honestly.

I also owed it to Pop, now aged 78, to share a time of calm. Mum had kept on reasonable terms with him since the divorce, and I saw her sometimes at the home of relatives in an outer suburb. Much of the time she was ill in bed. The family told her I had been overseas. Knowing the truth might have killed her. Young brother Tom was the foreman at a brass foundry and still shared the home with our mother.

Pop had always stuck by me. In the dear old fellow's wonderfully sparkling eyes, I was an innocent victim of circumstances. I knew from the looks sometimes in Pop's eyes that he was happy and had confidence in me now going straight.

Larry and Johnny were of that rare type who belied the maxim that there is no honour among thieves. They had copped plenty of pain from the hands and weapons of the police. But neither had ratted on a pal. They were my pals but I was not interested in their proposals. They wanted me, master cracksman who could handle an emergency without panicking and shooting someone, to be their mentor in crime. They had several 'good jobs' lined up and, they kept saying, they needed me. Neither of them could handle nitro or even jelly properly. They were gunmen.

I was not surprised when several police visited me at home. I knew they kept an eye on ex-cons by paying unsolicited calls. Nothing could be done about that. And they soon accepted that I was going straight. The word had gone around. They assured me they were pleased about that. If there was anything they could do for me, just ask, they said. I thanked them politely, assuring them that I wanted nothing more than to live like other people, to be left alone.

Most of them did leave me alone. Two did not. These detective sergeants, whom I'll call here Gale and Malley, were frequent callers. They made it clear that they had scores to settle. They wanted my 'cooperation'. Which I call ratting, stooling on my former partners. I told them to forget it. They then offered me money and stressed how I could earn plenty if I was 'smart'.

'With all your underworld connections, Darcy, you'd have no trouble getting and passing on names to fit most major crimes,' Gale declared.

I repeated that I intended minding my own business, leaving others to mind theirs. They told me I was making a mistake, that squares had a duty to assist the police in every way. I did not dispute their claims, but could not do what they wanted.

'You'll change your mind,' said Malley as the pair left Pop's home. 'See you soon.'

A few days later, the detectives walked into the storeroom where I worked and spoke to the foreman. The foreman scowled at stacker Darcy Clare, looking surprised. Gale and Malley turned and grinned at me across the big room. The foreman gave me another dark look. He clearly now knew I was D. Dugan. I put down a case of butter and walked to the dressing room. I had not quite changed into my own clothes when a messenger told me the foreman wanted to see me in his office. Not wanting to be fired, humiliated, I walked off the job and never returned.

Feeling hollow and an outcast when I returned home to Pop, I could not at first tell him about it. Numb depression persisted. Eventually I told the dear old fellow. After getting over the shock of it, he was full of fight.

'I'll go to the bloody Police Commissioner,' he threatened, clenching his fists until his knuckles looked like white pearls. 'And I'll tell the newspapers. Those bastards can't get away with this. You've done your time for your crimes.'

Complaining would be useless, I told him. I had taken care not to let the police know of my new name and where I was working, but it was sometimes their job, I conceded, to let an employer know when a criminal was on his staff. Gale and Malley simply had been doing their jobs. Strictly speaking, I should have told my employer when I applied for the job that I was Dugan and once a crim, I soothed.

But really, I knew those scumbag cops were wreaking revenge because I refused to be their informer, denying them the chance to get some arrests.

Pop knew nothing of the detectives' entreaties to me to become a stool pigeon. I did not look for another job. It would result in the same sort of termination. Maybe, I thought, Larry and Johnny were right. One thing at least was clear: I was a marked man.

I began going out at night. I had saved a reasonable amount of cash, nearly enough for the truck. But who, I wondered grimly, would entrust his cargoes to D. Dugan?

Still as Darcy Clare, I became a regular at several dance studios. It was at one of these that I met a magnificent girl, June. She was a curvaceous but slim brunette, with clear, olive skin that had no need of cosmetics to enhance its bloom. A small patrician nose, lovely hazel eyes under elegant black brows, sweet and rosy lips just made for kissing. It was all set in a heart-shaped face. I was attracted instantly.

I am far from good looking, but found that sometimes a woman looks for more in a man than a handsome face. I suffered from no inferiority complex, either, so I had no hesitation in pursuing this lovely creature. I can't say cupid's arrow pierced my heart the first time I looked on June's loveliness, but it must have been close. And I had plenty of rivals for her attention. It helped that I was a good dancer. And I dressed well. I knew that clothes did maketh the man.

My motives in trying to win June were not absolutely noble. Every time I looked at her, my pulse leapt and I thought of bed. We danced many times during the evening. She had a fine, relaxed style. She had it all.

At the end of that first evening, I offered to escort her home. But she politely and firmly said no.

'Will you be coming to the studio again?' I wondered anxiously.

'I'm not sure, Darcy.'

'Well, I'll keep coming here just in case. Could I take you out some time?'

'I'm afraid not, Darcy,' she said, smiling gently. 'I don't know you well enough.'

'Well, could I write to you? Or phone? Surely there's no harm in me phoning just to say hello.'

'Well ...'

I got the phone number! I rang it every day and asked if she would go out with me, anywhere. At last she said yes, I could take her to the theatre downtown. This Cinderella had to be home by midnight.

This exhilarated pursuer did not realise at the time that he was falling in love. I simply wanted to get that sweet-smelling bundle of loveliness into a bed with me.

June was a lady in the true sense. I played the game cautiously; quietly confident I would bed her. I did not even attempt a goodnight kiss after our first few nights out. Just, 'Thank you for such a lovely evening, June.' Then, saying good night, I kissed her quickly and lightly on the lips. She did not object. Later, it was not so quick; then there were several kisses, affectionate ones. I was proud to be seen with the bright beauty.

One night, as she returned my kisses with sweet warmth, I waited for her to erupt in a volcano of passion. I had enjoyed reading some Shakespeare in jail and believed his: 'A woman's nay often means yay.' I respected a woman's right to say nay, but when June said that, I lovingly persisted.

Suddenly I got a sharp tongue-lashing. She proved she had intelligent control of herself, based on a sound, moral upbringing. We quietly walked to her house. It struck home that June meant more to me than a sexual conquest. Maybe I had lost her. Would she ever trust me again? At her front door, I stumbled out an apology.

June turned a clear gaze on me. 'It's all right, Darcy. I'm as much to blame as you.'

'Then everything's okay?'

'Yes,' she said and smiled, flashing those hazel eyes. 'But you must understand that I'm not *that* kind of girl. If *that's* all you have in mind, it's better if we don't see each other again.'

Soberly, I assured her that *that* was not what I had in mind. 'I think more of you than any other woman in the world, June. I love you. I always will.'

Of course, I still wanted the sweet delights of possessing June's body, but that night I knew I wanted more: a lifetime of the love and companionship that could be shared only with her. June responded so warmly that when we parted, we were secretly engaged to be married. She was 19, nine years my junior. I decided to get another honest job somewhere. One the cops would not find out about. I walked home to slummy Ultimo in an ecstatic daze.

Then in bed, I began to worry again. June was a truly decent girl. What would she say when she inevitably found out that Darcy Clare was Darcy Dugan, the Houdini, India-rubber man crook? One day we would be walking down the street and a detective would stop her and ask if she was aware she was in the company of a notorious criminal. They had done that before. It was part of the job.

I saw June every night at her home for a week. Her parents were warm-hearted people who made me feel welcome. But I had no illusions as to how welcome I would be if they learned of my past. At last I gathered courage and told June who her secret betrothed really was. I made no excuse for myself. June listened quietly.

Then she gazed into my anxious eyes and said, 'It doesn't matter, Darcy. It's in the past. It's the future that counts. I just hope to God that you don't do anything like that again.'

She pondered for a while and added, 'I still love you, but if I ever know you've returned to crime, our marriage will be off. I couldn't live that kind of existence.'

I was jubilant. We discussed our future together. We could get married very soon, we agreed. 'We can find a couple of rooms to live in,' she enthused. 'And I could keep working as a dress designer.'

I was awfully tempted, but I wanted to be in a position to care for her properly when the time came. And my recent splurging had taken most of the money I'd saved to buy a truck.

'I'll work and save like hell,' I vowed. 'With luck, we'll have enough cash in a lot less than a year.'

My parents were able to lend me enough money to add to what I had and buy a used truck. D. Clare worked it and began to do well. Maybe, I thought, we would not have to wait those 12 months.

June and I spent as much time together as possible. We would have enough kids to field a cricket team but accepted the probability that we would never be rich. One thing I had to accept was that she would remain a virgin until we wed. Sometimes this hot-blood carefully, but fruitlessly, tried to talk her away from that notion.

'Why wait? We're going to marry. I'd be careful, see that nothing happens. Do you know about contraceptives? Don't you love me?' And so on, and on.

June would gaze into my shifty eyes in a searching way, then laugh and play her trump card. 'Yes, dear, I love you and I'll marry you as soon as we get some money. Unfortunately for *you*, fortunately for *me*, I'm strong willed.'

All I could do was fall deeper in love, and work and save.

About this time, my mates Larry and Johnny pulled off a diamond robbery worth £5,000. It was a neat job with no loose ends. They were quick to point out to me that I ought to have been in on it. A third split of the take would be the means of immediate marriage. But I reneged when they invited me to be in another job being planned. I had something more precious than diamonds — June. I would keep my promise to her.

The police were running around, looking for the diamond robbers. I was the sole outsider, they were aware, who probably knew who had pulled the job. Stoolies could not tell the cops a thing. There was not even a possible lead from a fence, as the boys had the rocks stashed away, cooling off.

I copped another visit from detective sergeants Gale and Malley. Gale did the talking. 'There's a couple of hundred quid in it for you, Darcy, if you tell us who's got the diamonds.'

I knew nothing about it, I assured them.

'Maybe you don't know,' Gale persisted, 'but you could find out.'

I repeated that I was all through with the game. I wanted no part of it.

Then Gale got tough. 'If that's the way you want to play it then, Dugan, come with us to the CIB. Now.' There was no point in remonstrating. I thanked God that Pop was not home. At the CIB, I was taken to a private room upstairs.

'Dugan,' Gale said, straight-faced, 'this is the way we see it. We don't think you were part of the job but you know who did it. Even if you don't, you could find out quicker than any man in Sydney. You're going to find out for us, or ... see *this*?' He produced two jewelled rings and laid them on the table before me. 'These came from the same place as the diamonds that were stolen. We just found them in your pocket when we searched you.'

He grinned at Malley. 'Didn't we?' Malley nodded.

'And,' Gale said, 'you have just admitted that the rings are part of your share of the jewellery. That's how it is, Darcy. How do you want it? Easy or hard?'

They were not bluffing. I had been planted with hot stuff and verballed before. I would never be a stool pigeon. I had to have time, so I put on an act. I said, 'Look, you two have cost me my job and I'm still living honestly. I don't know anything about that jewellery job. I'm going to hate doing it, stooling on robbers who I just might know, but I guess you've got me. I'll do what I can to find out something for you. Drop the charge and I'll cooperate, dammit.'

After some considerable debate, I was told they would not drop the charge altogether. They would slap on me a minor holding charge of being in possession of goods suspected of being stolen. That would allow me out on a small bail. If and when I told them who stole the diamonds, they would withdraw the charge. If I failed to cooperate, to find out what they wanted to know, they would charge me also with being an accessory to the crime. They unnecessarily pointed out that, with my record, four or five years of jail would follow. I was gripped by a much worse fear — of June saying goodbye.

I was bailed out. There was nothing I could do. Who would believe me if I claimed I was being pressured illegally by two upholders of law and order?

When I told them, Larry and Johnny were sympathetic but thought my predicament was rather funny. They were not worried. They knew I was not a squealer. Their simple solution was for me to come in with them, get a few grand and shoot through. With June. I was a bit inclined to agree. I would think it over. When I told Pop about the coppers' blackmail, he was furious and worried but could do nothing. I was too afraid to tell June.

On every one of the next few days, I telephoned Gale at the CIB and told him I had not been able to find out a thing but was trying. No one in my community of crooks knew who had done the jewellery job. 'Try harder,' Gale would snap. 'Or else!'

After three weeks had passed, I knew there was only one way out. I saw my solicitor, Mr Abe Brindley. He listened to my story then sadly shook his head. There was nothing new in what I had told him. Years of experience of the police's modus operandi had taught him. He knew I was telling the truth, but there was little he could do to help.

I had a plan, though. I detailed it to him and, with an amused shrug, he told me to go ahead. He would help. I knew now I would never be allowed to go straight in New South Wales. The police would not leave me alone. I would have to go to another state, preferably Victoria, and with June. But first I had to clear myself of the jewellery charge.

If I skipped out on bail, I could be arrested on an extradition warrant. So Gale and Malley had to be conned into dropping the charge. I would have to make myself mighty scarce afterwards. Gale and Malley would fume at being outsmarted.

I had some cash, although I still owed money on my truck. I could sell it and pay what I owed. Then I would have to tell June the score. She was intelligent, and I would have to do a good, honest job there. She just *had* to believe it. And how could we start in Melbourne with practically no money, me with no particular trade other than safe-cracking? Yep, I had to get more cash quickly. One or two jobs with Larry and Johnny, then skip. If things worked out in Melbourne, June and I would settle down in our own home.

It was a gamble. At stake were the love of June and our future. I felt there was no other choice. I told June what the detectives had done and how I planned to con them and skip the state with her.

Yes, she said, she would marry me and go wherever I went. She accepted that it would take a few weeks to get things settled.

I continued to stall Gale and Malley, and at last the charge was to be heard. I arrived at Central Court of Petty Sessions with solicitor Brindley. I had told Gale and Malley by phone the day before that I had learned who pulled off the diamond snatch. I would tell them outside the courthouse. The two minions of the law were ready to do a tap dance when they saw me arrive there. I stepped aside from Brindley, who had his instructions, and began to confabulate with the law.

'I've got the names,' I confided. 'But, even when I tell you, what's the guarantee that you'll drop the charges?'

They looked indignant at my doubts about their integrity.

'I can tell you where the diamonds are right now,' I continued, spicing the bait. 'But first you have to withdraw the charges in court.'

'We can't do that,' said Gale. 'You tell us now. Then we'll keep our word. You can trust us. You know we're men of our word.'

Oh, yeah? I did not bother suppressing a doubting grin. Malley shuffled awkwardly on his feet and looked at the pavement. Clearly, these two skunks craved departmental hero worship from getting the diamond robbers, and subsequent promotions.

'Sure, I know you're worth trusting, I suppose,' I said. 'But you have my word. And you know I keep *my* word, too! Don't you trust me? What's to stop you picking me up on another manufactured blue and bodgying me again?'

They conceded the point. Finally, the pair agreed to my terms. Before the bench, the detectives gave evidence that they had investigated my explanation of how I came into possession of the rings and that they were satisfied with that explanation. I was not guilty of a crime. The police prosecutor supported them. It went off beautifully. The magistrate said his piece, commended the police on their prompt handling of the matter and dismissed the charge.

Gale, Malley, chuffed solicitor Brindley and I stepped outside. I stuck to Brindley like adhesive tape. The detectives stopped on the footpath ahead of us and waited. Abe Brindley and I walked on by. I turned back, raised a thumb and gave them a slight wave. 'I'll see you later, men.'

Looking furious, they muttered to one another. Perhaps they were promising one another that, yes, they sure would be seeing me. Mr Brindley thought it was a great joke. I suppose it was, for the moment.

Part one of the plan had worked. Now, to keep out of sight, get money fast, get married, flee the state. Out of their jurisdiction.

My first task with Larry and Johnny was to raid a large food-production plant, but not the one where I had worked. An informant, who worked at the premises, had drawn a floor plan of it and assured us that at least £5,000 cash was in the safe. He would get a quarter of the take. My share would be the stake for Melbourne.

At night, the three of us climbed in through a skylight over the third floor. All was quiet. Scattered lights cast dark shadows about a labyrinth of stacked foodstuffs. The three of us, handkerchief masks over our noses, padded cautiously through the maze to the top of stairs leading to the second floor. Here we paused. We did not have to go looking for the watchman. He would come to us.

He had to ring a bundy on each floor every 30 minutes or so, we knew. Soon, we heard the thud of his feet mounting the stairs. As he reached the dim landing, Larry grabbed him from behind around the waist, lifting him off his feet. Johnny applied a stranglehold to prevent him crying out. I stepped in front of him and let him see my automatic. He didn't know it wasn't loaded.

'Listen,' I said quietly in a doctored voice. 'We don't want to hurt you. Do as you're told and you'll be okay. Play games and you know what to expect. Understand?'

The watchman, a prudent man, knew when he was beaten. He nodded and I asked Johnny to ease the stranglehold. The watchman drew deep gasps of air as we quickly tied his arms behind his back.

'Keep your mouth shut,' Johnny warned as the four of us walked to the ground floor, where we believed we would find the maintenance engineer. Larry and I went first, then the watchman, shepherded by Johnny. The engineer was in the engine room. He appreciated the situation at a glance and gave us no trouble. His arms were tied behind him.

The five of us went to a large office at the front of the building. There were three large, new safes with up-market locking mechanisms that challenged a certain tank cracker, so Johnny and I loaded them with gelignite. Larry guarded the staffers.

The safes blew together, revealing a lovely collection of ledgers! Not a pound note was in sight.

The three of us vacated the premises, leaving the watchman and engineer tied up. The watchman was smirking. We were angry and disappointed, anxious to confer with our informant. Especially when we read the newspapers the next morning. They reported how armed cracksmen had missed £7,000 in a big vault.

Said informant had told us the money was in a safe, so we had looked for safes. As he later explained, to him a safe and a vault were the same thing. We thieves had not known of the existence of a vault in there. It was not a very good vault, either, I later learned. I could have blown it in jig time. Strangely, it was in a part of the building well away from the safes.

Our informant was terrified we would trash him but we simply dismissed the matter as part of the luck of the game. For a while, though, I found it harder to think the episode was as funny as my two colleagues did. They had less to lose.

10

Two days after the abortive break-in, I got out of bed and set off for Larry's home in the Eastern Suburbs. I had some matters to arrange. I arrived at 11 a.m. and entered the house through the kitchen door at the back. Larry's mother and sister, Liz, an old flame of mine, told me he was still upstairs in bed. I went up the terrace house's narrow stairs and walked into Larry's room.

Larry was on the bed, and not alone. The bedclothes had been thrown back, and kneeling on the mattress was his girlfriend, naked. She was leaning down on her elbows, facing the wall. Larry, also naked, was kneeling in behind her, his hands gripping her by the thighs. His back, too, was turned to me. They were oblivious to my entry.

I was about to make a risqué remark when there was a crashing sound from downstairs. The front and back doors were being battered. Next, screams from the kitchen. 'The cops!' Larry's sister yelled. 'Coming in the back.'

Larry and the girl twisted around in a hurried tangle of dismay, seeing me standing thunderstruck at the door. Larry's jaw dropped. The girl dived to the floor for her panties.

It sounded like bedlam downstairs. The police were on the rampage, bursting into the homes of all underworld characters who might have done the hold-up at the food factory. I had walked in at a hell of a lovely time. I thought fast. It would be distinctly unhealthy to be found in Larry's place. I ran across the room, ignoring Larry and his girlfriend, who were scrambling for clothes, and went through an open window onto an upstairs verandah.

Three patrol cars were parked along the street. Directly below, two detectives stood on the pavement. The rest of them were already in rooms downstairs. I heard feet pounding up the stairs. They were in for a treat if Larry and the girl had not finished dressing.

A grin left me as I sprang onto the verandah railing, gripped my fingers around the edge of the galvanised-iron guttering on the roof, and pulled myself up. It was an old house. I prayed the guttering would hold. I prayed, too, that the detectives on the footpath did not look up. It would take only one noise from me, a creak from the guttering or a yell from a passer-by.

So far, so good. I swung out onto the roof of the verandah. From there, I scrambled to the roof proper, which was mercifully flat. It was of tin, coated with tar. And the tar had melted to jelly in the hot Sydney sunshine. I wore a light-grey suit, but I smartly flattened myself onto the sticky, black goo. I was out of sight, unless the police climbed to the roof. Considering the scene they would have walked into, I doubted whether the cops would suspect that a third party had left through Larry's bedroom window. I would wait out the raid, hoping Larry's girl, outraged by my untimely intrusion, would not give me up.

Somewhere behind me, I heard a lot of animated talking. Looking down at me were 30 or 40 girls! They were at windows of a lingerie factory overlooking the terrace houses. The girls would have seen the police arrive. I looked up at them, crestfallen, limply waved an arm. Any minute they would yell out to the police about the man flat on the roof. It would provide a good show for them. Then I realised that the girls were signalling me to keep flat. Their conversations ceased. I watched them intently, and they me. Occasionally they pointed to police in Larry's backyard and out front.

About 90 minutes later, I heard cars leaving. 'They've gone now,' one of the girls called. 'You're in the clear, chum.'

Wow! The girls cheered as I waved to them and climbed back down to the verandah, feeling sheepish. I now sported two jackets and pairs of pants. The outers were of tar. Larry's bedroom was empty.

Those girls would have been from working-class families. They had demonstrated as one that they had no respect for the constabulary. I have found that, generally, working-class people sympathise with the underdog. Still, it was an extraordinary business. For all they knew, I could have been a mass murderer or rapist.

Downstairs in the kitchen, Larry's girl was disconsolate and alone. The coppers had taken Larry to the CIB. His mother and sister had gone for a solicitor to free him. I muttered an apology for walking in on the love scene. That, sadly, made her burst into tears, poor kid. I made myself scarce.

Later I was told what took place at the CIB. The police rounded up a dozen or more suspects, including Larry, and other men and put them in an identification parade. Now, as the three of us had been masked and it was fairly dark in the factory, there was no possibility of a legitimate identification by either the watchman or the engineer. But the police tried.

Both factory employees recalled that a *big* robber (really, little yours truly!) had called one of the others Joe. All of the men in the line-up had handkerchiefs over their noses. Quite a sight, it must have been. When the watchman confronted Larry, he stopped and had a good, long look. He was unable to say, however, that this big man was a culprit.

The police prompted him. 'You said the big chap talked a fair bit,' an officer said.

The watchman said, 'Yes, I remember him saying, "Look, Joe, here's a tank."'

The police officer instructed Larry to say, 'Look, Joe, here's a tank.'

Larry had a deep, rumbling voice. A distinctive one. It now could have been his undoing. Sombrely, he recited the line, in a voice as high-pitched and feminine as Popeye's girl, Olive Oyl. Like a canary, I was told. The entire line-up and several coppers erupted into laughter. An unamused officer obliged Larry to repeat the line a dozen times but the high pitch continued. The watchman was not able to identify the voice. Larry's solicitor arrived and the suspect was released.

Thank heavens, I reflected, that the diamonds from that earlier heist were not hidden at Larry's place.

Confident of a change of luck, Larry, Johnny and I had another job lined up. It was to be at a large soap factory, patrolled at night by an armed watchman. There was also a small group of night-shift workers. If things went as planned, the staff would not know a thing was amiss until the two tanks were blasted open. We three would empty them and scarper in a minute.

Inside the factory, all went as planned — at first. We trapped the watchman, disarmed him and tied him up. We had no sooner done this, though, when along came another shiftworker. We tied him up. Then along came another. He, too, was secured. Then came another, and another.

At least there was plenty of rope about for binding them. We put all five staff members in a storeroom and told them they would not get hurt if they kept quiet. I left Larry and Johnny to watch over them and collect any more staff who happened along.

In the office block, one tank was charged with gelignite and the other was half loaded, when Johnny burst in. 'Another bloody worker came in!' he cried. 'He's run off.'

The three of us were armed, but we had no intention of shooting; my gun was again not loaded. Consequently, Johnny had let the man escape. We had to get out of the place, fast. We were not worried about anything the workmen might do. A shot over their heads would keep them at a distance. But the police would be here in minutes.

'You two clear out,' I told Johnny. 'Have the car ready to move. I'll blow these tanks and be right behind you. Quick, man.'

I quickly set the fuses and lit them. I stood away as they blasted. The first tank opened beautifully. The second remained shut. Our luck was still bad. I grabbed the few £100 notes in the safe and ran.

The papers the next morning told us the other safe contained £5,000. Hell, at this rate, I would never get that stake for Melbourne. In this far, I had to go on. Just one good job, and finish. Finish crime forever. I prayed June would not find out.

* * *

We were lining up another job in mid-1949 when Larry said a tough gunman had told him an easy haul was waiting, providing the tough got a share of the take.

'Who is he?' I asked.

'A Balmain crook, now living at Gladesville, I think. Lennie McPherson.'

'Jeez, *that* bugger!'

Leonard Arthur McPherson was one year my junior. We had knocked about together in Annandale and Balmain as kids, shoplifting, stealing food and pursuing girls. He was convicted of stealing, aged 11, in 1932. After his fourth stealing conviction two years later, Len had spent a while at the Gosford boys' home, where he was raped and bashed. He had warned me before I went there of Gosford's sadistic regimentation.

I had punched him to the ground years back, when, full of arrogance, he attacked a lass who had told him to piss off. His brutal streak ended our friendship but I had kept an eye on his career.

He had even done a few months way up the coast in the viciousness of Grafton jail. McPherson had told me that he bribed a politician to get him out of there. Not yet 30, he had strong connections in Sydney's underworld, and he fenced stolen goods. He had scored some big hauls around town since he was paroled out of Long Bay the previous December. He had served only ten months of an eighteen-month sentence for receiving stolen goods.

'Lennie's a bit of a rival of mine,' Larry the Linkman continued. 'He specialises in finding jobs for others and getting a slice of the action. Sure, Darce, he's maybe a sneaky bugger, and the word is, he's killed one or two. But Lennie's info is pretty good. He pulls some weight, all right, and he's damned lucky.'

'Yeah,' I said. 'He's put me onto a job or two through Dick Reilly. So, what's the job he's got?'

'He won't say until we agree to do it, and he shares in what we get. I told him I'd consult you and Johnny first. Oh, and Lennie sends you his regards. You're a good old mate of his, he says.'

Besuited Lennie McPherson greeted me with a hug when he joined Larry, Johnny and me in a pub in Rozelle, the suburb where seven years back he married 16-year-old beauty Dawn Allan. Thick and curly brown hair topped a broad forehead, a broad and smiling face; he had a solid build and was taller than me now.

And that brutal streak seemed to have mellowed. I was prepared to forgive his viciousness of the past. He was, after all, one of *us*. Not *them*, the labouring mugs and law enforcers.

'It's a shit-easy one,' said Len, keenly downing a middy of beer. 'Easier than stuff I know you boys had a go at lately.'

It entailed taking over a large, luxurious house in a top-flight harbour-side suburb, the residence of a rich businessman. He was a big punter and owned racehorses. I was not surprised when Len told us his informant was Dicky Reilly, who would want a slice of the action. Reilly, he said, was a 'friend' of the punter and knew the mansion well. A large safe in the study held at least £10,000. After a good day at the races, there was £50,000.

It took us only ten minutes to agree to do the job and give him a quarter of the take, to be shared with Dicky. We were ready to move at short notice. Melbourne with June loomed.

Living in the mansion with the businessman were his wife and several children. The servants slept out. Len had decided that five men would be needed for the job. It was essential that we simultaneously moved in on the house from all sides to ensure no one slipped away and raised the alarm.

The night came for us to move. Reilly had said £19,000 was in that safe.

'Darce, I wanted you in on this because you're Sydney's bloody best tank cracker,' Lennie said in the car on the way. I was surprised that he went with us.

We surrounded the house about 9 p.m. Lights burned on both floors. Larry and Johnny went to the back. McPherson, an accomplice mate of his called Jack and I went to the front and rang the bell. It was a waste of time. No one was at home. I quickly slipped back the lock and punched a knife through the edge of the woodwork, and we walked in. Johnny and Larry were inside. The safe was simple to open, but it contained only £2,500. It worked out at £400 each, allowing for Reilly's £500. Not good, but handy. Most men would work for months for my take.

I could have taken June away with me at this stage but, I confess, I was getting damned greedy again. I now wanted at least £2,000 for June and me to settle down with in Melbourne. I told myself this run of bad luck could not continue. Just one good job … And before those two verballing detectives I had tricked got worked up enough to lumber me again.

Things by now were hot. Amid publicity about a crime spree, CIB men and women were running around making things uncomfortable for the underworld in general. But I was not concerned. On every job, we had been masked sufficiently to make a positive ID impossible. We had taken care not to leave fingerprints. We did not mix, I believed, with possible police informers. The only way the police could legitimately get an arrest and conviction, I figured, was to snare us on a job.

A few days later, Reilly said through Lennie that he would make amends. He claimed we could get £12,000 to £15,000 from the wall safe in a millionaire real-estate owner's penthouse. I was a bit sceptical but, like the rest, would give it a burl. My share of even half that much would be enough for me to take June away.

Detective Sergeants Gale and Malley, I now knew, were keeping an eye out for me.

The penthouse was on the second floor of a new block of apartments right by the water at Elizabeth Bay, near Kings Cross. There was only one entrance to the building, so the five of us simply walked up at 10 p.m. and rang the door bell. We walked in as the door was opened by a departing resident. We masked our lower faces with hankies. Each of us carried an automatic pistol. Mine was not loaded, to Lennie's mild annoyance.

A woman opened the apartment door in response to my knocking, and she put up no resistance. The occupants were the woman, her husband and their son, a legal luminary in his early 30s. We sat the three in the lounge and searched the penthouse. Once we found the wall safe, we brought the owner and his wife and son over to it and sat them down in chairs. It was a combination safe, and although it could be opened by force, that would take some time. Too long for us as we had not brought safe-breaking gear.

'You are going to open that safe for us,' Len told the owner. 'Otherwise you'll get this.' He pushed the muzzle of his Colt .45 into the man's belly.

The man sat there, set his face, and said, 'No.' Len smashed the heavy pistol across the man's face. Blood spurted from above his eye. It ran down his cheek, staining his shirt. He groaned and cried out as he clasped his hands to his face. Len grabbed him by the throat as the man's wife cried. I began to feel ashamed as two gang members held down their son.

'Do you want more?' Len asked quietly. 'Are you going to open that safe?'

That millionaire had guts. He shook his head. I did not want to see the bloke bashed any more. And I was the senior man here. Len was about to lay into him again when I spoke up.

'Fucken hold off a bit, Harry mate,' I said to Len in a deep and slangy voice, and stood before the bloodied man. 'Look, you's only makin' this harder for every bugger here. You keep on sayin' no and a real belting's com'n. If ya stay bloody stubborn, ya son here'll get it.'

That did it. The man got to his feet and opened the safe. Before I could see inside it, I saw a look of amazement on his face. The safe was empty. And the man did not seem to be acting. He looked more surprised than we were.

'It was *in* there, I tell you!' the poor devil cried as Len grabbed him again. 'I swear it! Thousands of pounds.'

Len did not hit him again. We quickly searched the place and questioned the man's wife and son. Both denied that there was any money in the house. After disconnecting the telephone, the fallible five stormed outside.

A couple of days later, we were told the money had been there all the time. The son had taken it out of the safe only a few minutes before our arrival. Why, we never discovered. Maybe, out a window, he had seen five devious-looking blokes entering the building. He put £17,000 in cash in the study's wastepaper bin and covered it with newspapers.

This last fiasco satisfied me that we were going about things upside down. We would do over a bank. There would be no guesswork or faulty information to contend with. Banks had money, period. We would get some of it.

I told the boys what I had in mind and all four were willing to go along with me. They, too, were sick of the uncertainties. What we wanted was a medium-sized bank in an industrial suburb. I had one in mind. I said I would look it over and decide whether and when to act. I spent a month checking. I lived in a room I rented in a house at Balmain rather than live with Pop, whose home would be visited by those two angry detectives. I seldom went out at nights — except to visit June, whom the police did not know of.

The bank had a staff of 15. We could handle them. They made up quite a number of payrolls for nearby factories. Just one payroll would total more than £50,000 in cash. If a hold-up was timed well, we would get at least £150,000. I outlined the setup to the boys, who agreed that it looked good. It was only a matter of when.

When? We could have done it straightaway but for an unexpected contretemps. The coal miners had been on strike for weeks. Coal shortages had reduced Australian industry to a trickle. Factories were closed or closing everywhere. No payrolls. We decided to wait out the strike.

Many people sympathised with the miners' cause but a certain five did not. To our cockeyed thinking, the miners were greedy, inconsiderate. Weeks went by, and the strike continued, as the police tried to get a lead on the hold-up gang. I continued keeping out of sight as much as possible, as some of the boys got unwelcome attention.

The whole underworld was unsettled, Lennie said, but the police could get nothing to go on.

With a few exceptions, the detectives of the Sydney CIB had little initiative. Their stock in trade was informers, who were mostly underworld characters. In return for worthwhile stooling, the police would choose not to press charges against these informers for crimes they had committed, and often gave them cash. If the detectives wanted someone badly enough or wanted an outstanding crime cleared from their books, but the accused would not confess, commonly they would verbal that person. That is, the interrogating cops would write the accused's confession themselves. At times, if the cops got hold of their victim's signature, they would forge it on the confession. Otherwise, they would swear to the judge and jury that the accused had admitted to the crime but refused to sign the document. From a police point of view, they were putting a crook in jail, where he or she belonged.

I guess the information that stool pigeons sell to police is often right, but I know of numerous occasions where it was wrong and men and women went to jail on the strength of it. (No, sir and madam, I do not believe jails are full of innocents. Most jailbirds deserve to be there. As, usually, did I.)

Many judges in New South Wales had previously been criminal barristers who fought court battles against the use of manufactured police evidence. Strangely, these men had not done a thing about preventing this method of gaining convictions since they gained their judges' robes. One excellent barrister gave a certain detective the title Verbal Kelly.

Once he became a judge, the gent blandly sat on the bench and repeatedly heard and accepted Detective Ray Kelly's accounts of how assorted accused people had verbally confessed — made statements they would not sign. Ho hum.

In my case, following the hold-ups, we knew a couple of stoolies had been commissioned to get the names of the bandits.

The coal strike continued. I saw my fiancée several times a week and marvelled that such a paragon loved me. They were sublimely happy days for me — but, as some oracle said, true love never runs smoothly. Our love had its ticklish patches.

The cause of disagreement between June and me was, in itself, a little thing — one of her girlfriends. I did not like that girl. She was a decent enough person but was notorious for her meanness with money. If she, June and their other girlfriends went anywhere together, this girl always had an excuse for letting the others pay for drinks, fares, etc. She was always going to fix it up later, but never did. (Yes again, I was a fine one, a hypocrite, to sling off about slyness with money, but there it is.)

June, on the other hand, was easy-going and generous with her limited wages from dress designing. I resented this other girl exploiting my June's good nature. I often advised her not to advance cash to the girl or tell her where we were going dancing. I liked June's other girlfriends but tried to bar the cheat.

June did not consider the girl's selfishness sufficient reason to dislike her. She refused to terminate that friendship. This girl had the uncanny habit of turning up at the same dances we attended, always joining our party. I knew June must be telling her where we would be. Finally, one evening, June insisted on attending a dance at the Paddington Ballrooms. The girl I detested was going to be there. I declared I would go elsewhere. Would she come with me?

'But I've told all my friends we'll be there, darling,' said June. 'We must go, Darcy.'

I said, 'No.'

And June stood firm. I stalked off in a temper. I felt, probably unfairly, she should put her fiancé before her girlfriends. Pride prevented me from capitulating. Some of the girls disliked the plundering offender but, reflecting now, I should have been more accommodating.

A party would be on that night at Larry's place, where I had hidden in tar on the roof. He hosted a party every Saturday night. There was always plenty to drink, this general abstainer was told. Plenty of girls, plenty of fun. I had an open invitation to drop in any Saturday. But those sorts of soirees usually bored me. Also, there was good reason to keep social contact with my partners in crime to a minimum.

Still annoyed about June's mean friend, I decided to drop in. I needed some cheering up. The party was in full swing; couples singing, dancing, drinking and necking. I tried to get into the groove and fastened onto Larry's sister, my old flame. Liz was married, but it had not been a success. She was voluptuous and had a generous nature towards men she liked. The way I felt that night, it was time we got together again. Since I had fallen for June, I had had no sex. Understand, I am a pretty virile type. Liz told me she was leaving her husband. I was thrown an invitation to renew our affair, which had ended when I went to Bathurst jail.

Sure, I wanted her right then, but I thought of June. I left the party before I weakened. I headed for the ballroom where June and her girlfriends were. I hankered to make up.

Looking as indifferent as possible, I sauntered around the room until I saw June standing with a group of her pals. She looked beautiful. I mouthed greetings to all of them. I was certain she would not have talked about our disagreement, so I was not feeling self-conscious. I made myself talk and joke with the other girls, even the one I disliked. I was conscious of every flick of June's eyelashes over those hazel eyes as she stood there cool, collected and silent. I ached for her to say just one word to me. I suppose she was waiting for one *from* me. My stupid ego would not let me break.

June's friends saw that something was amiss but the well-bred fillies did not show it. For the rest of the evening, June and I might have been strangers. When the dancing ended, I collected my topcoat and stood talking at the ballroom entrance with a group of acquaintances. June and her pals walked past us and stood nearby talking among themselves, stealing quick looks in my direction.

June looked across at me and our glances locked. I turned my back, pretending to be absorbed in the banal chatter of my new companions. June and co. moved off. What a twit I was.

In the group was an attractive young and little doll who was cheeky and playful. The constant flirter gave me the impression she would be easy. She was. If I had seen June with another man, I would have hit Mars. But little blondie caught me in an inexplicable 'I'll show her' mood.

As I was taking her to her home, blondie said she was 19. We stood on the dark verandah there and I gave her a half-hearted kiss. Suddenly it was not half-hearted. She pulled my face to hers and, for a moment, I feared I might lose my tongue. Blondie's busy little hands moved quickly to another department. She had me partly undressed and took what she wanted before I really knew what had happened. Boy, was she a hot-pants. That lovely little doll with blue eyes gave me the quickest going over I ever experienced.

I was in no mood to stop. As her parents were in bed, she smuggled me into her room on tiptoe. It was obvious I was not the first guy she had sneaked in. We made love until dawn. When I left, I had arranged to see her later in the week.

I woke at home because something was irritating me. My pyjamas were stained. A vital part of me was sore and discharging. VD! In 90 minutes, I was being treated at Sydney Hospital, knowing I deserved the impediment. A mate later told me the nymphomaniac was aged only 16. I was the third he knew of who had caught venereal disease from her.

No more stray stuff for me. My June had all I wanted. I would wait until we married. At least in one respect, I was reformed.

11

The coal miners' strike went on. My four confederates and I were determined to get that £150,000 from the bank, so we impatiently waited. We kept in touch through Larry the Linkman. When I walked into his place one day, he was sitting talking with a chap I had gone to school with. It was William Cecil Mears, who was the same age as me. He and Larry had been mates in jail.

Since 1932, aged 12, Mears had frequently been in court and had several convictions. His crimes were breaking, entering and stealing, being an uncontrollable child, causing malicious damage, illegally using a motor car and a motorbike. Mostly minor crimes, they were.

He seemed tickled to see me. As he stood and gripped my hand firmly, I saw that Mears was more than six feet tall. My head was about level with his shoulders. 'I've just been telling Billy about an easy little job,' said Larry. 'I've been put onto a place at Edgecliff owned by an old girl who keeps £2,000 in a hatbox.'

'The box is in the upstairs bedroom,' Mears chipped in. 'On a wardrobe.'

Our intended victim was 62-year-old Mrs June McNaughton Simpson. One of her old cronies, who said she drank with Mrs S. most afternoons in the saloon of a nearby pub, had told Larry about it. The woman informant had been promised £200 for her disloyalty.

'All we've got to do is wait outside the place until the old girl trots off to the pub,' Larry told us enthusiastically. 'Then just walk in and take the dough. A pushover!

'Come along with us, Darce, and we'll split it three ways.'

Mears nodded encouragement, although Larry could easily have done the job alone. Mears was fresh out of jail, and broke. Larry knew I was still trying to get that stake for Melbourne. Letting us in on such an easy job was Larry's way of giving a helping hand. He was a gunman, a hard man in a rough and tumble, but he was generous to his friends.

I had planned to avoid crime until the bank was ripe for plundering. This, however, seemed too good an opportunity to pass up. The £600 share would be handy. Half an hour later, the three of us were in Larry's car, parked where we could see Mrs Simpson leave her home for the pub. After three hours without seeing her, Mears was impatient. 'She's already gone out,' he said. 'I bet we've been watching an empty house.'

He volunteered to knock on the door and find out. We opposed that. There was no hurry and, as the police would be called when the money was missed, it was just as well not to risk showing our faces. Mears argued and finally we let him have his way. It would be his own blue if it brought him trouble.

Mears knocked on the door and Mrs Simpson opened it. He inquired after a Mrs Smith, was told no Mrs Smith lived there, and left. It was now late in the afternoon. The old girl apparently was not going to the pub that day. We drove off.

The next afternoon, we parked near the same spot. Mrs Simpson remained indoors. Mears again insisted on knocking to see if she was home, and went there against our cautions. At the door, the woman recognised Mears from the day before. This time he told her the elusive Mrs Smith was his runaway wife. He had been told she was living there.

Again we drove off and returned the following afternoon. Quite soon, Mrs Simpson left the house and walked up the street.

'She's off to the pub,' Larry said, grinning. 'It's going to be an expensive session for her.'

In the company of our woman informant, I guessed.

As planned, Larry remained in the car as watchdog while Mears and I hurried down a back lane to enter the rear of the house. As we went, Mears stopped and picked up from the ground a child's water pistol.

'I'll give it to my girlfriend's kid,' he said, putting the toy in his pocket. The back door was not locked. We walked in just as Mrs Simpson came in through the front. I saw her before she spotted me, and I quickly whipped a handkerchief over the lower part of my face. Mears was caught unawares. She had a good look at his face.

Mears and I had little alternative now but to go ahead with the robbery. I imagined that Larry, outside in the car, would be in a bit of a state. Apparently the woman had returned for something. Perhaps to lock the back door. She looked scared as we walked towards her.

'We're not going to hurt you,' I said as soothingly as the circumstances permitted. 'Just you do as you're told.'

Mrs Simpson was as brave as a terrier. She tried to push past us to get to the backyard. Mears and I stood together, barring her path. She stepped back, tripped on some wooden blocks and landed on the floor on her bottom. I bent down to help Mrs Simpson to her feet. She picked up one of the blocks and made a slow swing at my head. I snatched it off her.

'Now, you're being very naughty,' I told her and, feeling singularly unchivalrous, shepherded the old dear into an inner room, where she sat in a chair.

Mears went upstairs but returned empty-handed. 'I can't find the bloody box,' he said anxiously. The pair of us went upstairs, taking the woman with us. Mrs Simpson was now quite cool. She seemed to realise, from the assurances I had given her, that she need not fear physical harm.

'Now, tell me where the hat box of money is,' I demanded.

'There's no box of money here,' she said, glaring. 'And even if there was, I wouldn't tell you where.'

At this, Mears, in an attempt to frighten her, took the water pistol from his pocket. He flourished the toy in such a way that she could not get a clear view of it. 'You'd better tell us,' Mears warned.

Mrs Simpson gallantly stuck out her chin, squared her shoulders and looked Mears right in the eyes. 'I won't,' she announced.

I told Mears to put the pistol away, but it was then too late. Technically, if you point even a lump of wood at a person who thinks it's a gun, while you rob him or her, it is the same as if you in fact had a loaded gun. By his action, Mears had made the crime armed robbery.

I told Mears to get on with the search. Still no £2,000! A lot of valuable articles were scattered about the house and big Mears began putting them in a suitcase. I saw what he was doing and, for the moment, lost my temper. I grabbed one of the articles from him and tossed it to the floor. 'We didn't come here for this sort of stuff,' I told him. 'Go and look for the money!'

Mears resumed the search. I picked up the article I had thrown and wiped away my fingerprints. I was still angry with Mears, and did not wipe it enough.

Mrs Simpson sat by unperturbed as the pair of us searched the house room by room. I left Mears to search a small room Mrs Simpson evidently used as an office. I was waiting in the adjoining room watching Mrs Simpson when Mears called to me to help him move a large roll-top desk.

I told Mrs Simpson to get up from her chair and accompany me to the office. 'I can't,' she pleaded. The strain of the ordeal was showing. 'I feel too ill to move.'

I hurried out of the room to help Mears. I had barely cleared the door when Mrs Simpson took off out the other door like a frisky rabbit. She darted from the front of the house. By the time I reached the front door, she had legged it across the road and was entering a factory. Watchdog Larry in his car apparently had not seen her. Mears and I ran to the car and an unamused Larry drove off.

A few days later, Mears and I were arrested and charged with armed robbery. Mrs Simpson, when shown a rogues' gallery of photographs, had identified Mears. I had left a fingerprint on the article I had thrown to the floor. Larry was in the clear.

We were taken to Paddington police station. When the pair of us was standing in the charge room watching the charges being registered, a detective sergeant produced an old Webley Bulldog revolver. He placed it in Mears's pocket, then withdrew it, saying, 'My, my, what's this, Bill?'

Mears turned green. Serious though the situation was, I could not help laughing at Billy's look of dismay. Mrs Simpson had said he had a gun, so the police had given him one to tidy things up.

The next day, Saturday, 20 August 1949, we appeared in Sydney's Central Court of Petty Sessions, along with the usual string of morning remand cases. Drunk drivers and the likes.

My activities in Mrs Simpson's home had been far from angelic. But Mrs Simpson said in evidence that I behaved like a thorough gentleman, had helped her from the floor before she swung a block of wood at me. Strange words from a woman who had been robbed.

But I felt desperate. Standing in the dock with Mears, listening to the police prosecutor's sonorous monologue, watching newsmen taking notes, I mentally upbraided myself. I had been a fool of fools. Why had I worried so about money? June loved me without it. Now, because of my criminal stupidity, I had almost certainly lost her. June had not been bluffing when she said she could not marry me if I returned to crime. And all of it was over an attempt to rob a little old lady.

Somehow, I had to see June, with whom relations had warmed grandly. Perhaps I could still work out some way to hold her love. By God, I was going to escape again. And quickly.

The stipendiary magistrate, Mr Earls, remanded us on the armed robbery charge to appear in Paddington Court on 21 September. Bail was refused. We were among 22 prisoners filed into a Black Maria headed for those familiar old walls of Long Bay jail.

During the ride, I looked with frustration at the screws fastening the van's panelling to a grille over the air vent. No screwdriver today. I looked for the slightest chance to break out. The guards, however, were paying me a great deal of attention.

When we remand men arrived at the penitentiary, we were taken into the reception section to await the end of the lunch hour and the reopening of the cells. We were in the charge of two turnkeys. Of course, other warders were within calling distance and there were armed men on the towers atop the walls. Most of the warders were dining, though, or guarding the eating inmates.

I already knew the layout of that jail pretty well and realised straightaway that I had been given my opportunity. Behind the reception centre was a small room, which was built onto the jail wall. The door to it was heavily padlocked. But, I believed, if I got in there, it should be possible to rip out a hole in the timber ceiling. Then get up on the roof. From there, I should be able to climb over the main wall.

It was a desperate chance. But I had to see June, beg her to forgive me. There was a guard tower no more than 30 yards along the wall from the spot where I would perhaps emerge through the roof. I would need an assistant, so Mears could go with me.

The guards in the tower would be less alert than normal, I figured, with the regular inmates locked up for lunch.

If my reasoning on this scheme was wrong, I would finish the day on a slab in the morgue with a slug hole through my skull. First I had to get the two turnkeys guarding us out of the main reception area, a long and wide corridor with two annexed rooms at the end farthest from the entrance.

By the entrance, an officer sat behind a desk to receive personal property from new prisoners. Prison shoes and hats for new prisoners were in an open room at the far end. At the back of this room was the bolted door leading to the room I had to get into. A turnkey stood on guard at each end of the corridor while we waited for the end of the lunch break.

I nudged Mears and quickly told him what I had in mind. Was he coming?

'Fucken oath,' he whispered.

'Well, hold it there for a moment.'

A fellow new arrival was William 'Joey' Hollebone, a Surry Hills-based murderer who could have cut half a dozen notches in his gun. He was one of the most dangerous men in Australia, yet one of the quietest — unless you did him an injury. Then he would get you, unless you got him first.

Joey was mates with the notorious crook John 'Chow' Hayes and my longtime associate Lennie McPherson. I had briefly met the arrogant and clever Hayes, who was 18 years older than me and a fellow graduate of the Gosford boys' 'reformatory'. Hayes was a busy thug, thief and contract killer. I knew that back in '45 he shot dead one of his rival crooks, Eddie Weyman, and had avoided being charged for it.

I knew big Joey pretty well. He was not on a serious charge this time and would not try to escape, but I knew he would help me. I sauntered over, motioned him aside and told him what I wanted him to do.

Joey nodded. 'Now?'

'Yep, now.'

Joey walked straight along the corridor to the entrance.

'Where are you going?' a warder yelled. 'Come back!'

Joey kept on walking. He stopped in front of the warder at the reception bay and crashed a big fist on the desk. The two warders who had been watching the rest of us chased after him.

'When the hell are we going to eat?' Joe demanded angrily. 'What's the bloody delay? Is this starvation tactics?' He continued ignoring the warders who had run after him, and maintained an impressive string of abuse.

I quickly picked the lock on the door with a gadget I had secreted on me. The other prisoners saw what was going on. I winked at them. They turned their backs to Mears and me and said nothing. A few of them walked over and stood between me and the turnkeys so I could not be seen.

Once the lock was sprung, I wrenched the long lock bolt from its housing. I took it with me as Mears and I slipped into the small room, closing the door behind us. The prisoners, I later learned, stayed in front of the door to mask the absence of the bolt.

Hollebone would not be able to keep the turnkeys distracted for long. We had to work quickly and silently. We carried a couple of wooden crates to below the spot in the ceiling where I would rip the hole. I jumped up on them while Mears steadied them. He excitedly urged me on as I went to work on the timber slats. With some of them removed, I used the bolt to prise up the roofing iron.

How much noise was I making? Any second, warders could burst in here. In the distance, I still heard Joey's tantrum. Good old Joe. He'd know he could cop a complicity charge.

I struggled up through the hole, onto the roof, and looked along the top of the jail's wall. Luck was with me. The sole guard up there was walking away along the catwalk towards his tower on the wall's southwest corner. An automatic shotgun was slung over his arm. He was no more than ten yards away.

How the blazes had he not heard the roofing iron being prised up? I signalled to Mears and he shot up beside me, quietly flattening the roofing behind him. I pointed to the guard, still strolling away.

'Come on,' I muttered and swung up and onto the top of the thick stone wall. Mears followed. We flattened ourselves. The guard had halted. If he turned around, we were dead men.

I peered over the outside edge of the wall, facing Botany Bay. We swung over the edge and dropped 22 feet, side by side. The grass cushioned our fall. We had been in jail just 25 minutes.

There was still no wailing of an alarm. Mears started to run to the small outer wall 70 yards away. I grabbed his arm.

'Take it easy,' I snapped. 'Don't attract attention before we have to.'

We walked casually towards the outer gate, glad to be in civilian clothes. At the first sound of alarm, I would break into a sprint. With luck, the guard on the wall, plus the guard at the small outer gate, would assume we were visitors. I fought off an urge to look up at the wall guard, although for a while we had to walk parallel to his wall.

As we drew level with the wall tower, a warder walked around the corner dead in front of us. My heart jumped to my throat. He looked at us as we kept walking.

'Morning,' he said, and smiled. 'Been visiting?'

'Yes,' I said, smiling weakly. 'I'm pleased to be out of there!'

Mears was studying the ground before him. The warder, probably reporting for work, walked on towards the main gate. Our luck held.

We walked through the open outer gate unchallenged. Outside in the street, we mounted a tram conveniently heading for the city. We sat together and anxiously looked back at the jail, waiting to see it erupt with pursuing turnkeys.

A £5 note was the only money we had. For years I had kept a fiver in the inside lining of one of every pair of shoes I had. One never knew when it would be needed. But the conductor who came to collect our fares refused to accept such a big denomination, which he could not change. So we had a free ride from Long Bay for a few miles to Maroubra Junction! There, we transferred to a taxi.

I told the driver to take us to Erskineville railway station. He would soon be hearing of an escape by two men and it would not be difficult to connect us with it. As we left the cab at the station, I told the driver to keep a £2 tip. A damned big one, it was, in those days.

'And forget you've ever seen us, mate,' I said, and winked like a confederate. He smiled over his tip and assured me he had already forgotten us. That, of course, would make the cabbie remember me.

The police, on being informed, would assume we had caught a train. Which we would not have. Time proved, incidentally, that the cabbie was as good as his word. The police never knew we took the taxi ride.

Billy and I walked rapidly to nearby Alexandria, where I got change and telephoned Lennie McPherson. He arranged to pick us up by car after sunset. We were safe enough where we were for a few hours.

Back in the penitentiary, Joey Hollebone proudly told me later, the two turnkeys assigned to watch the new arrivals were engaged in placating him for quite some time. They did not notice that Mears and Dugan had gone. Nor did they see that the bolt on the back door was missing.

The jail returned to normal business after the lunch break, some 30 minutes after we escaped. The other warders returned from their meals, and the receptions were lined up in the corridor to be counted.

'Twenty,' the checker reported.

His colleague looked hard at the delivery sheet from the police. 'There's twenty-two listed here.'

The checker counted the men again but could not get to 22. A senior warder was called. He checked the warrants and, after counting the prisoners himself, made the portentous announcement, 'There appears to be two missing. And one's bloody *Dugan*!'

The warrants were checked again as the line of prisoners chuckled. The turnkeys looked at one another incredulously. They still had not noticed the missing bolt. Each man was checked off by name.

Then things began to happen.

All prisoners were returned to their cells and locked in. The whole jail was searched. Jail Governor Harold Vagg was, like Drake, playing bowls at the time. But, unlike Sir Francis, he did not finish his game. After taking a phone call, he hurried back to Long Bay. The Comptroller-General of Prisons, L.C. (known as Elsie) Nott, rushed out there from his city office.

Police assigned to the Saturday races at Rosehill were about to watch the second event. Many of them joined the scores who converged on the jail — more than an hour after Mears and I had strolled away.

It was some time before the authorities were convinced Mears and I had left the place. The guard at the outer gate remembered two men walking by him. Interestingly, the warder I spoke to must have kept mum.

While police ran up and down sand hills surrounding much of the jail property, Comptroller-General Nott vented his spleen on the staff.

'As God is my judge, that swine Dugan will pay for this,' he raged.

Meanwhile, the prison grapevine buzzed. Dugan had been in and out in less than half an hour. Governor Vagg went up to the tower, near the spot from where we had leapt, and confronted his minions.

'There's a hundred of you on duty here today and not one of you had his bloody eyes open,' Vagg shouted. 'Those damn two must have passed under your noses!'

I'm told that finally the tower guard told Vagg, 'Stick the job up your arse,' and stalked off. He was one of three warders dismissed because of the escape.

Rumours publicised at the time suggesting that we had bribed warders to turn a blind eye were not correct. But the mass media had a ball ridiculing the system.

Police hurried to Pop's home at Ultimo. Over bewildered Pop's protests, they snatched up a used shirt in the main upstairs bedroom. A police car took it to Long Bay. The shirt was placed before the quivering noses of a couple of bloodhounds to give them my scent.

The dogs headed across open country near the jail. I'm told that at that stage the pursuing police were confident. They theorised that, once through the outer gate, Mears and I had cut across there for the coast. The bloodhounds, however, proved useless.

They never found out, but the shirt the police grabbed at Ultimo and scented the dogs with belonged to Pop!

At dusk that evening, a passer-by reported seeing Mears and me in bushland a couple of miles from the jail. The police rushed in, still with the falsely scented hounds. Some 200 soldiers were camped at a rifle range near the jail that night. They, too, joined the search, treating it as a sort of manoeuvre. The troops advanced in patterns to the beach, with fixed bayonets.

Some soldiers spotted a man huddled in a hole by a sand dune. Stealthily, they surrounded and closed in on the sleeping figure.

'Right,' a sergeant yelled, turning a spotlight on their target. 'Hands up!'

The sleeping man was an old derelict with a white beard to his waist. The poor devil lived in the hole. Most of his food came from rubbish bins. He jerked bolt upright. His eyes boggled at the sight of bayonets. He yelped in horror as the soldiers sheepishly tried to placate him.

I understand the derelict was taken to the jail, charged with vagrancy. So they got someone for their trouble.

Soon after dark that evening, Lennie drove Mears and me to a temporary hide-out in the Western Suburbs — the home of Len's friends Eve and Wally, whom the police would not connect with me or Mears. I was safe, but I did not intend staying there more than a few days.

I desperately wanted to see June but did not dare just then. And her parents did not have a telephone.

The Sunday papers carried banner headlines: 'Hunt for desperate criminals after break from gaol. Underworld combed; city search'. The Sydney *Truth* said: 'High walls did not a prison make for Darcy "Houdini" Dugan.' There were pictures of the jail, and police mug-shot photographs and descriptions of Mears and me. Feature stories inside the papers related the known career of 'Escapologist Dugan'. The police and prison authorities were irked.

Motorists were warned against their cars being stolen. Key transport points, even the seaplane base at Rose Bay on Sydney Harbour, were watched. The media quoted police saying Mears and I could by now be armed — that we would 'fight it out' if cornered.

They were at it again, making me more uneasy and it less likely that members of the public, like those girls at the window when I was in the tar, would help us. And a trigger-happy cop would be all the keener to blast us to death.

The propaganda would also further humiliate my darling June. Her friends, knowing me as Darcy Clare, would recognise me from the pictures and probably tell the police about June and me. The pictures also ensured that Mears and I would quickly be identified in public.

* * *

Len's wife, Dawn, was a gorgeous and honest brunette. She could not reform Len, however, so she lovingly took him as he was. For then, anyway.

When I asked her to, Dawn eagerly contacted June. On the third day after the escape, Len brought June to the hide-out. After introductions, the others at the house, including hosts Wally and Eve, tactfully left the room.

At first June and I just looked at each other. I lacked the courage to speak or put my arms around her. June looked terribly upset. I could see she had been crying.

Then I blurted, 'My love, I've got myself in a nice mess. I just had to see you, June, and ask if you'll give me another chance … Or have you finished with me?'

June stood facing me silently. She slowly shook her head, and I had her in my arms. We did not speak for a long time.

When the emotional turmoil had subsided, I outlined my plans. If I went quietly for a few weeks and evaded capture, I would have little difficulty leaving Australia. We would go to Britain for a few years, ideally Ireland, then return to Australia. I would give myself up, with proof that I had turned over a new leaf. I should get a light sentence. Even, possibly, a bond!

'Are you game to give it a try?' I asked. 'Would you come with me?'

Yes, June said firmly. Yes, she would.

We agreed not to see each other until I had completed arrangements to go to Melbourne, where friends could organise a quiet wedding for us. From Melbourne we would cross to Adelaide, lay low for a few months, then slip out of the country.

Police were watching the homes of Pop and Mum, but I was able to send them messages assuring them I was okay. I heard Pop in a radio interview. Sobbing, the poor old fellow announced that he had found a note from me under the back door (delivered by Wally). He had burned it so the police would not get it. Pop pleaded with me to contact him and give myself up.

Meantime, the cops, working day and night (overtime pay!), were chasing up all sorts of false leads on Dugan and Mears, who, they claimed, loved the notoriety. The search extended to Melbourne and Brisbane. They raided the homes of several innocent folk, following anonymous phone calls from practical jokers.

The police shadow squad tailed our known associates — who, it seemed, did not include Lennie McPherson.

Mears and I did not want to further endanger kind hosts Eve and Wally, so we moved to a new hide-out. It was a small house, isolated atop a cliff in rough bush country at Lugarno, near the Georges River in Sydney's outer southern suburbs. Friends rented it for us.

I wrote a letter to the editor of the *Daily Mirror*:

If cornered I will give in quietly without any bother ... I deny that I am dangerous or that I am a gunman. I have never fired a pistol in my life, have never been found with a gun and never will be. I have escaped from adult custody on three occasions, but at no time did I injure or assault anyone while doing so.

If I had not escaped, I would have had to wait four to six months to come before a judge and jury, locked up 16 hours out of 24 in a stone cell 12 feet by 8. The other hours would have been spent in a small yard, like an animal pen. And given one meal a day, of which the less said the better.

If people think bad of me for attempting to keep my freedom, I am sorry, it can't be helped. But I resent being presented to the public as a gunman.

Darcy E. Dugan

I had the letter posted at the GPO.

The police, after declaring it authentic, said they believed I would give myself up in a few days.

Eight days after the escape, Len again brought June to see me, after travelling by a long and circuitous route to ensure they were not followed. I detailed to her the final arrangements for our trip to Melbourne the following night.

She was to bring no more than one light suitcase. She would have to leave her parents a letter to try to alleviate their inevitable worry. It would say she was going away for a short time, making no reference to me or her destination.

I felt selfish making June go with me.

The next day, 29 August 1949, would be my twenty-ninth birthday. The prospects looked good.

'What a terrific birthday present,' June said, beaming.

The same night, however, the police had learned of our hide-out. A Detective Fred Krahe took the credit. The CIB's chief, Superintendent Thompson, Detective Superintendent Gorman and Detective Inspector Joe Ramus immediately planned a raid.

(I knew Ramus. In the following years, I was unfortunate enough to come up against him several times. Ramus was an honest, relentless and courageous policeman. I consider this man — who, unlike most of his colleagues, shunned publicity — the only detective I have ever met who possessed integrity and an intelligence to respect.)

I learned later that at two in the morning, 16 police, heavily armed and led by Ramus, quietly drove to Lugarno. They left their four cars two miles from our hide-out and walked in single file through the cold, still night. Some wore rubber-soled shoes. The others walked barefooted across the rugged country. Smoking was forbidden. They spoke in whispers.

By 4 a.m., they were hidden behind trees, rocks and bushes around our dark and silent house. The detectives waited for dawn, their feet growing numb. Some had cut their bare feet on the rocks. Dew settled over them.

A watchman passed by the house on his way to work. In the half-light, he saw a detective crouched silently behind a bush. The watchman flashed his torch and saw half a dozen others, silent and motionless. Pistols, rifles.

'Oh, good night,' he said nervously.

No one answered.

'Er … chilly, isn't it?'

Still no reply! He hurried off, nearly falling over more police. The watchman ran into the scrub.

At 5.45 a.m., Ramus led his men to the house. He gave a low whistle. Flashlights were turned on. Police crashed through every door and window. An officer ran into the bedroom where Mears and I had been asleep, in single beds. We jerked upright. Guns pointed at us from all directions. Glass from a window had showered on us.

We gave Ramus and his men no trouble and we were not armed. It was a well-executed raid. I would not be seeing June today.

Happy birthday, Darcy!

After extensive questioning at CIB headquarters, Mears and I were returned to Long Bay and paraded before Comptroller-General of Prisons L.C. Nott. I was his chief target in a torrid barrage of verbal abuse, which I had better not report on. I took it silently, feeling contempt for my keepers.

Someone, I ruminated warily, someone must have fizzed, grassed, told the police where we were hiding. The place was known only to our few helpers and June. Billy and I had never gone outside that house and risked being seen by neighbours. Had someone ingratiated him- or herself to the authorities to avoid possible prosecution as a collaborator?

In the following three months, conditions were as tough at Long Bay for Mears and me as the Department of Prisons and its turnkeys could make them. I was told that if I attempted to escape again, I would be shot down like a mad dog. And also, the treatment I faced would break my spirit. Because of the escape, three warders had lost their jobs.

Mears and I had a small exercise yard each. Intercourse with other prisoners was forbidden. We spent seven hours every day pacing our yards. Then we were in solitary cells, under heavy guard, for the next 17 hours. As I had anticipated in my letter to the *Mirror* when we two moved to Lugarno.

I was allowed nothing to read or otherwise occupy my mind. I walked up and down the yard. Up and down the cell. Torturing myself with the realisation of what a fool I had been. I had had my chance with June and again lost it, on the very day we were to celebrate my birthday by going to Melbourne. Losing June would make me fret until I died.

The police or prison authorities told her parents she was writing to me in jail, and her parents made her promise to stop it. She was barely 20; she had been brought up to love and respect her parents. I certainly did not blame them, or the authorities who told her parents. It was their job.

In Sydney Quarter Sessions on 2 December 1949, Mears and I faced Judge Adrian Curlewis. We were convicted of robbery in company, eight years; escape, two years. Accumulative. We faced ten years each. Judge Curlewis said he was giving us such a severe sentence to 'make an example and provide a deterrent to others of your ilk'.

Occasionally I still received a letter from June. Writing for her was now a sordid, surreptitious business and those letters were heart-rending. They indicated that she was desperately unhappy. She loved me. She would wait for me. And we would marry. The letters had been read by prison authorities, of course.

A screw tossed one to me through the bars. 'This is from ya stupid bitch,' the bastard said.

I dreamed so often of being with June, in Melbourne, Adelaide, London. And especially of living in a law-abiding way in a village in Ireland, the land of my ancestors. Those mental meanderings were splendid breaks from the nightmares.

Again, I made up my mind to take a risk so I could be with June. The chances of success were slim under this tight security, but now there was nothing to lose by trying. Nothing other than my life.

I had a plan and would get out again.

12

Mears still had to appear at Central Court of Petty Sessions to face the charge from having the pistol that was planted on him at the Paddington police station.

He was not likely to cop more jail time, but the matter had to be cleared from the police books. I sent Billy a message to subpoena me as a witness and conduct his own defence.

I was able to use the jail grapevine to have two hacksaw blades smuggled to me. Mears and I were to be in court on Thursday, 15 December. I had bragged to a couple of cons I trusted that I would be out by Christmas.

Early that morning, I threaded a blade with string and hung it between my shoulder blades. The other blade was hidden in a yard for possible future use.

Some 30 prisoners were going to assorted courts that morning. Each was to be searched at the jail, but, as the turnkeys neared me, some prisoners at the head of the queue, as arranged, began a loud argument. Punches were thrown.

As the turnkeys tried to placate the prisoners, I skipped along the queue to join the men already frisked.

Mears and I arrived at Central at 9 a.m. and were placed in a cell together for the hour until he was due in court.

It was what I had hoped for. We had not been able to talk together in private for months. Prisoners waiting to appear in court at Central were housed in six cells off a corridor. Two armed warders were assigned to watch over us that day. They stood talking to a police sergeant at the entrance to the corridor.

'Want to make another break?' I asked Bill quietly.

He looked at me curiously and said, 'Bloody oath!' Just as he put it the last time.

I told him the plan. He would prolong the hearing as much as possible. If he ran out of questions when cross-examining the police, he was to repeat the questions in different words. Ask them the time of day, even, but keep the court in session for three hours, until it was time for the lunch break. He had to delay calling me as a witness.

I showed him the hacksaw blade. 'By the time you come back in here for the break, I should have sawn through those bars up there.' I pointed to a high window set in the far wall. Across it were two horizontal bars of steel, one and a half inches in diameter. Billy looked at them, then at me, bewildered.

He did his stuff in court:

MEARS: Isn't it a fact that you put a gun in my pocket?
DETECTIVE: No, I did not put a gun in your pocket.
MEARS: You deny you put the gun in my pocket?
DETECTIVE: Yes.
MEARS: Are you sure you did not put the gun in my pocket?
DETECTIVE: Yes, I'm sure.
MEARS: Are you positive?
DETECTIVE: Yes.
MEARS: You didn't put a gun in my pocket?
DETECTIVE: No, I said.

And so on, and on.

Back in the cell, while most of the guards were in court, I busily sawed away at the top bar that blocked my passage to freedom. It was tough, hard work on tough, old steel. I had to hold myself up at the window with one hand and saw with the other. And I had to keep noise to a minimum. Heavy traffic in nearby George, Liverpool and Pitt streets drowned much of the noise.

The one warder left to watch me apparently felt I did not need close scrutiny, as the corridor which led to my cell had a dead end. I heard him at the corridor's entrance yarning with the police desk sergeant in charge. They were only about ten yards away.

Shortly before 1 p.m. — lunch time — I had all but cut through the bar at each end. It was not likely that the cuts would be noticed, the window being nine feet from the floor.

It was a long ten-minute wait for Billy. We were given lunch in the cell, and the turnkey went away for his meal, leaving one to hold the fort, resuming his position at the corridor's entrance. We heard him talking to the sergeant.

For a lark, I think it was then that I scrawled on the wall 'Gone to Gowings'. Gowings was a big department store down George Street that sold menswear and, importantly, camping gear.

I sprang up and removed the bar, while Mears watched for the guard. I slipped through the space and pushed back an iron grille. I had noticed this grille years before. It had been faultily constructed. I was able to push it back far enough for even big Billy to squeeze between it and the wall. Once through, and still in the building's attic, I looked down on a warder a few yards along in the corridor, as Mears followed me out.

This escape was damned dangerous. That turnkey's .38 was not an ornament. If he saw us, we would be blasted down. The pair of us crept further along and climbed through a skylight onto the roof of the cells.

We crossed the roof, right under a window of CIB headquarters. If a detective looked out of it …

Still no outcry. We dropped to the roof of a building adjoining the CIB, then jumped down into Central Lane, by Central Street. We sprinted 50 yards into busy George Street, jumped on a tram, and ten minutes later had cleared the city.

I called an astonished Lennie McPherson from a public phone box and arranged to be picked up by car after dark.

I rang June at work. I heard the telephone click, her heavenly voice.

'It's Darcy, darling. I've escaped again.'

She gasped. 'Oh, Darcy! Where are you?'

There was not much time. I knew the police would head straight for her, so I told her to expect them.

'They'll watch you night and day, love, so it'll be impossible for us to meet. But I made the break only so some time I'll be with you.'

I quickly added that I planned to leave the country. Did she still love me enough to join me if I could get to England or Ireland?

She forthrightly declared, 'Yes.'

'Right, I'll try to see you in a month or two, before I leave the country ahead of you. I love you so much. Don't lose hope.'

Meanwhile, the guards discovered that Mears and I were not in the cell. In minutes, the news flashed over the police radio and hundreds of police throughout Sydney were looking for us.

On commercial radio, CIB Chief Superintendent Thompson warned the public that we were dangerous criminals. We might try to get weapons, he said.

At 2 p.m., Central Court of Petty Sessions reconvened and the magistrate was informed, in front of an amused gathering, that Mears and his witness Dugan had escaped. The case was adjourned.

Later that day, 100 police were assigned to catch us.

The next morning's newspapers again ribbed the police. Under banner headlines, the papers told how we had sneaked away under the eyes of our guards and the whole CIB. One newspaper's police roundsman called it the most audacious escape in Australia's history. That, Mears and I thought, was a bit rich.

The media loved reporting my cheeky message on the wall: 'Gone to Gowings'. The store's management, however, was less amused. Gee, it was free advertising!

There were pictures and diagrams of how it was believed we got out. Also, of course, mug shots again of Mears and me.

The papers also reported that the police and prisons departments were launching an immediate inquiry into how we got away. The *Daily Mirror* had more of Houdini, and claims that Dugan was trickier, smarter than that bushranger of Irish ancestry, Ned Kelly. Again, I didn't like it.

After a telephone tip, dozens of armed police fruitlessly searched a residential building in the inner-city suburb of Surry Hills from top to bottom. Another caller claimed we had stowed away on the freighter *Cobargo*, which had just sailed from Sydney. Detectives from police launches boarded the freighter on Sydney Harbour and went over it with searchlights. Again the tip was a hoax.

Newspapers reported that by Saturday afternoon — 48 hours after the escape — the police had received more than 50 hoax tips to where we were.

Police with drawn guns raided the homes of dozens of innocents. Incidentally, I was told that via the remarkable grapevine at Long Bay, prisoners there had the news within 30 minutes of our scarper.

Scores of crooks were constantly followed because the police believed they could be my or Mears's acquaintants. Sydney's underworld was disrupted. The police were frustrated and furious. They warned that no mercy would be shown to people found harbouring the escapees.

The following week, as Billy and I laid low, newspapers reported a police theory that we were masquerading as women! They had information, they said, that we had been given women's clothing the day after we escaped. How the hell could that be so? I was said to be a blond, Mears a brunette.

The police checked out a report that I was working in a city store dressed as Father Christmas. Two outraged Santas, in front of crowds of children and their parents, had their beards pulled off.

General ridicule of the police mounted. Newspapers said Pop was making a pencil mark on the wall inside the front door every time the police called. By 20 December, there were 30 marks.

Another tip to the police had it that we were hiding by day in the bush near Lidcombe State Hospital and spending nights in bed posing as patients. At 3 a.m., a big party of armed police sneaked through the hospital grounds and rushed into the wards. They frightened the daylights out of patients and nurses.

I sent another letter to the *Daily Mirror*. It noted that again the police were claiming Mears and I were armed and would shoot it out if cornered. I denied this, adding that certain police had threatened to shoot me if they got a chance. The letter, run at the front of the paper, further said that, if caught, I would never make a statement to police. This was my insurance in case arresting sods in court one day tried to verbal me.

The media subsequently asked the police for assurances that Mears and I would not be shot if encountered unarmed. The police complied. It did not make me feel much easier, though. What was there to stop them planting weapons on our bodies?

I sent a newspaper another letter, accusing police of coercing me back into crime, getting me sacked from an honest job, after my release from Bathurst jail. Enclosed was a note from Mears.

A joke went round CIB headquarters that Mears and I were ringing newspaper editors complaining about the way subeditors were cutting our letters. A paid informer one morning reported that Mears and I planned to stow away on an aircraft that afternoon. The police vainly searched five planes about to fly out loaded with passengers.

We hiders had a quiet Christmas; and on 29 December, the state Public Service Board dismissed three warders after a two-hour inquiry into our escape. It was found that the men had not properly carried out their duties. There were also rumours that the warders had been bribed on Mears's and my behalf.

One fired warder said he had attended, along with Comptroller-General Nott, a demonstration of the sawing of a bar in the cell we had escaped from.

'I pointed out that the noise the saw was making could have been heard across in Liverpool Street,' the warder said in a prepared statement. 'When the full facts are found out, it will be discovered I think that the bar was not sawn through on the day of the escape, but days before.'

Mears and I were red-hot. We had to get out of the state but, in the circumstances, we needed plenty of cash to organise it.

Lennie said the crack jockey Jack Thompson kept in his home a safe containing £10,000. We could try for it if we wished. Masked, we broke into Thompson's home on the night of 8 January, bailed up the jockey and his wife while they were in bed. But Len's information was wrong. We got only £170.

Little Thompson, by the way, showed a lot of guts during the robbery. And, as Mears and I hurried to Len's car near the house, Thompson raced to the door and blasted at us from both barrels of a shotgun. The shots missed us.

After that debacle, I decided that the surest way to get plenty of cash was to raid a bank — a small one that two men could handle.

The Ultimo branch of the Commonwealth Bank, near Pop's home, seemed to fit our requirements. It was all in one large room and staffed by only three men. We estimated that it would hold about £20,000.

Len, true friend, made the necessary arrangements.

Every day, newspapers still carried reports on the hunt. Often when they reported a decent sort of crime, they fatuously inquired whether Dugan and Mears were the culprits.

The CIB announced that we had held up Jack Thompson and his wife. Desperate, and in my first-ever lie to the public, I sent the newspapers another letter, denying any knowledge of the hold-up. The searching police were now enraged. They had not got one solid clue to our whereabouts.

Lennie provided us with a stolen car, fitted with stolen number plates, for the bank job. On the morning of 13 January 1950, 29 days after our escape, Mears and I drove to the bank. Len, driving a car behind us, acted as scout. Mears and I stopped in front of the bank just after it opened at 10 a.m.

Len cruised around the block to ensure that no police were nearby. As he passed us again, he nodded the all clear. He drove off to meet us a few miles away, where we would abandon our car.

Driver Mears was jittery. 'I think a bank's too hot,' he said.

The men in the bank would be armed. And, yes, desperate Dugan and Billy were also armed. Billy was unaware that my gun was not loaded.

I did not want to go in there with a man jumpy enough to begin shooting at the slightest provocation.

'Don't go in if you don't want to,' I told him bluntly. 'If you're losing your nerve, say so now, for God's sake, and we'll forget it. You can go your way, I'll go mine.'

Mears swore that he was not scared. If he kept calm, I assured him, we'd be all right.

'And, again mate, there's to be absolutely no shooting unless someone goes for a gun,' I instructed. 'Under no circumstances, none at all, are we to kill anyone.'

I got out of the car and said, 'Come on!' Mears said he wanted to wait a while. I was tense, too, but there was no point in hanging about. Only a few pedestrians were in sight.

I turned back to my accomplice. 'Look,' I said angrily, 'are you going to do this or not?'

Mears followed me to the swing door. We pulled masks over our faces, pulled out our guns and burst in.

Four people were queued in front of the sole teller. I flew across the room and bounded onto the teller's counter, legs straddling the grille. My .32 automatic pistol covered him and his customers.

I yelled, 'Hands up, everyone.'

Mears had sprung onto the other end of the counter, which stretched the width of the room. His .38 Webley revolver covered bank manager Mr Leslie Nalder, a woman cleaner standing nearby and a 19-year-old male clerk.

It was going well. We would soon have the £20,000. I reached down with my free arm and pushed the teller to the rear of his cage, out of reach of a shelf that probably housed a handgun or an alarm.

The hands of all the staff and customers stretched for the ceiling.

The sound of a shot shattered the tense silence. I looked over to see Nalder slump to the floor behind his desk. Mears's gun was smoking, now aimed point-blank at the clerk by the counter. Mears fired again and the youth fell.

Another quick shot from Mears just missed the teller, who dived away. The customers had flattened on the floor.

'You stupid bastard!' I screamed at Mears. 'You shouldn't have done that.'

Mears was not listening. He ran out through the door, leaving me straddling the teller's grille.

With the others still on the floor, I suppose I could have herded them all into a corner and cleaned out the place. But there was no time. The shooting would have been heard and there was a police station only a quarter of a mile away.

Mears was not waiting. I had to leave.

Had anyone been killed? Nalder did not look well, and Mears could not have missed the clerk. I quickly bent down and scooped a handful of notes from the teller's drawer before running out. The whole fiasco took less than a minute.

Mears was entering the car. I jumped in beside him and, as he drove off, called my big accomplice quite a few uncomplimentary names.

'But Nalder went for a gun,' he protested. 'He was going to fucken well shoot you. I had to get him first.'

I did not believe him. Mears, I was sure, had panicked. Now we might be murderers. I hoped sorely that the bank manager and clerk were going to be okay.

He drove to Jubilee Oval, at Forest Lodge, where we left the car, walked across the oval and were picked up by Lennie in a safe car.

When I told him of the fiasco, that at least one staffer might be dead, Len snorted at Mears. 'You gutless cunt,' he said, seething. 'I shoulda got seven grand out of that. Instead, there's a murder rap. We oughta be done with you.'

When Mears left the car to urinate, Len actually told me my accomplice was such a liability that we should shoot him dead. On finding the corpse, the police would have their murderer. I laughed, thinking he was joking. No, I assured my childhood mate, Billy was okay. Ultimo was a one-off, an untypical failure.

An hour after the robbery, we learned from the radio that Mears had hit only Nalder. There was a .38 slug in his chest. Doctors feared he would die. How Mears missed the clerk, I shall never know.

Another debacle and I still needed cash.

Despite what I told Len, I was reluctant to plan another hold-up with Mears. But I needed some sort of assistance. And Len was generally not one to participate in a crime. He was the job spotter, the aloof supporter who shared the spoils.

None of the regular boys would assist me. They were being watched too closely. Even Len said he had been paid a couple of calls by police. He was sticking his neck right out by helping us. I asked, but he was not willing to be in a stick-up.

I resolved to have one more try with Mears. If he botched it, that would be the finish. I would go it alone.

Len knew of a payroll that had possibilities, and he began investigating it for us.

The police were blaming us for the bank robbery. Nalder's condition was no better. We had stirred up the proverbial nest of hornets.

Leaving Mears in Sydney, I adopted a minor disguise and, under a hat, went to Melbourne to arrange a hide-out for June and me as soon as the next robbery was over. Despite a road, rail, water and air blockade, getting there was not difficult. If you had the right contacts, there was always a way.

I spent seven days in Melbourne before everything was nicely arranged. The day before returning to Sydney, I posted from the Melbourne GPO a letter to the *Daily Mirror*. It was a flippant, inconsequential note denying that Mears and I had held up the Ultimo bank. What an awful thing that was, lying again to the media — like, however, the cops did regularly.

I was back in Sydney by the time the police examined the letter and saw the postmark from Melbourne. For a while, the search centred there.

After this next stick-up, there would be another letter. This time from Sydney, but not until the eve of going back to Melbourne.

On 18 January, the state government offered a reward of £500 [more than $22,000 in today's money] for information leading to our capture. Premier James McGirr and Police Commissioner Scott said they hoped it would tempt one of our helpers.

Posters featuring pictures of Mears and me and offering the £500 reward were displayed about the city, even at the Art Gallery of New South Wales. The search was estimated to be costing the government £1,000 a day.

Newspapers reported that kids were no longer playing cowboys and Indians — it was Houdini Dugan.

Some wag entered D. Dugan and W. Mears in a lawn bowls tournament at Armidale, in the country. The club member who entered us later admitted that perhaps we could not play bowls, but we played a neat game of hide-and-seek.

A wit went around city pubs hawking, for a shilling each, envelopes branded 'The History of Dugan and Mears'. On opening them, the customers found the envelopes empty. The salesman would look astonished. 'Gone again, eh?'

Sydney radio actor Ken Wayne closely resembled me, and he had a taller friend who could have been mistaken for Mears in disguise. Some folk they passed in the street 'recognised' them. Some looked horrified, some smiled confidingly. A few silently gripped the actor by the arm and squeezed it encouragingly. Both men carried identity papers, which they showed regularly to suspicious police.

The police still chased scores of false leads to the escapees' whereabouts. The reward did not worry me. The few people who knew of our hide-out could be trusted, I thought.

In Adelaide, police boarded and searched the passenger liner *Orcades* following a tip from the Sydney CIB that Mears and I might be on board. The search was fruitless, but the ship's officers were given photographs of the fugitives for the coming voyage. Police again searched *Orcades* when she berthed at Fremantle, Western Australia.

Fifty armed coppers combed the liner *Oarangi* when she arrived in Auckland, New Zealand, from Sydney, following another tip.

Roadblocks were set up on the Hume Highway, the main artery between Sydney and Melbourne, after a report that Mears and I were in a dark-coloured car speeding south.

The situation was out of hand. The police were exasperated.

I had a woman friend fly to Melbourne for the day, all expenses paid. While there, she mailed a letter from me to the newspapers. Again the search intensified in Melbourne.

Scores of police surrounded Sydney Airport one morning, soon after a pilot leaving Melbourne flashed an urgent radio message saying that two of his passengers were Mears and me in disguise.

Armed cops boarded the plane when it landed. The crew had mistaken two innocent businessmen — one short, the other tall — for us.

Lennie McPherson meantime checked out the scene for a likely big job. Every week, he learned, a payroll of £12,000 was delivered to the Mort's Dock shipbuilding company's works. It was on Sydney Harbour, in the inner industrial suburb of Balmain, Lennie's old territory. Two men, Len said, could pull it off pretty easily.

Our plan was to be on the spot when the payroll car came to the front gate and stopped at the office there. We would be dressed in denim overalls to look like workmen. As the car stopped, Mears and I would run up behind it, covering the five men in the car from each side and behind.

We would order them out of the car, unarm them, take the two money bags and drive off in their car. In case part of the plan went awry, an emergency car would be parked across the street from the dock gates.

I felt uneasy about how Mears would handle this, but there was still no alternative accomplice.

Len suggested to me that, instead of me, Mears handle the Thompson sub-machine-gun we had for that job. The gun's drum took 50 bullets. Five rounds belched from it at every press of the trigger. The Thompson, Len felt, would intimidate the payroll guards sufficiently for them not to resist.

'The Thompson ought to give Mears confidence,' said Len. 'Steady his nerves.'

I agreed. Mears was happy with that.

As I handed him the Thompson, I said, 'Remember, this is for show. Fire it only if *they* shoot. And shoot over their heads. No more bloody action like at Ultimo.' Mears eagerly agreed to comply with that.

On the morning of Friday, 3 February, we two were hiding behind a nearby shed when a cream Dodge stopped at the front-gate office. The payroll car. We ran to it. We had covered only about ten yards when, out of the corner of an eye, I saw Mears stop in his tracks.

He had yellowed on me! I cursed, but by now my mind was in top gear. I could stop, too, and we could take off empty-handed, like a pair of mongrel dogs. Or I could go on alone.

I kept running for the pay car, the .32 automatic drawn. I stopped at the rear and to one side of the car and bellowed at its five occupants.

'Get out with your hands up or I'll start shooting.'

Mears still stood just inside the dock's front gate, 25 yards away. I concentrated on the five armed men pouring out of each side of the car.

From where I stood, I could cover only one side of it properly. The guard who was carrying the bag that I reckoned contained most of the money took advantage of this and ran. With the bag. I had to go after him. As he sped towards the dock's main office, I shouted at him to stop. He kept running.

I took careful aim. He was no more than 20 feet in front of me. For the first time ever during a job, I fired. I deliberately aimed above his head. Even so, I had a chilling mix of fear, desperation and guilt. The man spun around but still clutched the bag. He regained his balance and started off again. I was not prepared to shoot him squarely in the back. I let him go.

I turned around and realised things were warming up. The other four guards were huddled behind the car and began shooting at me. Mears still stood by the gate, rigid as the Statue of Liberty, hugging his Thompson.

To get back to the gate and the emergency getaway car, I had to run past the shooters by their car. I ran at it, ducking and weaving, as bullets whined about me. I gave myself little chance of making it.

I shrieked at Mears, 'Use that gun, you bastard!'

I snapped shots above the guards as I ran. Then the pistol clicked. I was out of bullets. Mears let go a blast of machine-gun fire. It went some 12 feet above the guards' heads, as the bullet marks on the walls showed later. The guards ducked, though. Long enough for me to race by.

I followed Mears out through the open gate. We headed for the getaway car across the street. The guards behind us were still firing. The bullets seemed to be going well astray, however.

Then, more strife. A uniformed police constable jumped from the entrance to a shop in front of us. Mears was running helter-skelter 15 yards ahead of me. Both his hands gripped the Thompson.

The constable took one look at the machine gun and ducked back into the shop. His .32 against a Thompson? I did not blame him. Mears ran past him.

The constable then saw me, with more his match in armament. At least, I thought as I sprinted towards him, he did not know my gun was empty. I aimed it at him but the constable stood his ground. He took steady aim from about 20 feet away as I passed.

I well remember thinking, 'You've had it this time, boy. This is curtains. He can't miss.'

I kept going, waiting for a thud of lead blasting my body. But nothing happened! He must have missed. Plenty of shots were being fired at me but they all seemed to come from the payroll guards back at the gate.

I reached the car as Mears clambered in behind the steering wheel. I grabbed the Thompson from him, swung around and aimed at the copper. He saw what was coming and streaked back into the shop entrance, just beating a burst over his head.

He had tried to kill me. If he had another go, I would lower my aim. Fury surged in me. I fired a burst above the dock gates to keep the payroll guards down.

The copper was only 15 yards away. He put his head and arm out of the doorway and snapped a shot. He had guts. Not even a Thompson would stop him. He faded fast as I drove another burst of five shots his way.

Mears was revving the car's motor but it was cold and would not start. He looked at me in despair.

'For God's sake, keep trying,' I yelled. 'Start it!'

The guards at the gate fired a few more shots. I let them have another blast. The copper in the doorway immediately snapped one at me, too. I drove him back with a burst that splintered wood at the bottom of his door. Four bursts left. I jumped in the car's back seat.

Mears was still revving the motor. 'It won't go!'

'Keep at it. It *has* to!'

Glass from the back window showered on me as the brave constable put a bullet through it. Any moment, police reinforcements would arrive.

The car's engine roared to life and we lurched away. The Battle at Mort's Dock was over. It was a miracle that I and Dangerous Dan, the constable, were alive. Either of us could have been shot from the hail of bullets coming from the gate. I later checked the Thompson's drum. Eleven bullets were left.

I later learned that, as I ran by him, the constable pulled his trigger three times. Every time, his .32 pistol had misfired!

I did not merit their attention, of course, but the angels must have been watching over me that Friday. The constable was wounded, but by a shot from the gate, I was sure.

Lennie had a cabin cruiser awaiting us at a bay a mile up Sydney Harbour from Mort's Dock. We abandoned the stolen car, cruised down the harbour and moored beside a buoy half a mile from the scene of the battle. Many other craft were moored around us.

I cursed Mears for his chicken-heartedness. Len was not amused, either. The way he glared at Billy after roundly abusing him, declaring again how gutless Mears had cost him thousands, I felt that Len was thinking again of shooting our chicken.

Mears, looking chagrined, said nothing.

'Struth, I heard the gunfire from the bay,' said Len. 'It sounded like a couple of armies having a go.'

It was decided that Mears and I would remain hiding in the cruiser's cabin. Len rowed away in the dinghy to see how things looked from the shore. All being well, he would pick us up late in the afternoon.

He had been gone from the craft about 45 minutes when, through a porthole, we saw something that made us worry. Two large, black police launches went speeding up the bay past the 30 or 40 boats around us. Heavy machine guns were mounted on their cabins.

They must have been told we had gone by boat. But by whom?

We had to wait in our hot spot. The launches would probably check every craft in the vicinity. If so, we were dead ducks. We would not even be able to make a decent fight of it. We had little ammunition for either weapon.

If we tried to get ashore, either swimming or in the cruiser, we would surely be spotted. Maybe, if Len did not front, we could swim when it was dark. Doubling back in the cruiser towards Mort's Dock had seemed a cunning idea at the time. Not so now.

We sat tight and sweated it out.

I closed the cabin doors and we watched the black launches in the bay. One came towards us. We watched it turn into the anchorage and crouched low out of sight. The launch cruised among the boats, but it sounded as if none of them was being boarded.

The low hum of a motor came nearer. We flattened on the cabin floor. The launch came alongside our boat and slowly moved by. Someone said, 'We ought to search this lot.'

Another said, 'They wouldn't be here. They're miles away by now.'

The men on the launch evidently looked about for a while, then their deadly looking craft roared away up the bay.

They had not been gone more than 15 minutes before we heard a craft bump against our cruiser's hull. We'd had it!

Then Len yelled, 'Quick, you've got to get out of here. The coppers must know we used a boat and they're searching the harbour.'

As we climbed out of the cabin, we told him we knew that.

'Well, they might come back,' Len said anxiously.

Chicken Mears and I piled into the dinghy, lay flat and accompanied rower Len on the short trip to the shore.

From there, his car took us to his home in the Eastern Suburbs. Here we heard radio newsflashes about the gun battle and the hunt for us.

Hiding at the home of Lennie McPherson and his wife, Dawn, was reasonably safe. Len was a crook gaining notoriety, sure, but we understood our cunning organiser was not known to be an associate of ours.

This time, though, Mears and I had stirred the police to a maximum of effort. There would be a new wave of police raids on the residences of known and suspected criminals. It was on the cards that they would visit Len. But even if the police did come, Len and Dawn were prepared to chance it.

Len had a false wall in one of the rooms of his plush home. The wall concealed a space eleven feet by three and a half feet. We hid our weapons in there.

We had been in the residence only two hours when there was a knock on the front door. Mears and I scrambled into the secret compartment. Len and Dawn opened the door before it was battered off its hinges.

Three carloads of coppers, some toting Thompsons, had surrounded the house before moving in. Mears and I heard the police noisily enter the premises, Len asking what they wanted.

'What do you mean, barging in here with those guns?' Dawn asked indignantly.

'By what right do you do this?' Len demanded. 'Do you have a search warrant?'

'No,' a copper snapped. 'Any trouble from you two and we'll give you a vacation at government expense. We're after Dugan and Mears.'

'Well, you're just as likely to find Ned Kelly in here,' said Lennie, mustering a laugh.

The police swarmed all over the house, emptying cupboards and drawers. Through a spyhole, I watched two of them search the room that housed the entrance to our compartment. Neither Len nor Dawn was in the room. The flatfoots talked as they ransacked.

'I'd like to know how the hell that bastard managed to pay for a place like this,' said the younger detective. 'He's got plenty of form.'

'A smart crook,' the other disclosed. 'He hangs on to all the money he gets his hands on. I think he's got powerful friends.'

'His wife's a decent sort,' the youngster observed. 'But she'd do anything for him. I'd like to get into her pants.'

The other said, 'Some of the boys have tried but she won't play.'

The policemen began discussing Mears and me. They did not seem to think Len really knew much about us, or anything about the gunfight at Mort's Dock.

Len let us out of the compartment well after the police had left. His beautiful home looked as if a cyclone had struck. Dawn, who kept it tidy, was upset. Mears and I helped them clean up the mess, but it was still only partially tidied hours later.

It was not unlikely that the police would be back. Len confirmed that they seemed satisfied that he knew nothing of us. But we could not be certain. Mears and me being there was risky, a strain on young and gorgeous Dawn.

The next morning's newspapers dramatically described the Battle at Mort's Dock. There was well-merited praise for the constable who kept firing at us. The police were quoted saying Mears and I were the culprits.

* * *

I was quietly ashamed of that crazy shooting near people at Mort's Dock. And about Ultimo bank manager Leslie Nalder still being critically ill in hospital. Doctors did not dare try to remove the .38 slug from beside his heart. Such an operation, they said, might kill him. The slug had entered his body near his left shoulder blade, blasting a tunnel ever so close to his heart.

It was revealed that, contrary to Mears's claim, Nalder had not gone for a gun. When I yelled out for everyone to put up their hands, Nalder had got to his feet from behind his desk.

The movement had unsettled Mears, and my nervous accomplice had begun shooting.

There was general criticism of the police. Editorials demanded that the £500 reward for our capture be increased. The police made fruitless raids again after getting tips from people who thought they had seen the desperados.

Len came home one evening to report that Sydney's underworld was in further turmoil. Many well-known Sydney gangsters had 'gone into smoke' because persistent police following and questioning made them afraid their associates might brand them police informers.

So, Mears and I had cut Sydney's crime rate!

Dawn rented on our behalf a house in sloping Alexander Street, a few minutes' walk from the beach in the northern suburb of Collaroy. It was a large double-fronted place with four bedrooms, two lounges, two kitchens, and verandahs on two sides. It was in a pleasant and quiet neighbourhood. But not too quiet!

By now Mears and I did not look much like the pictures of us in the newspapers almost daily. I had dyed my hair raven black and grown a neat moustache. I also wore glasses. Mears had also dyed his hair and changed its style. It made a remarkable difference to him. He, too, wore specs.

13

We moved into the Collaroy house about 10 February. I did not intend spending more than a few days there. Arrangements were being finalised for me to slip alone to Melbourne. To be joined by June.

There would be no more damned robberies for me with Mears. In fact, no crimes with anyone or alone! I would make do with the little cash I had. Every caper with Mears had made us awfully notorious.

I wondered anxiously how June was taking the news of our escapades. Not too well, I guessed. I would soon try to contact her.

The weather at Collaroy was warm and sunny. Len and Dawn, and former hosts Wally and Eve and their children, were daily visitors. They gave the place the right atmosphere for the neighbours, with whom we got on well. Sometimes I played in the backyard with the neighbours' children.

Billy and I never went out together. A few times I went to nearby shops and the beach. On these outings, I wore sunglasses, a panama hat, shorts and sandals. Not one of the hundreds of people I moved among showed a hint of recognition.

At the Collaroy rockpool, I won myself a girlfriend. Annette McKilliam was a blonde, with laughing blue eyes and rosy cheeks. I spent a couple of hours teaching her to dog paddle. Annette was four years old.

One day Mears said he wanted to see one of his sisters and his girlfriend, and asked Len to bring them out to see us. Mears said he would ask the girls to stay with us to 'add to the atmosphere'. I agreed with that. As Bill knew, I was not going to be at Collaroy much longer.

Both girls stayed over for the first night. They were attractive and friendly brunettes, whom I liked. However, the girls slept together and, contrary to newspaper suggestions later, there was no hanky-panky.

The following evening, Len collected the girls a block away from the house and drove them home. They would return the next day with clothes and other necessities for a longer stay.

That night Mears and I sat in the lounge talking and listening to the radio. He drank a couple of bottles of beer. We went to bed late.

Crash! I was out of bed and moving before I was fully awake, but there was nowhere to go. It was dawn, 14 February. Police were pouring into the house like a stampede of buffaloes.

Searchlights beamed through smashed windows as men piled through them. Doors burst open. Artillery was behind the searchlights. I heard other men running along the hall.

I crouched beside my bed, hidden from the window and doorway. Mears, in another bed, sat upright, his hands held high. Police entered the room.

'Mears is here,' yelled a detective holding a Thompson. 'Don't move, Mears, or I'll blast your head off.'

Another detective yelled to his colleagues outside, 'We've got Mears. But that other bastard's gone again!'

A moment later, however, they spotted me. After two months, my liberty had ended.

Detective Inspector Flint, ably assisted by Detective Sergeant Aldridge, plus 'Verbal' Detective Raymond Kelly, led the 22 raiders.

In a few seconds the light was on and the room was crowded with police. They carried sub-machine-guns, automatic shotguns and tear-gas containers. Neither Mears nor I was armed with even a peashooter.

Glints in the policemen's eyes told me that Mears and I faced a torrid time, especially with Kelly here. I had a stampede of dread at a graphic memory of Kelly's merciless bashing, his squeezing my nuts at the Burwood police station after accomplice Harry and I were arrested trying to crack the safe at the dentist's surgery on Christmas Eve '45.

We were handcuffed and taken to the lounge room. Flint ordered two detectives to take me to the basement while he, Kelly, Aldridge and Detective Maurie Wilde 'questioned' Mears. I wore only pyjama shorts and a T-shirt as the police stood over me in the basement, guns drawn.

The lounge was above. Going on the noises from up there, Mears and the police were having a gymnastics session. Mears cried protests amid thudding, crashing sounds. A few times Mears screamed but his cries were quickly muffled.

The hubbub continued for at least 40 minutes. What, I wondered, would I cop? My two guards stoically stared at me. Then, silence from above. I waited ...

Half an hour later, big Kelly strode into the basement. He placed a piece of paper before me.

'You'll remember me, Darcy,' he said, and grinned thinly, blue eyes narrowing behind round spectacles. 'Now read that. It's all there. All about the Ultimo bank. Holding up Jack Thompson. Mort's Dock.

'Your mate has told us all about it. We've got you cold, Darcy. You can make a statement yourself and make it easy all round.'

I made no move to touch or read the 'statement' before me. I looked deadpan and said nothing. I had been around too long to fall for that ruse from Verbal Kelly. Mears had been verballed. Or at least tortured into a confession.

Kelly knew as well as I that the paper could not be used as effective evidence in court unless I testified to its truth. Surely, I thought, they wouldn't verbal me in the light of those letters I wrote to the press declaring that I would not make any statement to the police without my solicitor present.

The eyes behind the specs glared. 'Look, Dugan, you bastard, you've played merry bloody hell. Well, it's *our* turn now. We're going to hang you! In fact, you'll write a statement here now or I'll shoot you down like the rat you are.

'Nobody's going to miss you or make a fuss. You'll be shot trying to escape again.'

He put a hand to his shoulder holster and drew out a .32 revolver. 'Well, how do you want it?'

I knew a lot about this man, also nicknamed Gunner Kelly, Machine Gun Kelly, and considered as corrupt as any on the force. He would have no compunction about putting a bullet in a prisoner's head. And not for the first time.

I was suddenly pleased I had told the newspapers that certain police would shoot me if given the chance. This, I hoped, would cause Gunner to hesitate, possibly on orders from on high. And surely the cops would prefer the pleasure of getting me hanged for attempted murder.

Kelly would know it was pointless trying to bash me into submission. He spun the revolver's chamber with his thumb. Was Russian roulette coming? *How many empty chambers are there?*

He went to the door and whispered briefly to another CIB man, then loudly addressed his juniors. 'All right, this is the way Dugan wants it. Let's get it over with. Put him in the shit house.'

They pushed me into the bathroom behind me. They made me stand with my back against the far wall. Kelly stood before me, gun raised. Two others stood at the door.

Kelly banged the barrel of his gun into my gut. 'This is your last chance, rat. I'm going to count to three, then I'll put a bullet in your rotten brain.'

He must have seen the sweat on my brow as I straightened, straining the cuffs on my wrists behind me.

'One …'

Was he bluffing? God, was he? I'd not be even the second man he had shot dead, close up.

'Two …'

I would rather die here than ceremoniously hang or get a life sentence. *If he's going to shoot, let him!* There'd be plenty of witnesses to the murder. But they were cops.

One of Kelly's eyes closed. The other stared behind the black hole of the muzzle.

'*Three!*'

The gun went to my head. And belted me under the chin.

Cursing and swearing, he knocked me into the bathtub. His size 11s stamped hard on me for many minutes, and his spittle sprayed on me. I was still cuffed and could not get up to defend myself.

I did not care. I had beaten him.

However, someone must have informed on us. Lennie McPherson later told me the £500 reward for our capture had gone to Bill's girlfriend.

From Collaroy, Mears and I were taken to CIB headquarters, now very familiar. We were tossed together in a cell to await a magistrate to hear the charges. Skin was missing from Mears's forehead. He looked dazed and sick. He looked at me uncomprehendingly.

'How are you, Bill? Are you all right, Billy?'

He nodded. 'I'm crook. Fuzzy. Aching all over.'

'Now, listen hard,' I said slowly. 'In court, tell the beak they forced that statement out of you. That's the truth. Deny what you might have said — or we're sunk.'

In Central Court of Petty Sessions, the police prosecutor laid several charges against us. They included attempted murder and armed robbery. The prosecutor asked that we be remanded in custody.

I jumped to my feet and addressed the magistrate. 'Your Worship, they tortured Mears to get him to make a false statement. He's ill because of the brutal treatment they gave him at Collaroy. Look at him! Look at me! It speaks for itself.'

Mears groggily slumped in the dock beside me.

I added, 'Detective Kelly's in here. He bashed me with a gun at my head and told me he would verbal me so they could use the statement they forced from Mears.'

I informed the beak I had made no statement, answered no question. I was innocent of the charges.

During this, several of the arresting detectives conferred with the prosecutor.

When I finished speaking, two of the detectives testified that Dugan and Mears had apparently had a fight before being arrested. Hence our visible injuries!

'Dugan abused Mears before entering this court,' one swore, 'telling Mr Mears he would blow his brains out if he, that's Mears, didn't deny making his confession.'

Mears regained his feet and made an inarticulate effort to deny this. He was too dazed to really know what was going on. Those casual acts of perjury by the police to get what they wanted were jailable offences. Standard stuff, it was.

We were remanded for a later hearing. The police had paved the way to verbal me, but I was not going to sit and take it. The best I could expect now was a sentence of life in jail. And damn tough treatment during it. I had made a lot of enemies in the police and prisons departments.

I had little to lose by breaking out again. On the way back to Long Bay, I tried to figure out how to do it.

14

Mears and I were watched like bugs under a microscope, treated like vermin, for several weeks at the Bay while waiting for our committal hearing in the court of petty sessions. Turnkeys regularly reminded us that our last escape had got three of their colleagues the sack.

Three more had been tossed out because of the one before that. We were going to pay here at the Bay.

'Then, you'll swing at the end of a rope,' a turnkey predicted.

Or perhaps we would go to Grafton jail, they said. The Bloodhouse. They implied that that would be worse than execution.

The screws loudly gloated over that thought. From a revenge point of view, they would rather have us at Grafton than see us hanged.

I had heard plenty about the place of horrors from former inmates like Lennie. The mongrel sadists there would want us as playthings.

I never bothered answering my moronic antagonists. My silence, though, made them all the more savage.

I was delivered, cuffed, to the office of the penitentiary's governor, Mr Harold Vagg. From behind his desk, Vagg sent the turnkeys outside.

After expressing some preliminary niceties, he leaned forwards, smiling confidingly. 'Now, Darcy, I'm very interested in the escape of yours from the lockup at Central.

'The three officers have been dismissed now, so it doesn't really matter. But, Darcy, just for my personal interest, it's been claimed that you had that iron bar cut through a few days beforehand and that you paid an officer £300 to turn the other way as you got out.

'It'll go no further, Darcy. Did you bribe him?'

I grinned back at the governor and answered, 'Sir, if I told you I had bought off one of your men, you wouldn't believe me, would you? And if I said I *hadn't*, you wouldn't believe that, either. Would you?' I shrugged. 'So what's the point of me saying anything?'

Vagg scowled. 'You're a sly fellow, Dugan. *Very* sly — now get out. Guards!'

Not long after the Central lockup escape, and if I got a chance, I had decided to pull the carpet from under a particular turnkey who guarded us at Central.

He was outstandingly abusive and brutal, but not bribable. And I did not want him to be on guard when we were back at Central.

I placed in the jail postbox a letter to a friend of mine. On the way, it would be read by both prison officers and the police. The letter thanked my friend for offering me money while in jail to buy off 'the screw'. But, I wrote dishonestly, I had got hold of £300 and given it to the brutal screw, whose initials I inserted.

The letter reached my friend four days later. No doubt the police passed it on to the Public Service Board. The board could prove nothing from the letter, but no doubt it helped get the turnkey sacked from his job. Vagg would have enjoyed reading it.

The authorities were finally ready to proceed with our committal hearing, at which the court would decide whether there was enough evidence for us to stand trial on the charges of holding up gutsy jockey Jack Thompson and his wife, attempting to murder Nalder at the bank, and the hold-up and attempted murders at Mort's Dock. It would take at least a week for them to get through the evidence.

Mears refused free government legal aid. He would represent himself, he said. I was represented again by solicitor Mr Abe Brindley. I had no money to give him. My few friends were now too hot to come out of the smoke with money.

My distressed pop offered Mr Brindley a few pounds he had scraped together, but Brindley declined the cash. Brindley came to the Bay and told me of a favour I had done him many years before that I had forgotten about.

I had come across a few thugs picking on a man, who I later learned was Brindley. The thugs were going to bash and rob him. I sent the thugs packing and walked away.

'No way will I take any money from you, Darcy,' Abe Brindley said. So I had all the resources of one of the best criminal lawyers in the nation, free of charge.

As the hearing drew closer, I wondered what Mum, Pop and Tom were thinking. The Ultimo bank's Leslie Nalder was hanging in. I had no illusions, though, about how hard it would be to toss the police once they verballed me. Even if Brindley beat them in court, I still had that ten-year sentence. But I had not been as idle as the Bay's turnkeys figured.

I would probably be handcuffed to Mears going to and from court. There would be plenty of armed screws and police about, but there was a bare chance of eluding them. Trying that would be stupid, though, if I could not first slip out of the cuffs.

I knew a lot about handcuffs, had found two means of springing their locks. Both ways were surprisingly simple and could be employed on even today's latest cuffs. One required a sliver of thin razor-blade-style steel. The other required an elementary one-tooth key.

I do not want to give here a guide for would-be escapists and had better not go into detail. The steel sliver method involved a lot of manipulating, attracting attention from nearby guards. But not so method number two.

I got hold of a small brass belt buckle, cut it at certain points and flattened it between a steel cap on my boots and the stone floor. The result was a key half an inch long. I had gauged the required size by pressing a lump of wet bread against the keyhole of a pair of cuffs and taken an impression.

The flat key fitted neatly between two natural grooves in my upper gum, inside my lip. After a while, it felt a normal part of my mouth. It would survive searches. When thoroughly searching a prisoner, turnkeys made him strip. They examined his rectum and peered down his throat. They did not pull back his lips.

When Mears and I went from the Bay to Central Court of Petty Sessions, two screws and a special escort of four police never let us out of their sight. All carried revolvers. They continuously watched us through an observation flap in the door of the Central cell. They all came along, two in front and four behind, when Mears and I went to and from court.

In there, three detectives were added. The nine positioned themselves around the dock in which we accused stood. Other police, usually including detectives Aldridge and Wilde, were also in court. Verbal Kelly was curiously absent.

That first day in the Central cell waiting to go to court, I motioned Mears to the back wall. 'I'm going to clear out of here,' I said quietly. 'It's risky, but come if you want to. Do you want to?'

'You're incredible! Bloody oath, yes, mate.'

That was positive oath number three.

He may not have deserved the chance. He might freeze again and shatter it all, but I was sorry for Bill. It was my fault for agreeing that his girlfriend, now evidently rewarded with £500, go to Collaroy.

I related the plan.

When we and our guards were entering and leaving the court, it was necessary to stop at a narrow corridor on the right usually used by only police and magistrates. It led to two swing doors to the court lobby.

On the lobby's left was another corridor. This led to a door opening onto the side of the court building, near public toilets. The door was usually open. Only 20 yards away was busy Liverpool Street.

I planned to break away from the guards as we halted at the first corridor. Most of the guards would be behind us. Mears and I would sprint along the lobby, through the swing doors, down to the toilets, out the window and into Liverpool Street.

I had kept fit. Once I was running at top speed, not one of those guards would catch me. We would cross the street, pass through the L-shaped Woolworths store opposite, and go into George Street.

I would try to contact Lennie McPherson, whom I had not heard from since Collaroy. Not that I expected him to write or visit me in jail. Len was too wary for that.

'But those first 30 feet to the turn before the swing doors will be the touchiest,' I warned. 'We'll have to get around the corner before they start shooting.'

I told Bill I could slip out of the handcuffs at will. 'Be ready to go every time we head back for the cell through the door from the courtroom,' I said.

For the first two days of the hearing, I attempted nothing. I studied the behaviour of our nine regular guards. Initially, both Mears and I had our hands cuffed together in front of us. My right wrist was further shackled to Mears's left by another set of cuffs.

The police reluctantly removed the two sets of cuffs locking our hands in front of us after solicitor Brindley, who had no inkling of my plot, protested to the magistrate. This left only the cuffs shackling Mears and me together.

Hours went by, me frowning at deceitful claims by coppers.

On each following day of the hearing, just before the 1 p.m. lunch recess, my hands went to my mouth to cover a manufactured cough.

I tongued the cuff key into my free left hand, unlocked the cuff on my right wrist, slipped the ratchet to the last tooth and re-locked the mechanism. I could then slip out of the cuff. I tensed, ready to go.

I decided to go for it at lunch time on day six — the last day. As the mob of us approached the court exit door, the two turnkeys ahead of us stepped into the corridor. One stood at each side of Mears, and I stepped between them. Before they had a chance to turn and face us, I slipped off the cuff and yelled, 'Now!'

I smashed into the turnkey on my right, rocketing him onto the wall. I took off. Mears did not move. Again, he had yellowed!

Police and turnkeys squealed, 'Quick! He's going. Get him. Shoot him. *Dugan!*'

A couple of police chased me. This prevented others, guns drawn, from getting a bead on me down that narrow corridor.

As I raced to the corner, I was confronted by an enormous police sergeant. He must have weighed 17 stone.

He crouched and spread his arms like a rugby tackler, ready to take me.

I was in full flight. I bounded against the wall, then bounced off, thrusting with all my might an open-hand stiff-arm. It landed on the point of his chin. The sergeant was lifted off his feet. He thudded to the floor on his back like a sack of potatoes.

The police and turnkeys were still yelling. Some were close behind me. I rounded the corner and bashed through the first swing door.

I hit the next, and was stopped in my tracks. The thick timber door was hinged to swing the other way.

My shoulder burst through a small glass panel. I recoiled and opened the door, then ran to the lobby and around to the left. The whole building seemed to be in pandemonium. Police were braying, women screaming.

The door before me, and leading to freedom, was closed. I grabbed its handle, turned it and pulled. It did not budge. The footfalls behind me came closer. Above the handle was a small bolt. I wrenched it back and pulled the door half open.

I do not recall what happened then. I went down under a ton of policemen. They hit me with everything but the magistrate's gavel.

I'm told I was carried unconscious back to my cell. There, I was also told, I was further punched and kicked as I lay on the ground.

I had been within an ace of freedom. The big sergeant, the door that swung the wrong way and the final door being bolted had slowed my progress enough for the police to catch me. They no doubt realised that had I got away, they faced the sack.

Consciousness returned as I lay face down and naked on the floor of the cell. I struggled to my knees, saw legs everywhere. Detectives stood all around the walls.

A heavy shoe crashed into the side of my head. Another dug into my ribs. Another into my back. I slumped to the floor, out cold again. I must have been out for only a couple of minutes that time. I woke to hear them cursing me.

'The fucking cunt,' said one. 'We oughta kill the bastard.'

Like snarling dogs, they waited for me to recover enough for another pounding. A shoe pressed on my right ankle, grinding it against the floor. Probably to see if I was awake. It hurt like hell, but I remained inert. It seemed an age before the detectives left, still cursing me. I got to my feet, shaking with pain and fury, and screamed obscenities at them.

A uniformed police sergeant and three junior constables, the regular guards, also the two turnkeys, peered through the slot in the door at the sorry-looking mess. I put on my clothes. Every limb was on fire.

The sergeant, known as Snowy, cleared his throat. 'Are you all right, Darcy?'

He spoke with astonishing aplomb but it was a silly question in the circumstances. Still, Snowy seemed to mean well.

'I'll be okay, I suppose.'

'I'm sorry, son, for what happened.' He turned to the three uniformed constables. 'We had no part in it. It was those bloody plain-clothes bastards. I couldn't do anything about it — can I get you a glass of water?'

I nodded gratefully. Two turnkeys were officially in charge of my custody. By rights, they should have prevented the detectives from pounding me.

'Let the miserable swine suffer,' one said.

Snowy apparently saw red. He turned on the two of them. 'Swine?' he roared. 'You two are the swines! You and those bloody sadists in plain clothes. It's our job to keep him in here. It's *his* job to get out.'

Sergeant Snowy continued abusing them as the turnkeys backed off. Then the tall, rangy man with greying hair told one of his constables to fetch a mug of water. After nodding my thanks, I drank the water. Snowy proved that there were humane men in the police force.

Everyone, Mears included, wanted to know how I had opened the cuffs, the latest type available.

Newspapermen questioned locksmiths, who were also baffled. Moments before leaving the court to try the break, I had asked to see a sheaf of depositions on a table. Before returning them, I removed a pin that held some papers together. Police later found the pin on the floor of the dock. They believed, as I intended, that this had keyed open the cuffs.

Even after the bashing in the cell, the cuff key remained against my top gum. Perhaps it would be used again.

In the six days at Petty Sessions, Mr Brindley was able to discredit important evidence from Mrs Thompson in the case of the Jack Thompson hold-up. The charge was dismissed.

With the Mort's Dock hold-up and shooting, the only concrete prosecution evidence was from a man who claimed he could identify Mears as the masked man standing by the dock gate. Under cross-examination by Brindley, the witness claimed he had identified Mears by his eyes. Brindley moved so that he was standing between him and Mears.

My lawyer said, 'What is there about Mears's eyes that enables you to be so sure they are the ones you saw at the hold-up?'

WITNESS: I recognised them by their shape and colour and the bushy eyebrows.
BRINDLEY: What colour are Mears's eyes?
WITNESS: Dark brown or black.

Without taking his eyes from the witness, Brindley softly asked me over his shoulder, 'What colour are they? Quietly!'

I looked at open-eyed Mears and whispered, 'Bluey green.'

Mr Brindley feigned disappointment, then readdressed the witness. 'You can't swear that the eyes of the man you saw at the dock were dark brown or black, can you?'

WITNESS: Yes.
BRINDLEY: You could be mistaken, couldn't you?

The middle-aged witness had made himself judge and jury. He was not mistaken, he swore. He had fallen headlong into Brindley's trap.

The witness repeated his claim that the eyes were dark brown or black and that they were Mears's eyes.

I thanked the Lord the witness could not see Mears smirking in the box, let alone his eyes.

Mr Brindley stepped aside and asked the witness to look at Mears's green and twinkling eyes. As the witness squirmed uncomfortably, Brindley told him he must admit that the man at the gate could not have been Mears.

Astonishingly, no one claimed to have recognised my masked face. The charges relating to the Mort's Dock affair were also dismissed.

The prosecution said Mears and I were equally guilty of attempting to murder the Ultimo bank manager. In law, and correctly I suppose, an accomplice in a crime in which someone was shot is just as much at fault as the shooter.

Mears's Collaroy statement concerning Ultimo was our principal worry. In the bank, Mears and I had worn hats well down on our foreheads and handkerchiefs as masks over our noses.

No one from the bank claimed to have identified me. But two people, a man customer and the woman cleaner, said Mears had done the shooting.

One man said he had seen us abandon our getaway car opposite his home and could identify both of us.

Brindley asked for the man's address in order to make his own investigations. The police prosecutor objected. The witness, he said, must be protected from possible attack by Dugan and Mears.

One minute, the witness claimed we left the car by the witness's home. The next minute, they refused to say where the witness lived. Apparently the police were not positive we had held up the bank and they were determined to limit the resources of our defence.

Leslie Nalder was still dangerously ill in hospital. If he died within one year and one day of being shot, and his death was because of Mears's bullet, the charge would be of murder.

Abe Brindley never tried to fool me. If he thought something was a lost cause, he said so. He considered the Ultimo bank charge the toughest to beat. But, with the evidence appearing to be thin, he was hopeful. He knew I dreaded going to Grafton jail as much as the prospect of being hanged.

Committed for trial, Mears and I spent four months at Long Bay in solitary confinement. Eighteen hours a day in a flea-ridden cell, six hours pacing about in a small walled yard. No reading matter.

Turnkeys regularly reminded us that we would hang.

On 5 June 1950, Mears and I appeared at Sydney Quarter Sessions before Justice (later Chief Justice) Leslie Herron, charged with attempted murder. The trial lasted five days.

Again, Abe Brindley defended me without fee and Mears defended himself. Brindley did what he could to help him. The Crown had a reasonable case against Mears. The man and the woman cleaner still claimed he was the one who did the shooting in the bank. And there was Mears's 'voluntary' statement of confession.

The case against me was weaker, especially as there was evidence that the non-shooting robber had abused the shooter for firing his gun. Brindley valiantly endeavoured to have Mears and me tried separately but that failed.

To prevent the police verballing me, claiming I had agreed that Mears's statement was correct, Brindley tried to subpoena the letters I sent to newspapers saying I would never make a statement to police. The letters, however, were not permitted as evidence.

Even at that stage, Brindley felt I had a good chance of acquittal. He defended me brilliantly for three days.

On the morning of the fourth, Mears cross-examined a police officer.

> MEARS: Why would I make a voluntary statement admitting guilt to this crime when surrounded by police, bashed by them, then deny making the statement now of my own free will?

DETECTIVE: You always make voluntary statements when arrested.
MEARS: That is a lie.

After that, I told Mears we would demand that the Crown produce statements written by him on previous occasions. If no statements were produced, the Crown would have to admit its police witness had lied.

'All such papers are kept for ages in the Crown Law Office vaults,' I told him. 'If they exist, they can produce them. Have you ever written a statement?'

Mears adamantly said no.

'Great! We've got 'em by the balls! Now stand up and demand that the statements be produced.'

Mears replied that he did not think it was a good idea. He preferred not to make a demand.

I gripped his arm. 'You demand them, or I will. But don't if you've ever made one. Have you?'

'No.'

'Then make the demand!'

Mears did his stuff. Justice Herron directed production of said documents.

During the lunch break, Brindley said that the way the trial was going, he only had to discredit police claims that Mears had previously confessed to crimes, and I, though probably not Mears, would get off. Some members of the jury of men and women sometimes had given me flickers of smiles. They seemed to be turning our way.

'So the fact they won't find any statements by Bill should win the day,' I said, looking across the cell at Mears.

Brindley nodded. 'There aren't any, are there, Bill?'

'Course not.'

Brindley's eyes shone. He would give the police a torrid time when no statements by Mears turned up.

When the court reconvened, the Crown prosecutor stood. 'Your Honour, the documents demanded by Mears. I have them.'

He picked up from his desk a thick sheaf of papers. He dramatically held them above his head, then let them drop to the table with a thud like a death knell.

I watched Brindley. Not a muscle in his face moved, but it went pale. He knew what those documents meant. The jury knew. Everyone knew!

Defendant William Cecil Mears was a liar. I felt sick. I held myself outwardly calm beside my co-accused in the dock, tempted to belt him.

Most of Abe Brindley's good work had been destroyed. And now Mears would take me down with him. Mears did not move.

Justice Herron looked at him. 'The documents do not have to be offered to the jury as evidence unless you wish it,' he intoned, and ordered that they be handed to defendant Mears.

Mears was handed the papers, which he kept out of my reach. He gave them a cursory look, muttered that they were forgeries. Ignoring my demands to see them, he handed the papers back out of the dock.

Why did Mears lie? I am not a psychologist so will not venture an opinion.

Mr Brindley tried every inch of the way for me in the final two days of the trial but the cause was lost.

On Friday, 9 June, the jury retired to consider its verdict. In only a few hours, they returned looking sombre, avoided Mears's and my eyes. Before the foreman announced it, I knew they had found us guilty.

Mears and I appealed to the Court of Criminal Appeal, but it was hopeless. The three justices, led by Chief Justice Street, QC, gave Mears short shrift. I expected similar treatment. But when I fronted them, they listened attentively. However, they didn't change the verdict.

Mears and I were housed in Long Bay's Observation Section. Prisoners there were under tight security. The OBS housed the mentally deranged, suicide attempters, the physically sick, the dangerous. And yes, it was also death row.

The state had not hanged anyone in the ten years the Australian Labor Party had held power. If they continued to govern, the Executive Council would almost automatically commute our death sentences to life imprisonment. This, in practice, meant about 15 years' jail.

Despite its gory reputation, Grafton was what I wanted. I would have a chance of getting out of there.

But if Leslie Nalder died from Mears's bullet and our charge went from attempted murder to murder, the gallows waited.

Nalder could die any day, the turnkeys were only too keen to keep reminding us. Such words no doubt sound hollow, but I was truly sorry and contrite about Nalder.

The situation with June had to be faced. There was now only one sensible thing to do. We agreed — painfully, by mail, which the warders read — never to see or correspond with each other again.

Gleeful turnkeys taunted Mears and me for hours, cracked macabre jokes. I held a solid seal over the turmoil inside me, but several times Mears broke down under the jibing. He screamed and cried. I felt sorry for Bill. He was, to my way of thinking, a well-intentioned bloke. Spirit willing, but flesh weak.

Deranged prisoners in the OBS wailed and bellowed all night. This was punctuated by Bill's calls to me. There were two cells between us.

'They reckon Nalder's going to die. They reckon the Liberals'll get in. Will they hang us? Darcy, Darcy!'

The question of whether Mears and I would hang became an issue in the state election campaign. Nearing midnight on election day, turnkeys said the Liberals looked like winning. I doubt if anyone has ever had so much, er, *hanging* on the result of an election. I was a Liberal. Being a prisoner, I was not eligible to vote. But had I been eligible, I would have defected.

In the closest contest ever, after days of vote counting, both parties had an equal number of candidates elected to parliament.

Also elected were two independents. Both of them, thank God, sided with the ALP, which retained government.

A little more than three months after our conviction, the Executive Council commuted our sentences to life imprisonment. The prison authorities wasted little time in packing us off up the coast to Grafton.

15

'You'll stew at the Bloodhouse, Dugan,' said a turnkey, grinning across the aisle at his colleague on the train. 'They'll hammer Christ out of you, you bastard.'

The job of jail warder attracted sadists, bullies. Some of them had applied on the strength of having been bully boys at Gosford. This baiting was typical of the patter on the ride 400 miles north from Sydney.

The turnkeys and four CIB detectives guarded us in a special compartment. All had guns. Handcuffs locked Mears's and my hands in front of us. Another linked my left wrist to Mears's right.

A crowd of spectators, news reporters and photographers, along with the heavy police escort, had made a runaway from Central railway station hard. This train ride was probably the last opportunity to escape I would get for quite a while. There surely were ways of getting out of Grafton, however, if I failed to flee on the way.

Through the abuse, I wondered what my friends, my associates over the years were thinking about my fate. School buddy Jimmy, flirty girls, dear old Tilly and her prostitutes at the 'Loo, the cinema hosties, fellow robbers Larry and Johnny, Len and Dawn …

And … and June. I thought I saw a teary June, a scarf over her dark hair, near the back of the crowd at Central station.

To this prisoner on a respite from jail, the scenery out the windows was magnificent — forests, farms, streams, the ocean, cows and horses and sheep. I even spotted some rabbits and a kangaroo.

If I didn't break away from this train or from Grafton soon after arrival, this would be my last look at countryside for a long time. I imprinted the landscapes on my mind, to recall if or when I was stuck behind stone walls again.

I watched for the chance of a break.

If I could get near the window, past Mears, I would dive through it. I could free myself of both sets of handcuffs in seconds. My cuff key, the one I used in the dock at Central Court of Petty Sessions, was still inside my lip.

A couple of the police in the train were eating oranges. One of them, who clearly disapproved of the continual baiting by the turnkeys and other cops, gave me one. I sucked at that delicious orange, a luxurious change from Long Bay's awful fare.

Mears got a handkerchief from his pocket. My hands were dragged over with his as I felt an orange pip in my mouth.

I spat it out. Then, the tinkle of metal hitting the floor. I had spat out my key!

I looked dead ahead. But they heard it. In a flash, the whole lot of them drew their guns. They alternately stared at me and the little metal object on the floor beside me.

'Easy, Dugan,' one said anxiously. 'Easy … one move and you're full of lead.'

Mears and I froze. Never knowing about the key, Bill was as amazed as the guards. A detective gingerly picked it up.

'Bloody oath,' he exclaimed, examining the doctored piece of belt buckle. He held it up for the others to see. 'His cuff key. Clever cunt, aren't you?'

My mouth was examined in case it contained more non-regulation goodies. My hopes of clearing out of the train were gone. The guards watched me like hawks for the remainder of the journey.

Two enormous towers of grey brick stood each side of the big iron gates at Grafton jail. In through those gates had passed the most ruthless, dangerous and hardened men in Australia.

Many of them, upon finally leaving the place, had been reduced to fawning sheep. Mental vegetables, on their way to asylums. Others had become seething barbarians. Many had gone out through the gates in coffins. They were the victims of what was known as the 'intractable' system at Grafton.

In 1943, state Comptroller-General of Prisons Nott introduced this unique system for the most rebellious men in his department's custody — those who, in Nott's opinion, were 'unfit to associate with other prisoners in the normal activities of a jail', those who would never reform. If Nott decided a prisoner was intractable, he went to Grafton. There was no process, no appeal. The prisoner usually remained there until Grafton's officer in charge advised that the convict had been 'tracted'.

Nott turned back the clock to make his Bloodhouse. Warders noted for their aggression were selected to staff it. It was Australia's little Alcatraz. I knew, from men who had done time there, that the Alcatraz island prison in San Francisco Bay was a tough place for tough men. But it was much less tough than Grafton jail. The punishments delivered at Grafton, usually 'unofficially', were enormously harsher, physically and mentally.

Most intractables spent two to five years there before being officially broken. I knew a couple who were intractables for only a few months. One was Len McPherson, graduate of the Gosford boys' prison.

I've known Grafton to have as few as 11 intractables, as many as 22. The jail also housed 20 to 40 normal prisoners from the district, including a few women. They did most of the chores in the jail and had much easier lives than the intractables. The local prisoners shaved the intractables, cut their hair and prepared meals.

Never, but never, was a local allowed to talk to an intractable. Grafton also kept 'escorts', or short-term prisoners, from other jails to do maintenance work when there were not enough local boys in jail.

In other jails, it was funny to see prisoners' reactions when told they were going to the Bloodhouse for building maintenance work like painting a shed. They ran about trying to get cons on remand to subpoena them to testify at forthcoming trials. And they got a wonderful assortment of sudden illnesses. Even these men copped hard times at Grafton.

* * *

After nearly ten hours on the train, and still cuffed together, Mears and I walked with our guards through Grafton's front gate on the evening of Friday, 29 September 1950.

Just inside stood a solidly built man I had known years back when he was a warder at another jail. He was nicknamed the Bagman, because he always looked dirty and untidy. He bit his nails and picked his nose. Dandruff always covered the shoulders of his navy blue turnkey coat. At the other jail, the Bagman was considered a coward. He was never game to clobber a prisoner for fear of retaliation.

He stood in front of seven other screws. I learned later that they included a few who were not even on duty that day. They had come up to the jail to 'welcome' the two monsters.

'We've been waiting for you, Dugan,' said the Bagman. He strode up and crashed a fist into my face. I was sent sprawling to the ground, dragging Mears with me.

'That's only a start, Dugan,' he continued, smirking at his colleagues. His boot crashed into my ribs. Two other screws joined in, kicking us as we scrambled to our feet.

The handcuffs were removed.

Four of the turnkeys hustled Mears into a cell block. As I stood under guard outside, I heard Mears cry out. The sound of thudding filtered through two-feet-thick walls of stone. After five minutes of that, Mears screamed loudly and the noises stopped. I assumed he had lost consciousness.

Then it was my turn. Six turnkeys took me into the same block. On the way I was struck on the back, thighs and legs by batons. Only at Grafton jail did screws have batons. They were a foot long, made of hard, black rubber, with central spines of steel.

In the block, I saw for the first time the turnkey in charge, Smith. His looks did not inspire confidence. He had a heavy body, ruddy face and great sagging jowls. His small eyes were bloodshot. And, I later learned, he liked whisky.

'So, you're Darcy Dugan,' he said. 'Think you're a big man, don't you? You reckon you're tough. Well, we're bloody tougher *here*, Dugan. We're going to break you.'

I said nothing. Talk would be useless.

'What's wrong, Dugan?' chief turnkey Smith asked. 'Lost ya tongue?'

I did not answer. A turnkey batoned me on the back of the head, and I fell to the floor. I learned later that this pack of men specialised in delivering punishment to prisoners. They were the Football Squad.

'Get up!' the Bagman commanded. 'When the officer in charge addresses you, you reply "Yes, sir" or "No, sir." Understand?'

Remembering my first day at Gosford, I nodded. And was knocked flat on my back. As far as I was concerned, that was it. I was not going to take this treatment like a cur.

I bounded to my feet and got in one good punch on the Bagman's mouth. The Football Squad moved in, batons swinging. I went berserk, threw punches in a red fog, but did little damage. I was pounded to the floor, kicked from all directions. Then I knew nothing.

On waking a few minutes later, I was face down on the floor of a small cell. The Football Squad stood around me.

'We've searched your clothes,' one said. 'Now we search *you*. On your feet!' I stood up.

'Bend over and open the cheeks of your arse.'

I did. A boot crashed into my rectum. I shot headfirst into the stone wall. I groaned as the turnkeys laughed. My stern ached like blazes. Big joke.

The Football Squad again moved in with batons and boots. Skin was ripped from my knuckles as I tried to protect my head. They battered me unconscious.

When I woke an hour later, still naked on the floor, a pile of prison clothes was nearby. Blue denim pants and an army-style jacket. Short-sleeved cotton shirt. White cotton underpants and singlet. Heavy socks of grey wool. Green duck hat of canvas. Leather belt with, aha, a buckle.

Square patches of white cotton were sewn on the left breast and in the centre of the back of the jacket. On these were printed in black the number 3. This from now on was my name. Seldom again

Police 'mug shots' of Darcy Dugan track his criminal career. The first was taken in 1937, aged 17, when he was sent to the boys' reformatory at Gosford, from which he escaped twice. The later ones were taken in 1948 in the wake of Darcy's celebrated breakouts from a Black Maria and 'escape proof' prison tram.

Sydney's infamous queen of vice, Tilly Devine. Darcy met Tilly in front of a brothel at Woolloomooloo in 1935. Darcy was 15, and took the opportunity to expand his already thriving business selling stolen cosmetics to Tilly's scores of prostitutes. Darcy and Tilly became regular bedmates as well as dance partners. Among his many other talents, Darcy was a champion ballroom dancer.

A shoplifter with Darcy as a boy, later an organiser of some of Darcy's robberies, Lennie McPherson went on to become the Mister Big of crime in 1960s Sydney. McPherson's subsequent betrayals of Darcy to the police added 17 years to Darcy's time in jail. Gun in hand, McPherson warned Michael Tatlow never to reveal in a book what Darcy said about him.

The 'escape proof' jail tram Darcy Dugan escaped from by sawing a hole though the roof as the tram went along Anzac Parade, Randwick, in March 1946. This escape was just five weeks after Darcy escaped from a Black Maria.

The inside corridor of the prison tram, now on display at the Sydney Tramway Museum in Loftus.

Only 25 minutes after being jailed for alleged armed robbery, Dugan and William Mears pulled off this outrageous escape in broad daylight from Long Bay jail.

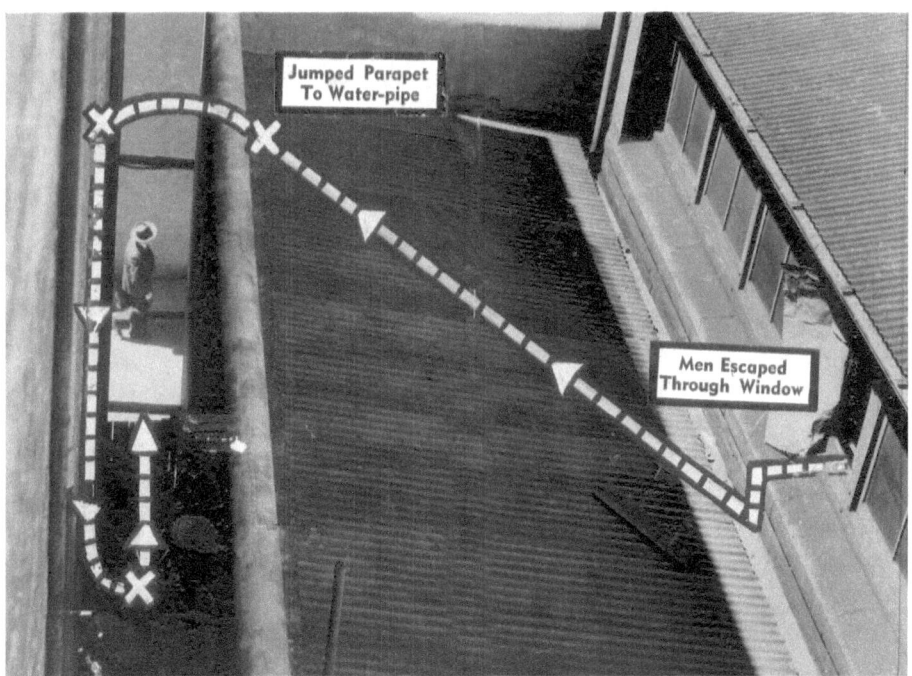

The escape route under the windows of the CIB headquarters after Dugan, followed by Mears, cut his way through a barred window at Sydney's Central Court of Petty Sessions. He left a cheeky message on his cell wall saying 'Gone to Gowings'.

ESCAPED FELONS
£500 REWARD

Whereas at about 1.30 p.m. on the 15th December, 1949, Darcy Ezekiel Dugan and William Cecil Mears, whose photographs appear hereunder, escaped from a cell whilst in lawful custody at the Central Police Station, Sydney.

Darcy Ezekiel Dugan.

William Cecil Mears.

Notice is hereby given that a Reward of Five Hundred Pounds (£500) will be paid by the Government for such information as shall lead to the apprehension of the said Darcy Ezekiel Dugan and William Cecil Mears.

This Reward to remain in force for a period of six months from the date hereof and the allocation of the said sum of Five Hundred Pounds (£500) will be at the sole discretion of the Commissioner of Police. Any information received will be treated in the strictest confidence.

Premier's Department, Sydney,
18th January, 1950.

JAMES McGIRR,
Premier.

In 1950 the police offered a reward of £500, big money then, for information leading to the arrest of Dugan and Mears after their daring breakout from Long Bay.

Escapees Dugan and Mears were arrested at their beachside hideout at Collaroy in February 1950 after being betrayed to police by a trusted 'helper'. Conviction for the bank hold-up they were originally in for, in which Mears shot and seriously wounded the manager, sent the two to the notorious 'Bloodhouse', Grafton jail.

Had a prisoner not 'ratted' to warders about Darcy's plan, the mutiny by prisoners he led at Grafton jail in 1953 would have resulted in a gang of escapees fleeing to Bondi Beach in a seaplane. Darcy planned the mutiny by his own 'wall talk' of tapping on cell walls. The mutiny led to reforms at the Bloodhouse and to Grafton residents and an Anglican bishop petitioning the government to stop warders' brutality.

The entrance to Grafton jail, the infamous 'Bloodhouse', where a handcuffed Darcy was greeted in 1950 by the 'football squad' of brutal warders, who kicked and punched him unconscious. During his record 11 years there, Darcy came close to pulling off two daring escapes and organised a mutiny of 'intractable' prisoners.

Detective Sergeant Ray 'Gunner' Kelly, who repeatedly sent Dugan to jail to stop the master escapist's public charges of police criminality. In 1975 Kelly's associate, corrupt Premier Robert Askin, made Kelly a Member of the British Empire.

Freed in 1968, a reformed Dugan went on to become a well-respected welfare counsellor at the Wayside Chapel, Kings Cross. Reverend Ted Noffs is said to have credited Darcy with reforming scores of young criminals, drug addicts and alcoholics. At the same time he also turned in champion performances at ballroom dancing competitions, became a popular public speaker and starred in a play.

In November 1969 riot squad police toting machine guns arrested Darcy and charged him with stealing $42,000 worth of jewellery from Kleemo's store in Sydney. He was convicted despite strong evidence he was innocent and that it was an invented charge to stop his public allegations of police corruption. Darcy also stridently denied the claim that he threatened a detective, and the charge was eventually dropped.

Darcy back in his natural habitat – in this case inside Maitland jail in October 1979 – with the ever-present prison guard pacing the walls behind him.

Darcy is freed in 1980 to join his bride-to-be, Jan Simmonds, who campaigned for his release. Two years earlier, Jan had sought Darcy's help at Maitland jail in writing a book about her brother, notorious criminal Kevin Simmonds.

Darcy weds Jan Simmonds in July 1980 at Sydney's Wayside Chapel, where he had been a welfare counsellor.

A tense session Darcy (seated) had in 1980 with his schoolboy chum and repeated betrayer, Lennie McPherson (left) and 'celebrity' criminal George Freeman. A gunman protector of McPherson stood nearby. When a fellow prisoner at Parramatta jail, Freeman had told Darcy of McPherson's betrayals and also helped Darcy in a dramatic attempted escape.

Criminal George Freeman showing off a book about himself to Darcy in 1980. Darcy had been the boyhood hero of George, who was also a former inmate of the boys' reformatory at Gosford.

Age and the effects of years of torture in prison, plus the disarray of his marriage, were showing on Darcy when he was admitted to Sydney retirement home Glebe House in 1981. Dugan had worked as a rehabilitation officer until his health deteriorated. He died on August 22, 1991, from Parkinson's disease.

```
                                        D.Dugan
                                        8 Moorhead Place,
                                        Latham,
                                        A.C.T.   pho. 549818.
       Dear Mike.
              Ienclose a manuscript thatwas intended for expansion. I used red
pencil to let you know the parts that I suggest you include in the rewrite of
the book. I know you will probably want to cut some ofit out,but sections I
think are musts are the parts that tell of "Jane". You do the best you can with
therest.
              The Shirley Briefman episode, as I recall, was she was the girlfriend
of ███████, a Brisbane cop. He used to take protection money from themolls.
Shirley was present when Krahe and ███████ were talking over the"setting up of
darcy Dugan."
              Shemade a statuatory declaration to this effect butit was hushed up.
              They found her dead in mysterious circumstances.She reputely had more
poiso-n inher body than wouldbe foundin the bottle they found beside her body.
              Ted Noffs was in Kerry Packers office when Perry was talking to the
Deputy Commissioner of police on the phone. Packer was told police had evidence D
Dugan was going to kidnap his kids. Noffs listened in while this conversation
was being carried on.
              It was typical mudslinging. No charges were ever made about this.I
was never questioned. Packers paper had generally been quite supportive regarding
me and this was onre way of ensuring this support ended.
              Anyhow read themanuscrip I amsending you and decide which sections
can be merged with yours.
              Let meknow what you think.
                                        Darcy.
```

The letter Darcy wrote to Mike Tatlow, accompanying the manuscript he had asked him to publish after he 'and the crooks we've exposed have turned to dust'.

would I be called Darcy or Dugan. It was either 'Three' or 'bastard' or 'rat', or worse. A prisoner's sense of identity had to be crushed.

Every part of my body ached. My face was swollen; head all lumpy but, surprisingly, not split open. I slowly dressed, groaning at almost every movement.

The concrete-faced wall of the cell was painted green to shoulder level, cream to the ceiling. At the end opposite the small steel door was a window three feet wide and a foot high.

Across that were two horizontal bars of steel, an inch and a half thick, painted white. It was the same sort of window as the one I had cut through at the Central Court cells. The bottom of the window was about eight feet from the floor.

The cell was twelve feet long, seven wide. Furnishings included a five-foot hempen floor mat, a hearth broom with no handle and a small wooden dust tray. No shaving gear or mirror. There was a plastic comb on a small triangle of timber two inches thick — my dining table. The chair was a two-foot-high slice of tree trunk, a foot in diameter. A small bucket made of tin, with a lid, was obviously my toilet.

The 'bed' was a six-foot slab of coir matting of the type one normally has at the front door to wipe your feet on. The 'pillow' was solid coir, eight inches thick. There were four woollen blankets, two sheets and a pair of cloth slippers.

As night drew near, I lay on the bed. My reception had taught me I could not score a goal for a while against the Football Squad. But my turn would come.

Dim light came through a narrow slit in the thick stone beside the door, which had a spyhole.

I did not sleep that night. No one had ever escaped from Grafton. But there had to be a way out.

I searched my mind for it. Perhaps, I mused, I would see one when I got to know this horrid place, had studied its security measures. There *had* to be a weak spot.

* * *

A bell rang at seven in the morning. The Bloodhouse routine began.

I rose from the bed, folded the blankets and sheets into an immaculately pleated pack, and rolled up the bed mat and stood it endwise against the rear wall. Then I washed in a small dish of water that had been filled the previous afternoon. Beside it was a small plastic drinking jug. I emptied the washing water into the tin lavatory.

We intractables had to be dressed at 7.20, when the cell door opened. Three turnkeys stood over me as I quickly and wordlessly placed my blankets outside the door, picked up my breakfast. That was a dixie of wheatmeal porridge, called mush, a quarter pint of milk and a half a loaf of bread.

I also picked up a spoon, a blunt knife and shoes, which had to be put out of the cell every afternoon when I was locked up for 15 hours.

As the door opened, the nerve war began. If an intractable was too slow bending to get his dixie, he got a boot in the face. Or, as he turned back into his cell, a shove in the back sent him sprawling on the floor amid spilt mush and milk. As a sort of a game with a prisoner the turnkeys had a 'set' on, they sometimes began to swing the heavy door shut before he was out of the way. If the con's body or arm was jammed between the wall and the door, too bad.

With the door closed, I sat on my block of wood at the corner table. If I was hungry enough, I picked ever-present weevils from my mush and ate the stuff. White, maggoty-looking grubs with black heads could also regularly be found sharing the mush. Hungry prisoners sometimes ate them.

Shortly after 8 a.m., the cell door opened again. I put out my sanitary bucket, the porridge dixie and utensils. Local prisoners emptied the buckets and returned them to the cell doors.

Every intractable was assigned to a particular 'yard' of usually four prisoners, who were locked together in a work cage. Mostly these cages were surrounded by vertical steel bars. The four men sat on wooden benches on each side of a table and sewed together shirts for convicts in jails throughout the state. Because intractables were given a minimum of contact with cutting instruments, the pieces of cloth for the shirts were cut at another jail, Maitland. For this work we were paid sixpence a week. It was added to our credit in the jail office.

We intractables sewed shirts all the working day; nowadays some of them convert books into Braille.

An intractable was allowed to speak only when addressed by a turnkey. If a turnkey saw a prisoner looking outside or talking, he was yelled at or received a pounding back at his cell. Still, we did manage to mutter between ourselves in the work cages when the patrolling turnkeys were diverted.

A screw never entered a cage unless other turnkeys were present. There could be no risk of prisoners grabbing him as a hostage.

At 11.40 a.m., we intractables were marched, a yard at a time, back to our cells. Going into the cell block, marching close together in step, we picked up our emptied shit cans, and dishes of lunch from a table. We were locked up alone until 1.20 p.m.

Lunch at Grafton was usually mutton stew. Sometimes we got beef, occasionally a roast. It depended a lot on the ability or interest of the local prisoner appointed to cook, but meals were not too bad. If, that is, you got used to first picking out the grubs and maggots.

It being a small jail, the food was not cooked so much en masse as at Long Bay. Once, I remember, we scored a professional cook. He lifted the standard of the meals gloriously. We got chipped, fried potatoes, little pieces of toast, slices of beef fat. And no grubs or maggots!

Then, one day the Bagman walked in and spotted the meals ready to be taken to the intractables. He glared. 'What's this? Chips, toast? What the bloody hell's this? Where's the maggots?'

The cook, knowing the Bagman's reputation, was terrified. 'Well, ah, sir, there was this bread left over, sir, and, ah, I thought a little bit of toast —'

The Bagman cut him short. 'Never you mind the fucking toast! And none of this other stuff, either. Give 'em stew! They get stew. With maggots from the bin of 'em here in your kitchen.'

'Luxury' food for intractables ended.

After the lunch break, we stood at stiff attention at our cell doors and waited for the bellowed order 'Quick march'. We stepped forwards, marched in double time with three others and halted in a queue at the cell-block door.

We were always tense as a screw inspected us. A button on a jacket might have come undone. A canvas hat might not be straight. A shoelace might have come undone or be hanging too far down the side.

If so, the con was belted across the face and told to smarten up. If he looked anywhere but at the ground in front of him, he automatically was slugged by a fist, boot or baton.

Usually at this time, one yard of four prisoners was told to strip for searching for non-regulation items. We never knew which yard would be searched.

Often this business was conducted by a big, fair-haired turnkey we called the White Rat, a lead player in the Football Squad.

The stripped prisoners' clothes were examined. Then mouths and rectums were examined. If the White Rat and his brutal colleague Bob the Dog felt jovial, they made vulgar cracks and suggestions of exploring anuses with their dicks.

It was humiliating.

The last man dressed received a cuff on the ear or a boot in the stern. Each yard of four prisoners was marched across about 120 feet of the jail's open courtyard to one of four work cages.

If I was marching too far from, or too close to, the prisoner in front, I was slugged. Slugged, too, if my nose was more than an inch from the wall when standing in my cell during a regular search. Standing within a few yards of the door also earned me a baton belt.

When a turnkey noted a spider, common in semitropical Grafton, on the ceiling, he said I was not keeping my cell clean. So, slugged.

Afternoons were spent back in the cages. At 4.30, we were quick-marched to the cells for the night, where we had dinner, mostly stew leftovers from lunch, with bigger you know whats. Certain yards were again told to strip and were searched on the way.

A critical time was when we stood at attention by our cell doors, waiting to be locked in. This was when we would cop punishment for any real or fabricated misdemeanour during the afternoon. We each had to stand midway along a mat that was a few feet long, with our noses an inch from the wall.

One day, standing at the wall, eyes dead ahead, I was punched from behind in the kidneys. It was a hard blow. My head hit the wall and I slumped to the floor. The assailant who booted me to my feet was freakishly tall, with gangly arms and legs. No chin. We called him the Praying Mantis.

'Stand at attention,' he bellowed. 'Number Three, do you know what that's for?'

'No, sir.'

'That's for not standing on the right place on the mat. Be on the wrong place tomorrow and you'll get worse.'

The Praying Mantis walked from the block sniggering with two other turnkeys. I thought I had stood on the correct spot. But maybe I had been an inch or so off it, to the right.

The next evening, I took care to stand two inches to the left of where I had been before. My eyes burned into the wall, the Praying Mantis behind me. A roundhouse swing from his fist struck the side of my head.

'Stand on the proper part of the mat, Number Three,' he roared.

The next day, I stood a few inches along the other way, to the right. And again that Praying Mantis was on duty. His hand slammed my head to the wall with sickening force. Skin was torn from my forehead. My nose spurted blood.

'Stand on the right place on the mat, Number Three.'

'Yes, sir. Where is the right place, sir?'

'Where I say it is! And don't talk to me unless you're spoken to!'

He walked off, giggling again. Happily for me, the Mantis was not working the next couple of days. This treatment was part of the nerve war, conducted to break a prisoner's spirit. When locked in at night, I surged with relief to be away from the war.

I once took a head count of intractables who had been at Grafton for two years or more. Half of them suffered from ulcers or allied peptic maladies.

Judges sentenced the (usually) guilty to terms in prison, locked away from society. Torture was not part of the sentences. I wondered how many judges knew about the torture at Grafton, and, knowing, how the fair-minded ones would respond?

Intractables were rebellious, aggressive men. In normal jails, they were usually heavies, who dominated other prisoners.

The man with the most guts usually runs all the other prisoners. A new prisoner had to show his guts early if he wanted to pull any weight in jail and be free of strife from other convicts, some of whom were always thugs and sadists. It was, and is, dog eat dog.

A new prisoner was watched closely by most of his fellow cons. At his first sign of weakness, they pounced and had fun at his expense. They needed only one chink in his armour.

When I arrived at Grafton, the other intractables knew me, or of me. My toughness was not doubted. From the outset, I was able to have my way with small, but to us important, things.

A con in my first yard was a lifer who had raped a hospital nurse. Dudley was a full-blooded Aborigine. I regard Aborigines as equals, but he was ugly, aggressive and stupid. He also had no scruples about informing to the screws about other cons' misdemeanours.

His low intelligence left him quite incapable of learning the ABC of Grafton. I finally pitied Dudley and tried over months to teach it to him, and failed.

He had commenced his life sentence at Goulburn jail. He was transferred to the tougher jail at Maitland after being caught having sexual intercourse with a 'cat' — a submissive homosexual prisoner.

At Maitland, Dudley poked on the chest a warder who was abusing him. The screw toppled backwards into a barrow laden with dixies of mush. Dudley was sent to Grafton.

In his first two weeks there, I worked across the table from Dudley but he hardly ever spoke. Then, with no turnkey nearby, the big black man came out of his shell.

'Hey, you,' he said to me, 'give me them scissors.' I noted his tone of voice but put it down to ignorance. I handed him the blunt scissors. Soon after, Dudley said, 'Hand me the bloody scissors!'

The two other intractables grinned quietly. The scissors were within Dudley's reach, where he had put them. I continued sewing.

Dudley snarled, 'You lookin' for trouble wiv me? You goin' to git it and git it fucken quick, Doogan. Hand me them scissors!'

I was dumbfounded for a second or two. This fool, in his slow, stupid way, was testing me.

The turnkey was loafing down the other end of the cages. I slowly stood. 'I'll give you a belt in the mouth, you cheeky bastard.'

Dudley sprang up. He adopted a stance reminiscent of the heavyweight boxer John L. Sullivan and bared his yellow teeth. I lunged at him. Dudley folded up without even throwing a punch. I took him by the throat and shook him. His eyes bulged.

'I oughta twist your head off,' I growled quietly. 'Never try that again with me.' I let him go.

From that day, I had no more trouble from Dudley. But I repeatedly baited him. He began it; I would finish it. The brutality of the prison was growing on me. I turned to a prisoner in the cage and said, winking, 'Do you know about Les Darcy?' The late boxing champ was thought to have been Aboriginal. 'He won't fight unless he gets a bit of sausage before he enters the ring.'

Dudley snarled. 'Yeah? You wouldn't say that if he was 'ere. 'E'd give you a bit of sausage up the arse, right 'nuff.'

I laughed cynically. 'If that bastard poof was here, I'd make him suck my cock.'

Dudley subsided, muttering to himself about white bastards.

A day or two later, when turnkeys were not about, I said to another prisoner, 'I don't believe what everyone says about Dudley.'

Dudley glared. 'What they sayin'?'

'You're my mate, Dudley, and I don't believe it, but in all the other jails, they're saying you didn't lay that cat at Goulburn jail. They reckon the cat laid *you*!'

The man frothed at the mouth with rage while I gravely assured him I did not believe it.

What I saw and heard Bob the Dog do to Dudley later made me punch the walls of my cell at night with frustrated anger. The Aborigine could not and would not fight. The unfortunate moron was all talk. Every time Bob the Dog searched Dudley in his cell at night, he found an excuse to beat him.

The sound of baton blows thudding on a man's body, and Dudley's screams and sobs, were regular when Bob the Dog was on duty. I got plenty of bashings myself, but the sound of other men's agony was noxious.

Bob the Dog had a psychopathic hatred of Aborigines. The bashings went on for years and years. Beating this helpless bloke like a dog was the action of a dog. A mad dog.

After Dudley was batoned and kicked, one of us in the yard sympathetically asked, 'What did the Dog do to you, Dudley?'

'Bob the Dog didn't bash Dudley!' he declared. 'No, boss. He didn't bash Dudley. Dudley bashed *him*! I threw him out the door!'

The poor devil, his body a mass of bruises and gashes, could never admit to being bettered. Sometimes I stole a glance at Dudley marching to his cell in the evenings when Bob the Dog was on duty. His face quivered; his eyes bulged with fear. He knew what was coming.

Intractables were allowed three books a week from the prison library. Illiterate Dudley was denied even the temporary calm induced by immersion in a book. There were no comic books. He was given the same picture books week after week.

Dudley served a then-unprecedented ten years at Grafton. He was returned to Maitland jail and died there from a brain tumour, induced no doubt by the battering to his head at the Bloodhouse.

16

The mental and physical stress affected me in an opposite way from what was intended. I grew more and more determined to one day even the score. And to escape. This was my mind's defence against weakening, becoming a brute or going insane.

Out of the blue, Pop turned up, after a train ride, for the entitled monthly visit of 20 minutes. He looked shaken, aged, but it was a thrill to see him.

Between us were two barriers of heavy wire mesh with a six-foot space in between, in which stood a watchful turnkey. I must have looked in bad shape. An eye was blackened and a baton swipe had cut my forehead.

'How is it, son?' the old chap asked. 'Have they been beating you?'

'Cut that out!' the screw snapped. 'Confine the conversation to family stuff.'

I looked over at Pop and nodded slightly. Emotion welled in me. I did not dare speak. Pop went away sobbing. Back in the cell, I was bashed for nodding to his question.

In Sydney, Pop issued a well-publicised statement about his visit and my condition. Some people demanded a formal inquiry but nothing resulted. Few, I suppose, believed him.

In July '51, after nine months at Grafton, I hit on a plan of escape.

Intractable Pinkie Moran was a safe-cracker who often bragged that his family ran a big crime gang in Melbourne. Pinkie, who I had known in another jail, had had some hacksaw blades sent to him, set in the hard cover of a book donated to the library. But the blades were found in his cell, resulting in weeks of bashing in the black pound, the jail's dreaded and windowless solitary-confinement chamber.

The word among us intractables was that someone had told the screws the blades were in Pinkie's cell, but fortunately they didn't find out how the blades got in.

We were allowed to mail one letter a week. I wrote to my old mate and accomplice Lennie. He, too, knew Pinkie Moran. He probably knew about the blade smuggle. Perhaps he had sent them. I asked him to send some books. 'The same type of reading Pinkie likes.'

Soon after, three volumes were donated anonymously to the jail library. I borrowed them. And in the cover of one, a hefty commemoration of the Australian Commonwealth Jubilee, were three hacksaw blades.

I hid them in a knife-thin slit in the floor of my cell, under the mat and covered with dust. Now I needed assistance — from a prisoner with guts and a cool head. Mears, whom I saw little of, did not qualify.

The con I settled on was Des Jones, aged about 23, doing a life sentence for murder and burglary. Des was about my height, strongly built, intelligent and not normally aggressive.

At 17, he murdered an Italian to whom he had sold stolen goods. After getting the goods, the Italian had refused to pay for them. So Des got a gun and shot the Italian dead. Des had been declared intractable after climbing over the wall at Goulburn jail. Not knowing the district, he had quickly been recaptured.

Des had been in my yard for a while but now was a member of another. Conversation with him was impossible. Even looking at a prisoner from another yard could earn a belting. But we intractables passed on to one another what little news filtered in. We did that by knocking on the walls of the cells at night.

When I went to Grafton, the wall-talk code was ludicrously slow. One tap represented A; two taps, B; three taps, C. For Z you had to tap 26 times.

I had introduced a new code by breaking the alphabet into five rows of letters. First row was A to F, the second one G to L, third

M to R. fourth S to X, fifth Y and Z. We indicated the rows by the number of taps on the wall with a comb or toothbrush. First row, one tap; second row, two; and so on.

A knuckle rap gave a different sound. After the comb taps, the number of knuckle taps told the required letter along the line. Thus, D was one comb tap and four knucklings. H was two comb taps and two knuckles. It was easily done with one hand.

I laboriously taught the intractables this code by tapping on the wall using the old method. After a while, we transmitted messages quite rapidly. Sometimes a couple of prisoners wanted to have a private conversation. They scrambled the rows of letters and reversed the knuckle and comb tapping by secret prearrangement.

But the several illiterates like poor Dudley never understood wall talk. Clearly, the screws did not learn the new code, either. I had expected them to beat the secrets of it from a susceptible prisoner. This stupid failure further confirmed my opinion that the screws were a rabble of dimwits.

I tapped away, addressing the message to Des. When a con began talking on the wall, others put their ears to the stone, the skilled among them passing it on to the addressee's cell.

Knowing the prisoners who would hear me were solid, would not squeal, I told them only Des was invited to join me in the break. He promptly responded, 'Yes.'

Sometimes the turnkeys heard the tapping. All-round thumpings came the next morning, as they never knew who did the wall talking. Des, incidentally, was barely literate when he arrived at Grafton, but a few prisoners, including me, taught him elementary reading and writing. At the risk of being caught and battered, during our lessons we wrote words on our work tables with chalk used for marking shirt material.

My plan of escape was to employ experience from when I got out of the cells at Central. I would cut through one of the two horizontal steel bars across the small window in my cell. Des would do the same in his cell, several doors away. We would signal our progress through the wall and climb through our respective windows at the same time.

First, I had to get a hacksaw blade to him. This was dangerous and difficult. Twice a week, intractables were allowed to have a two-minute bath or shower. We went to the bathroom a yard at a time. It seemed all I had to do was carry a blade to one and leave it there for Des.

Every bath day, however, when leaving our cells, one yard of men randomly had to strip and be searched. There was one chance in four of being caught with the blade. Also, the bathroom was searched after each yard used it. And some prisoners were searched on the way out.

Bath day arrived and I had the blade hidden on me. Number 1 yard had their cell doors opened. They marched to the bathroom. No search. There were three yards to go. The odds were in my favour. Being caught with it would get me a battering and weeks of black and solitary confinement.

My yard, No. 2, stepped out and filed to the cell-block door. We stood in line waiting to be told to quick-march — or strip. A turnkey ordered us to march. What wonderful relief that was.

A screw patrolled up and down by the bath and shower cubicles. When he was not looking, I thrust the blade in a crack in the floor under the bath. Wall talk had told Des where it would be. He was as lucky collecting the blade and getting it to his cell as I was in getting it out of mine.

I was anxious the following day when two screws searched my cell with rare diligence and unusual quietness. A tip-off? I wondered. But they didn't find the two blades slotted under the mat.

That night we each began cutting one of our cell window bars. With solid work, it would have been possible to hack through the inch and a half of steel in less than an hour. But our windows faced the front wall and gate of the jail, no more than 20 yards away.

Outside my window, the strip of no-man's-land, which we called the moat, was seldom patrolled at night. The outer wall beyond was also the back wall of the chief turnkey Skunky Smith's house. Sometimes we heard him and his wife brawling. That meant that they could hear a hacksaw working.

We could not put much pressure on the blades. We found we could cut little more than an eighth of an inch, even cutting all night. It was hard, tiring and risky stuff.

To reach the required height to operate the hacksaw, Des and I tightly bundled our coir beds and bound them in blankets. Then we placed them on their ends, atop our wood-block chairs, under our windows. We stood on top. We were in the dark, but if a screw happened to go to one of our peepholes …

Des and I worked 12 hours every night for ten nights. Tiredness caused me to doze off once in the work cage.

Time was against us. The cell bars were examined twice daily. We filled the cuts with soap, which blended with the white paint on the bars. Then we blew dust over them. Every night, sawing became riskier.

We had to stop work now and then while patrolling turnkeys strolled by outside. This night patrolling was a new measure. In the heat, sometimes they tired of walking and sat on a stone step near the front gate. We had to stop our gentle hacking until they moved.

The two of us cut through the ends of our lower bars at one o'clock in the morning. I tore a blanket into strips and plaited a rope, then tied it around my tightly wrapped coir mat. I attached the other end of the rope to the cut end of the lower bar. Standing on the coir provided enough weight to keep the bar down.

Just as I was about to crawl through, two turnkeys on guard out there stopped about 20 yards away. It was odd. They talked for a few minutes. One of them, the Praying Mantis, sauntered away. The other was a ruthless Irishman we called the Bog Trotter.

He strolled past my cell and Des's, to the corner of the cell block. After a couple of minutes, the Bog Trotter slowly walked back — and stopped with his back to the wall directly under my window. I was crouched on the sill. I looked down on the Bog Trotter's head, two feet away.

Of all the places to stop! He gazed towards the protruding steel cage inside the main gate. A long five minutes passed as I feared he would hear me breathing. I could have reached down and swiped his cap.

The Bog Trotter casually turned to face the cell block, and took a step away. Suddenly his head snapped up.

'Quick!' he screeched, jumping back from the wall. 'Quick, it's Dugan! *A break!*' He pulled out his revolver.

'Stay there, Dugan. Don't move, Dugan. I'll blow your head off.'

I leapt back into the cell, cursing my luck, and heard the Praying Mantis run up, then sprint to the main gate. I kept quiet. In a few minutes, a mob of turnkeys was excitedly talking outside my cell window, looking at the cut and bent bar.

I waited, disconsolate, in the dark cell. Weeks of planning and nerve-racking effort was shot to ribbons. If the Bog Trotter had walked around the moat just once more, Des and I would have been out and over the main wall.

Chattering turnkeys gathered outside my cell door. The grandaddy of bashing was coming, but this time I would not take it lying down. I picked up a length of timber I had ripped out and used to pry down the bar. It was three feet long.

I held it above my shoulder, like a baseball bat. The first turnkey in here was going to get it on the skull.

The door was flung open. The Football Squad was there, batons drawn. The sight of me with the timber pulled them up smartly. They exchanged grave glances. In front was a senior screw with an exceptionally large snout. He was the Beak.

He yelled, 'Put that down, Dugan.'

Blimey, wasn't I No. 3 any more? 'Come and take it off me,' I taunted. 'Or haven't you got the guts when I'm armed, too?'

The Beak stepped back and whispered to his squad.

I said, 'I'll put it down when you and your pals put down their batons and guarantee there'll be no bashing.'

The White Rat had clobbered me with his baton two days beforehand. He stepped to the doorway and looked in.

'Come and get it, rat,' I suggested.

He slammed the door shut. A while later, however, it was opened. There stood the Beak, again at the head of the Football Squad of eight. In his hand was a bucket.

'This is boiling water, Dugan,' he said. 'Come out or I'll throw the lot over you.'

So, had they gone away to boil some water? I did not believe the threat. The Beak was bluffing. I held my ground. The Beak stepped to the doorway and hurled the water at me. The bulk of it hit my chest. Some showered my face.

I screamed as it scalded me, and dropped the wood. The skin puffed up on my face, arms and hands. The pain was unbearable. My throat felt on fire. Blisters formed on my arms and hands. Had I not been wearing thick clothing, I probably would have lost the skin from my chest.

The Football Squad battered me unconscious. The Beak, the Bagman, the White Rat, the Bog Trotter, the Praying Mantis, Bob the Dog. And a latecomer, Skunky Smith.

When I came to, I was on my back in the Black Peter. The Football Squad, I realised, was standing around me. They carried flashlights.

I nearly cried out with the agony of my scalded chest, hands, arms, throat, face. I kept my eyes closed as the torches' light beamed down. As my brain cleared, I continued lying doggo. If they knew I had come to, the battering would resume.

I felt the heat of a torch close to my face. A hand was placed over my heart. The Beak said, 'Can't feel anything. I think we've killed him.'

'So what?' someone said. 'We were preventing an escape.'

I felt someone come to my side. His hand rested on the side of my neck. 'No,' the turnkey said after a minute, 'the shit's alive.' It was Skunky Smith.

'Will I call the doctor?' asked the Praying Mantis.

'No,' said the head screw, 'let the bastard put up with it. He'll keep till morning. The doctor can see him then.'

They left. I remained on the floor. I heard a commotion from elsewhere in the jail. The sounds were familiar — thuds and screams. They had discovered Des's cut bar and were taking 'disciplinary action'.

In the morning, three members of the Football Squad walked into my room. After receiving a few blows, I was told that I was to be charged with attempted escape, assaulting a prison officer and destroying jail property.

The jail's consulting doctor attended to my burns. My arms are scarred from that boiling water to this day.

After a few days alone in the pound, a visiting magistrate sentenced me to 14 more days' solitary in there, plus three months of 'coercion' — solitary confinement in the same Black Peter but with one hour a day alone in a small walled yard, pacing to and fro under the eyes of a turnkey.

The magistrate also fined me £12 for damaging government property, cutting the bars. One screw at the time said I could pay the fine from my personal cash the Department of Prisons held.

'No,' I retorted. 'Take it from my sixpence a week.'

It would take 20 years for my accumulated salary to pay the fine. Many months later, they dropped the debt. The paperwork recording each weekly payment made the whole business ludicrous.

Back in solitary, I pondered why those two screws had been patrolling outside my cell at night. Why it had been so carefully searched beforehand. Had I been betrayed again? Hell, only Des knew I had the hacksaw blades.

And supplier Lennie. An awful suspicion germinated.

About halfway through the coercion period, the solitude and rigorous discipline, combined with the effects of the scalding and beatings, spawned a serious reaction in my mind. Being mostly in blackness all day and night, it became increasingly difficult for me to stop my mind wandering into grotesque fantasies.

My legs paced me up and down the yard from memory. The

sublime landscapes of the train ride from Sydney now seemed like visions of another planet.

I was keen to learn how Des was faring. But wall talk did not reach the others from my isolated hole.

When my legs weakened and I dropped to the floor, regular guarding turnkey the Bogtrotter strode in and kicked me to my feet. If my walking pace slowed to only a few miles an hour, he harangued me. If I repeatedly fell down, a couple of turnkeys batoned me.

My diet was of alternate weeks of dry bread and water, and light rations. The only time anyone spoke to me it was in anger. I was not allowed books, or work to occupy my hands and mind. I lost track of the days. My clothes dug into the new skin growing over the burn marks. The stinking lavatory bucket was emptied about once a week.

Sometimes at night, I ripped a button from my jacket and hurled it against a wall. My mind faced the welcome task of finding it, fingers groping all over the floor. *I must not go mad!*

Every time I ripped off a button, I was bashed. What was happening in the world outside? I thought of June, of Pop, Mum. *Don't cry out loud. Those screw bastards'd love it.*

About this time, the Bog Trotter strode in, smirked and said, 'Ya bastard. Ya mother's just died.'

He revelled in my anguish. How could those screws, men from different backgrounds, collude in such vicious hatred? I asked myself, interrupting for a while my memories of dear old Mum. Mob rule?

My brother, Tom, had lived in the same residence as Mum for many years. He rode the 400 miles on his motorbike for a monthly visit.

After young Tom was let through Grafton's main gate, a turnkey went off to consult with his boss. Thirty minutes later, top screw Skunky Smith turned up and announced that prisoner No. 3 was denied normal privileges because he had broken regulations. So no visit.

'But our mother's just died,' Tom protested.

'He knows,' said Smith. 'Please leave.'

Curious and angry, Tom rode all through the night back to Sydney. There had been no public announcement, of course, of my attempted escape. A letter from Tom was withheld from me for weeks. It told me he had made the trip. That he had wanted to let me know that sickly, mostly bedridden Mum never knew of my last arrest, conviction or jailing.

I was also denied permission to send the normal weekly censored letter to thank him.

I tried to think of another way to get out of the Bloodhouse. It was as much for the want of something to focus my mind on as the desire for freedom. Not seeing Mum before she died still distressed me.

Previously I had considered feigning insanity. If I could convince them I'd gone mad, they would send me to an asylum. From such an institution, escape would be pretty simple.

Convincing the turnkeys that I had lost my wits would not, however, be simple. Several intractables had really cracked and become raving demons. Any such prisoner suffered five or more weeks of bashings that were more vicious than usual.

These were to test whether the prisoner was truly mad. If after this he still seemed mad, the intractable was sent to Long Bay's OBS for medical observation. Perhaps from there to an asylum.

A couple of intractables had faked insanity. They gave up their acts after a week or two of the 'special treatment'. Fortunately, I had read a few books on psychiatry and psychology, had seen in prison men whose minds had snapped. So I was armed with a reasonable idea of how to fool a medico.

And I was already in bad shape, had lost a lot of weight. I had not seen myself in a mirror since reaching Grafton but felt hollows beneath my cheekbones, under my short beard. When a local prisoner cut my hair and went over my chin with clippers not long before my attempted escape, grey hairs had fallen on my shoulders.

I had no grey hairs when I entered Grafton a little more than a year before. I probably looked like a madman. My predicament could easily generate madness. I would give it a try.

Next morning, the Bog Trotter, bringing my bread, found me lying still on my back, eyes open but unfocused, ears apparently unhearing. He prodded me with his boot but I did not move. The Trotter called another screw and the pair of them kicked me some more. Still no response from No. 3.

They lifted me to my feet, but I slumped back to the floor like jelly. A couple more screws turned up. While two held me, the Bog Trotter punched me. It was hard not to wince. They let me go and I tumbled down again.

The evident stupor went on for days. I did not wash. The screws came in each morning to find faeces scattered about the floor, the walls and my body. I ignored my blankets and slept on the stone floor. I repeatedly flung off my clothes and lay naked. I did not eat.

I got a batoning every day. Barely a spot on my body was not cut or bruised. I was filthy, stank of dry sweat, urine and faeces. Blood matted my hair and beard. Every few days, screws carried me to be washed. After I was lowered to the ground in the jail yard, a local prisoner had to strip and hose senseless No. 3 with water to expel my feculent coating. My entire body was scrubbed with a long-handled straw broom. Hell, that hurt! Especially where I had been scalded.

Every day, I was carried to a special exercise yard, where I was supposed to pace up and down for an hour. They propped me up and I sagged to the ground, remaining there for the hour.

After about ten days had passed without me eating, the jail doctor put a clamp in my mouth and slid 18 inches of black rubber hose down my gullet.

Through the hose he poured a mixture of milk and eggs. Hunger raged, but, as soon as I was hauled back to the pound, I put my fingers down my throat and heaved most of the food out. That continued for days.

After a while, I was able to get my stomach to throw up the mixture without using my fingers. Poundings from the Football Squad continued.

Some residue from the force-feeding kept me alive, I suppose. I had been playing mad and not eating for four weeks when four members of the Football Squad came in and stripped off my shirt and trousers. Three held my face against the floor. Not that I needed to be pressed. Skinny No. 3 was as weak as a kitten.

The Bagman produced a length of thick, heavy leather, apparently from a horse's harness. He held it at one end. On the other end was metal of some sort.

'Now we'll see who's faking, you bastard,' said the coward.

He flogged me with the metal-ended strap until my back and buttocks were bloody. I did not pass out but seemed to go numb after a while. My glazed eyes saw only mist. I was sinking.

I cried out. Then nothing. It must have been hours later when I regained consciousness, alone in a fog. I sobbed quietly. *I'll get out of here yet, you bastards. I won't crack. I won't!*

My body absorbed some of the milk–egg mixture but I did not eat as such for three months. The jail doctor recommended that I go to Long Bay, where there were reasonable facilities for treating me. I remember little about the trip. Screws carried me on and off the train. My inability to stand was genuine.

I had won the first round. Round two was coming. Then the asylum!

But how long could I keep this up? It required a great effort to even move my head. My heart thudded like a ponderous drum. I had not spoken since the ruse began and did not know if I could do more than mutter.

I was pretty sure, though, that I was sane. Thanks to the fantasies. I was with June. We were married and had children. I had a good job and a home as I was half dragged, half carried into Long Bay's OBS.

A big screw there with a reputation for brutality picked me up and hurled me into a cell. Still in Grafton handcuffs, it felt as if my every bone was fractured.

'You can't put anything over *me*, Dugan,' the turnkey yelled. 'I know how to deal with bastards like you.'

That warder and another were later and quietly sacked after a prisoner died from unexplained injuries. Details of the affair were never related to the public.

The thug's words to me seemed to come from a long way away. The handcuffs were removed and I was stripped and laid on a blanket on the floor. As the turnkey examined my shattered body, he said to himself, 'Jesus Christ.' He stopped the abuse and treated me almost gently.

Later, I was weighed. I am normally 11 stone. When they weighed me at Grafton, not long after I began the hunger strike, I was nine stone four pounds. Now at Long Bay, I had dropped to six stone two.

Doctors tried forcibly to pour milk down my throat. I was too weak to hold my jaws closed but contracted my gullet so my mouth filled and milk flowed out. The medicos left, cursing my stubbornness or shut-down body. *When will I get to the asylum? I can't keep this up much longer.* It was a bitter admission, but I was not going to kill myself. Suicide is alien to me.

My condition must have caused concern to the three government medicos. They apparently felt that if I did not eat soon, I would perish. Force-feeding with a tube through the mouth had largely failed, so they tried a variation.

They pushed a tube directly to my stomach through my nose. It was excruciatingly painful. I was too weak struggle.

Every time I was fed this way, my nostrils were left raw and bleeding. But I battled on. My stomach regurgitated much of every meal. After two days of this, the doctors added to the treatment. All they did was roll me on my stomach and inject something into me through a hypodermic syringe, jabbed into my bruised and scarred buttocks.

Breathing was difficult. My heart pounded faster, like a tom-tom. Everything looked dim and foggy. I was beaten. I cried when admitting that to myself.

I wanted to live, so I now had to eat. I would recover and try to escape again. And again. If, that was, I gained weight and some strength at Long Bay.

I consoled myself with the notion that, failed body and all, I had retained my spirit.

I thanked a constitution of steel. A month after the hunger strike ended, I could walk with the aid of other prisoners. In three months, I regained three stones' weight.

Still pretty weak, I was taken back to Grafton.

17

When I hobbled through the Grafton gates, I expected the usual knock-down, kick-along reception. But not a blow was delivered.

I thought about it alone in the cell, concluding that orders had been sent from Sydney that Dugan was not to be battered until he gained more strength.

In the following three months, I went about the intractables' routine, seldom receiving more than a cuff or a kick. My strength was renewing, as was my determination to get out of the place.

Good physical condition was vital. At night I tried exercising, but after about ten minutes of jogging or body-pressing, I trembled and gasped in pain. Prison hardtack was not ideal for rebuilding one's body.

I hit on a way out of this hell house. It needed only one item of gear — a key to fit the lock on the outside of the door to my cell.

Once I made it, the plan was to smash the edge of the cornerstone near the lock so I could squeeze my hand through. I would have to stretch my hand seven inches, from the corner to the lock. The good thing was that a turnkey was never in the block all night.

When out of the cell, I would wait in the corridor for the turnkey's arrival at 5 a.m. to let out the jail's cook. Then I would overpower the screw, take his gun and sneak outside, still in the dark. There was a way to clear the jail without being seen.

Then I would steal a car.

With the overpowered screw still out to it, my absence would not be noted until another screw arrived there at six, when I would be 50 miles away. At 6.15, I'd hide the car, continue cross-country by foot and lie low for a couple of weeks, living off raw farm stuff.

Ah, the thought of liberty! Open spaces!

Using a scrambled version of the wall-telegraph code so others would not know, I announced the forthcoming break to Des, my confederate in the last unfortunate attempt. For two nights, Des pleaded to go with me.

I wanted to go alone but relented. He had suffered badly after the last try. He was reliable. The locks on the cell doors were identical, so letting Des out once I cleared my cell would be easy.

First, to make the key for the complicated Jackson lock on the door. It had four levers that had to be pushed back before it opened. Such a lock could not be picked.

Every time I passed through a locked gate or door, I fastened my eyes on the bunch of keys in the turnkey's hand. Especially on keys for Jackson locks. For weeks, I was not able to get a good look. Then a look, for a whole 30 seconds.

It was impossible to memorise at one time the exact dimensions of the complicated key, so I did not try. I remembered one notch of the key at a time. As I got each step, I added it to an almost-invisible scratched diagram on the cell wall. After months of vigilance, the scale diagram was completed.

Now, I needed some metal, which was hard to get. A missing piece from the lavatory bucket would be noticed. But we used metal thimbles for sewing those interminable shirts. We were issued with them each morning, returned them every evening.

A relieving screw was patrolling our work cage when I reported that my thimble was too small. It was hurting. With a second screw posted outside, he obligingly brought in a box of them.

I was told to exchange mine for another. I dropped the box, scattering thimbles about the floor. This took the screw's eyes off me for a second. I was belted for carelessness, but had a second thimble.

Using the cage scissors, I cut the steel thimble into the required shape. I added the finishing touches to the key with the third hacksaw blade Len had smuggled in to me long ago for the abortive break-out. It was still slotted between stone blocks under the mat. (And, I understand, the blade is still in the jail. This book will probably prompt a search for it.)

By now the turnkeys had resumed their regular kicking, punching and batoning of me, gloating over the fact that I had failed to be declared insane. Not wanting to provoke them into paying more special attention to No. 3, or dumping me back in the pound, I was compliant. I heard a couple of turnkeys say Dugan was broken. They were going to get a surprise.

The small key ready in the cell, I waited for a windy or stormy night to cover the noise from cutting the stone. I had not tried out the key, of course, but I was confident. I had considerable experience behind me.

Heavy rain and wind struck Grafton one evening in August '52, soon after we intractables were locked up. Counting the Gosford two, this would be escape number seven.

The sole piece of metal in the cell to cut the sandstone was the quarter-inch-thick black-iron handle of the lavatory bucket. I bent it roughly into the shape of a brace and bit — a boring tool with a U-shaped handle that turns a drill bit — and went to work on the stone on the corner by the outside lock.

I bored a vertical row of closely spaced holes an inch deep and two inches from the corner. It was impossible to cover the damage, so the job had to be done in one night. I began drilling at 5 p.m.

Black iron is soft, and the going was heavy. Outside, the storm raged. By about 2 a.m., dripping sweat, I had a row of ten holes. Three more minutes, and I'd be out.

I bashed the rock from the corner, and it clattered to the floor outside the cell.

Although a screw wasn't posted out there full time, one usually peered through the hole in the cell door once or twice a night. If a screw turned up now, he would see the rock. Anxiously, but thanking Mother Nature for continuing her storm, I belted off some more stone.

Holding the key, I squeezed a hand through the gap, tearing skin from my knuckles. I groped for the lock's keyhole and fitted the key. Holding my breath, I turned it.

It worked! The lock opened and swung back on the clasps holding it to the bolt. My hand grabbed the bolt's lever and began lifting it. Thirty seconds to go.

I was astonished as the door flew open. I jerked my hand back inside.

'Stay there, Dugan. My gun's out. Stay, or I'll blast ya bloody 'ead off!' It was Bob the Dog.

He had come into the block at the crucial moment. I clenched my teeth and fists in frustration. I'd been so close! I could have cleared away the pile of rock and re-locked the door behind me. Des and I would have jumped him when the Dog came in at 5 a.m.

It did not take the Football Squad long to assemble. Not fancying being scalded again, I walked out to them. Half an hour later, I was unconscious.

A visiting magistrate sentenced me to 21 days in the black cell, then three months of 'coercion'.

'Obviously,' he said, 'you have been assaulting prison officers.' Battered No. 3 was not allowed to respond to that or, of course, get a defence attorney.

In the hell of the Black Peter, I was thrashed daily. To the turnkeys, my repeated attempts to escape were a personal affront. It was the only time a Grafton prisoner had got his cell door open. And, incidentally, metal handles on toilet buckets were replaced for all time by string.

I was told I was an animal and treated as one. I was a brothel-bred bastard. My mother had conceived me in a brothel to an Abo. 'We knew about her,' said the Bog Trotter. 'She liked Abos best.' He said the same sort of thing later.

I could take, and expected, physical brutality. But having to listen to those filthy lies about my dead mother, that virtuous angel I had loved, filled me with fury.

One definite achievement of this mental and physical torture was to turn me, in fact, into an animal. A twisted being lusting for the blood of revenge.

When I was eventually returned to my usual cell, I planned. I was sure going to escape, but that was incidental. The Football Squad was going to be butchered.

If I finished up a bullet-riddled corpse, too bad. Before that, animal Dugan lusted, my team and I would kill and kill.

18

All intractables became depraved to a degree. The depravity manifested itself, among other things, in us deriving pleasure from bullying and taunting any fellow inmate with a weakness.

Even more so than with Dudley, the illiterate Aboriginal, this was sordidly demonstrated through Jack Matthews. Jack was as mad as a hatter. A monomaniac.

Before Grafton, he was a prisoner at the big jail in the western Sydney suburb of Parramatta. 'They're out to kill me,' he declared. 'They' were Murder Incorporated, MI. It was controlled by King George, Winston Churchill, President Roosevelt and Prime Minister Menzies.

Cons there teased Jack about his obsession. He sometimes accused his antagonists of being representatives of Murder Incorporated, sent to kill him. A popular jokester at the jail delighted in making fun of Jack in front of other cons.

He would walk up to Jack and say gravely, 'Jack, MI says you must die. It might be tonight.'

Jack raved and muttered, 'They'll never kill me! I'll live forever.'

The big and powerful man had a quiet manner, except when baited about MI. He was considered a trusty prisoner — a well-behaved one, not likely to cause strife. He worked in Parramatta jail's walled farm garden, peeling and slicing vegetables for the kitchen. Jack's delusion was a joke to cons and screws alike.

Until, that is, he put down a pumpkin he was slicing with a big knife, ran up behind the jokester who represented MI, and plunged the 12-inch blade right through his back.

The jokester straightened from the ground where he was picking vegetables, exclaimed, 'You bastard,' and ran 20 yards before dropping dead. Several prisoners who saw it had described the event to me.

With the bloodied knife in his hand, Jack soberly had walked to a nearby tap. He washed the blade, sat down at his vegetable-peeling box and rolled a cigarette. As prisoners and screws clustered around the bloody corpse 30 yards distant, Jack nonchalantly resumed slicing pumpkins with the death knife.

The autopsy report said the knife severed the jokester's spine and split his heart.

The authorities were tipped that Jack was the killer. But psychiatrists were not able to find anything wrong with him. Jack had a sharp, rat-like cunning. He said nothing to the shrinks about MI. A charge of murder was dismissed through lack of evidence. No one testified to seeing the crime.

This lack of evidence was not from fear of Jack. His fellow cons knew he was nuts, but he was one of the boys. He was not an informer. So the boys, on instructions from Parramatta's heavies, saw nothing.

Jack was sent to Grafton, placed in the same yard as me and two prisoners I shall name here Ken and Don. This was not long after I returned to normal duties in the wake of my attempt to escape by making the key. Ken and Don also knew of Jack's blade work at Parramatta.

At the long work table in our cage, Jack sat opposite me. Ken was on my right. Don sat on Jack's left. For weeks, Jack was quiet and friendly. He copped the customary regular bashings from screws while 'settling in'. We helped him learn the intractable routine to minimise the torment. And he was a learner of our wall talk.

Then, one day, Jack confided to me that Ken was a member of MI.

'What the hell is MI?' I demanded, knowing full well.

'Murder Incorporated,' Jack muttered fearfully. 'They've planted Ken here to do me in.'

Glancing uneasily at preoccupied Ken, he added that every night from outside his cell window, Ken and other unspecified

MI agents 'put the powers' through him. The powers, according to Jack, was a form of electric shock. And the power machine was in Ken's cell!

'You run the jail, Darcy,' he said. 'You're our big heavy. I can rely on you to help me. As long as I've got you with me, they won't have enough powers to kill me.'

Jack further reported that that mongrel Ken had 'magic eyes' everywhere to spy on him. In the ceiling, in the wall. 'I was having a shit last night, Darcy, and I looked down, and there, in the bottom of the bucket, was a magic eye. That bastard Ken put it there to look up my arse.'

Jack had not lost his monomania. I warned Ken and Don. We did not want a repeat of the Parramatta slaying. There were no knives in our cage, but there were two pairs of scissors, which we kept out of Jack's reach. He had to ask for them and we would watch him until they were returned. Jack complained about this but after a couple of days accepted it.

One day Ken used the scissors and placed them on the table. The points happened to be aimed at Jack. Jack grabbed them. With a triumphant smile, he firmly returned the scissors to the table, pointing at Ken.

'You dirty, murdering shit,' Jack snarled at Ken. 'Don't think you can put the powers through me! Point the scissors at me, huh? How do *you* like it?'

The poor lunatic was convinced the powers, via the scissors, were electrifying Ken. Amazingly, no turnkey heard the exchange.

Ken was not impressed. Then, entering into the farce, he said with a serious face, 'All right, Jack, so you know about it. I've got orders to kill you with the powers. As soon as Darcy consents, MI will power you to death.'

Jack spat out with rage, 'MI can't kill me! Anyway, Darcy won't let you.'

Ken looked to ensure that no turnkey was listening. 'We'll fix that,' he said. He ceremoniously turned the scissors away from himself and looked at me.

'Mr Darcy Dugan, the heavy of this place, on behalf of Murder Incorporated, I am empowered to offer you one million pounds to let us murder Jack.'

Sombre-faced, I said, 'Money cannot buy me. Never, while I'm in this yard, will I stand by and see Jack killed.'

Jack's eyes had been darting between Ken and me. He jubilantly exclaimed, 'There you are, you filthy MI bastard. You can't buy my boss friend. He loves me.'

Ken grabbed the cue. 'Darcy, that's what the trouble is. MI loves Jack. Jack loves *you*! I love Jack, so he must die.'

'You don't love me,' Jack spluttered. 'What do you think I am — a nut?'

At this, Ken, Don and I could not contain ourselves. We doubled over, trying to muffle our hysterics. From then on, Jack was fair game. Every day, just for a laugh, we taunted the madman. Like animals, we were, preying on the weak one. Remembering that environment-induced brutality shames me today. At least I maintained a kill ban on MI.

We never doubted that Jack was dangerous, but could not have cared less if he was Frankenstein's monster. He was our source of amusement, a clowning outlet for the savagery we would have preferred to unleash on our keepers.

Most days, Ken went through a rigmarole of how, the night before, he had just missed out on killing Jack with the powers — in defiance of Master Darcy.

After that one day, Jack glared at me and asked, 'What's wrong, mate? You've sold me out!'

I assumed an air of injury. 'So that's the thanks I get for saving your life. I've kept you alive for months. You'd be dead if it wasn't for me.'

Turning to MI's rep, I said, 'Ken, you have my permission to murder Jack tonight.'

Ken raised his eyes to heaven. 'Thank God. As soon as I murder Jack, I can go home. But there's one thing I want before I kill him, Darcy. I love him. I want to take him in my arms, bend him back and kiss his soft, rosy lips. I want to dart my tongue into his sweet mouth.'

Sickeningly mad stuff it was. Ken gazed at probably the ugliest man in Australia. 'Kiss *my* rosy lips, Jack. Dart your tongue into *my* mouth. Then I kill you.'

Jack expleted, 'You filthy sexo bastard. You'll never kiss *me*.'

Ken continued. 'You'll be mine tonight, you beautiful boy.'

The language got more specific — to sodomy. Jack's eyes shone with fear. 'You'll never lay me, you homo bastard.'

He looked across the table at me. 'Darcy, are you going to let this bastard fuck me and murder me?'

I took my time about answering, sewing up a shirt, savouring the sweetness of his anguish. 'You said I sold you out, Jack. I've washed my hands of you.'

'Hell, I didn't mean it, Darcy. Please don't listen to that mongrel.'

After a while, I graciously relented. 'Ken, I've changed my mind. You can't murder Jack tonight.'

Ken looked bitterly disappointed. 'Foiled again, but MI will get him sometime.'

After more weeks of that, Ken stopped it, but Don, our other yard man, took over the taunting.

I told him to shut up. I did not like Don, who had sexually attacked and killed a little girl. He was a snivelling character, a potential informer.

Jack Matthews was at the Bloodhouse for about four years. He was insane before he went there. His time at Grafton ended when he was declared officially insane.

He was dispatched to an asylum, where he died. Jack Matthews, bashed regularly, was just another victim of the Bloodhouse.

19

I still planned the big break. It called for about a dozen confederates as determined as I was.

Deaths in this one were inevitable. In any case, I was determined that turnkey brutes would die. We would take over the jail and walk out the front gate.

A party of five men of the calibre I required had arrived as intractables late in 1952. They had almost succeeded in a daylight bid to go over the wall at Parramatta under the blazing guns of the guards. Their arrival made me selfishly exultant.

There is no point now in suppressing their names.

Antonio Martini, whom I called Art, was aged about 36 and serving life for attempted murder during a solo gun battle against 25 police. A small man, well proportioned, intelligent and quick to grasp an opportunity, he was also reliable. He was full of humour and normally unwilling to partake in brutality but was extremely dangerous if tested.

Eddie Gwilliams was about 40, serving life after a gunfight with police. Small and of solid build, he had proven his courage as a soldier in World War II, escaping a couple of times from German prisoner-of-war camps. A cool, cunning thinker who weighed the pros and cons of any deal before committing himself, he was capable of cold savagery if pushed.

Willy Burney, about 35, was serving 14 years for abducting a girl. Tall, balding and with a slim build, he was a quiet type given to moody introspection. A cracksman, he was potentially dangerous and had a record of attempted escapes, but he was quiet enough if left alone.

Sid Grant, about 30, was doing life for shooting dead a detective who was trying to arrest him on robbery charges. Slim, quick thinking and with plenty of guts, he had performed well in the attempted break-out at Parramatta.

Robby Moulds, who was also about 30, was on ten years for armed robbery, plus an indeterminate period under the Habitual Criminals Act. He had a long record of convictions for robbery and had also done well at Parramatta.

I was doing 'special solitary' when the five arrived at Grafton. I heard them being brought from the jail's front gate, one at a time. Each man was battered, stripped and battered again. I knew Art Martini and Robby Moulds well, the others by repute.

Art Martini was the only one of the five to clear the wall at Parramatta. On landing, he broke one of his legs. Now Bob the Dog repeatedly struck the plaster on Art's leg.

As I listened to the bashings, I gloated over the prospect of the intractables' revenge.

I knew they would join in the big break but there was no hurry to tell them about it. Each man had to first serve months of solitary.

Along with the Parramatta five, I planned to ask Des Jones, my fellow near-escapee, and three others, who were all in their mid-20s.

David Golding was serving ten years for burglary and escape from Bathurst jail. Of medium height and solid build, he had a record of violence. He was from the country and was a graduate of the Gosford boys' reformatory. From a broken home, he was poorly educated but ambitious and clever with his hands. He was given to berserk rages but loyal to a friend.

Max Williams was on ten years for burglary and escape from Bathurst jail. He had a long criminal record, from the Gosford boys' home to prison, and came from a slum background. He liked to write poetry, which showed an imagination that was rare in criminals. Max was easily led, but once he committed to something, he was in it all the way.

Ted Garling was doing a 'lifer' for assault, robbery and escape, again from Bathurst. Tall and solid, he had a quiet manner and was moody. He was a first-class bare-knuckle fighter.

Others would participate in the break, but these nine men would be my lieutenants.

Billy Mears, in the meantime, ended his term as an intractable. He went to another jail, where he was considered a cooperative prisoner. I'd had, and sought, little to do with Mears in Grafton.

While the would-be escapers from Parramatta were doing pound, I received an unusually vicious hammering from the Football Squad for some misdemeanour. During it, as I lay on my back, the Bog Trotter spat on my face. I tried to get to my feet, but my legs failed me. I almost cried with rage, being so helpless.

This act by the Bog Trotter sealed his fate, as far as I was concerned. It was also he who had smeared my mother's memory and sprung me on the window ledge when I first tried to get out.

When the big break came, I would personally slay the Bog Trotter. I hated the fact that he, like me, had Irish ancestors.

I knew the jail's layout well. The guards did not conduct their patrols to timetables, but there was a general pattern. And I had found a flaw in that pattern.

Every Sunday morning, if not ill or copping special punishment, fellow Catholic intractables and I attended Mass celebrated by visiting chaplain Father Rogers. When the priest could not get there, two Sisters of Mercy from the local convent ran a service for us. The intractables were afterwards marched four at a time from the chapel back to the weekend exercise yard near the front gate.

We were watched from afar by a guard who was armed with an automatic rifle and was posted halfway along the catwalk, on the top of the jail's back wall. Normally, the screw in charge, Skunky Smith, was in his office by the main gate. The office contained the jail armoury.

But Skunky lately walked into the courtyard to watch the intractables leave the church. Two screws trailed us. Another stood on the other side of the small iron-bar gate to the exercise yard. Through that gate and across the moat was the main gate. Only that screw was between the intractables and the armoury.

On Sundays, the jail had a skeleton staff of nine turnkeys. The only one carrying a gun was the man on the catwalk. Screws down in the jail in daytime were armed only with batons. It was a precaution against an intractable grabbing a gun.

The screw at the exercise yard let us in there one at a time. Happenings inside the walled yard could not be seen from the outside. With Skunky still in the courtyard, away from the armoury, this was the jail's most vulnerable moment of the week.

The plan was for two of us to knock the three screws in the compound to the ground. A third prisoner would fly up a steel ladder at the far end of the compound, drop into the moat and sprint to a position between the front gate and the screw at the small steel gate. At all costs, that con had to hold his ground, keep the screw away from the armoury of guns and the telephone.

Meantime, we cons in the compound would take the screws' keys, every set of which included the means to open the small gate leading to the moat, the gate through the cage surrounding the entrance foyer, the door to the senior screw's office, the main jail gate and every cell on the premises. Intractables still in the chapel would overpower the three turnkeys there and join us.

Under no circumstances were the nuns or Father Rogers to be intimidated.

We intractables idolised them. Those cheerful, dedicated servants of God were our sole regular contact with the world outside. And we knew that Father Rogers and the sisters abhorred the treatment dished out to us.

A regular nun at the jail had been Mother Marie Bernard, a reliable soul with a sharp wit. The final time Mother Bernard visited 'her boys', I noticed tears in her eyes. She was going, against her will, to take a more senior position in another town. Mother Bernard and I exchanged letters for years.

The sisters had gathered signatures from 5,000 Grafton residents — three-quarters of the population then — for a petition to the government. The petition said the intractables were treated like animals. It requested that brutality at the jail be investigated and stopped. That the whole business, a blight on the district, be removed.

The Grafton turnkeys strongly resented the nuns doing that. People living near the jail often heard prisoners' screams in the night. Former local prisoners had told tales of the savagery inflicted on intractables. The turnkeys were generally despised by the townsfolk. They were game to drink at only one pub.

Australia's general public, though, had no idea of the horrors of the Bloodhouse. And the government clearly wanted to keep them ignorant. No action was taken on the petition.

When the screws in the chapel were flattened by us mutineers, our priest and the two nuns were to be ushered gently into the jail's small adjoining library. They would be locked in there, away from danger. That done, the intractables would grab an axe and knives from a nearby woodshed and kitchen.

Armed with the keys and turnkeys' batons, we cons in the exercise yard would clamber up a ladder and drop to the moat, and join the con on duty by the gate leading to the senior screw's office — and the armoury.

A con would remain at the narrow entrance to the yard to repel 'intruders'. All this could be done in a minute.

A con who had been interviewed in the senior screw Smith's office told me the armoury consisted of a head-high cabinet of cedar. The double doors were secured by a huge Jackson padlock. The screws' keys would include keys to that.

If we did not get a key to the armoury, getting at the guns would not be difficult. Its lock was as effective as a lock on a matchbox. Once inside the office, we could rip off the cabinet's doors with our bare hands. Inside were automatic rifles of high calibre, shotguns and revolvers. And, surely, plenty of ammo.

Des Jones and Max Williams, both crack shots, would grab and load rifles. They were to sprint around the moat in opposite directions and peg, from each corner of the jail building, the screw on the wall catwalk. I hoped that at that stage no shots would have been fired. I did not want the neighbours, or the wall-top guard, alerted.

Meantime, I would take a revolver and grab a turnkey, who I hoped would be OIC Smith. I would march him to the back wall, shielded from the armed screw up there. I would order my hostage to command the screw to toss down his rifle. He would be told to lower himself into the jail. If Smith did not do as told, I would blow his backbone through his navel. If the screw on the catwalk played up, Des and Max would shoot him in their crossfire.

Meanwhile, one of the team, with keys, would release members of the ten still in their cells.

All the remaining screws were to be ferreted out, herded in a line with their backs to the wall of the cell block, facing the jail courtyard, for the butchering. We would not shoot them.

If no screw had been slain by then, seven of my colleagues would each have a turnkey to execute.

In my sick and avenging mind, I gloated at the thought of that moment. Each intractable would walk up to his victim with either the axe or a knife. We would make the turnkeys who had battered us grovel on the ground, pleading for their lives.

The turnkeys would be hacked to pieces. I would use a knife on the first of them, the Bog Trotter.

There was one screw who would be spared if he was on duty. Lawrence Freebody did his job conscientiously and well, but nothing more. Never did he take part in a battering. We had seen by the look on Freebody's face that he was revolted by those sessions.

A con had told me he heard Freebody accuse the Bagman of being the chief coward in a bunch of gutless wonders, the Football Squad. Freebody had pointed out the truism that, unlike screws at other prisons, a turnkey at Grafton had never challenged a troublesome con to a fight in a cell, man to man. Most Grafton screws had volunteered from other jails to go and brutalise intractables.

Freebody would be locked, unharmed, in a work cage. Sparing him would make a lot of people realise that we had not killed blindly.

Freebody would be able to testify in court against us, but we did not reckon on ever being captured alive. If we manufactured brutes ever re-entered Grafton, we would be in coffins.

We would recover our civilian clothes from the jail stores and go, leaving the Bloodhouse looking like a pork abattoir.

When the Parramatta five had served their introductory solitary, I cautiously sounded out my nine selected lieutenants, one at a time. I did not use the comparatively public wall telegraph. Several weeks passed before I had talked to all of them.

Art Martini, the most valued assistant, immediately realised that the odds were 100 to one for us surviving more than a few days. 'Yes, I'm in,' he said. 'Just so long as we can take the turnkeys to hell with us.'

Eddie Gwilliams nodded and grinned. 'They'll get the army after us, Darce. You know it'll be the finish of us.' He shrugged as I nodded back, and he added, 'That's the way it'll have to be, then.'

Willy Burney looked moodily at the ground. 'I'd just as soon be dead as stay in this hell.'

Sid Grant, quick as a flash, looked delighted. 'Yes, let me take the Bagman.'

Rob Moulds ran his tongue along his top lip in anticipation. 'With you a hundred percent, Darce.'

Dave Golding smiled slowly. 'Lovely. Give me an axe and Bob the Dog.'

Max Williams agreed without a flicker of an eyelash. All he said was, 'They asked for it.'

Ted Garling looked at me suspiciously for a moment. 'You kidding? Right, then. I'll slaughter every screw bastard in sight.'

My loyal break attempter Des Jones gave a low whistle. 'Let me get the White Rat in my hands first, and I'll die happy.'

Each of the nine was told of my special scrambling of our wall-talk code for later discussions. The walls of the cell block were busy for weeks. Several times the turnkeys heard us and all-round batterings followed. We ten did not care.

I felt a bit sorry, though, for the other dozen or so, who were utterly baffled by the new wall language and its popularity. Often they cut in using the normal code, asking what the hell was going on. It seemed funny tapping out to them, 'S – H – U – T — U – P'.

We agreed that the only chance of remaining alive for a while after the break was to get to a big city, Sydney or Brisbane. Brisbane was 250 miles north, Sydney nearly twice as far south. The army and the air force would soon rout us out if we went west into the mountains, or to the bush and the open plains beyond.

Brisbane was dismissed, its population of half a million being too small. Besides, criminal contacts there were sorely limited. Sprawling Sydney, two and a half million residents, was the only place to go. Most of us knew the city well.

But how to get there? We could take some of the turnkeys' cars parked out the front of the jail, but a roadblock would get us less than 100 miles from Grafton.

Rail travel was equally impossible. Every train would be stopped and searched. The open sea was only 30 miles from the jail. We would probably have time to get to the coast and commandeer a boat. But what then? We would be no match for the navy.

There *was* a way — by air. A twice-daily seaplane service operated between the Clarence River, which runs through Grafton, and Sydney Harbour.

Just after noon every Sunday, we heard the aircraft heading south. Its base was on the river, only two miles from the jail. If we took the jail before 11 a.m., there would be plenty of time to get there in a convoy of cars. It would be an hour or more before authorities outside the jail were alerted.

Their first alert would be when at least ten of us — armed to the teeth with automatic rifles, shotguns and revolvers — accounted for any resistance the small Grafton police force could muster. We agreed to try not to kill any of those country cops, who we knew also despised the screws.

One con suggested that we get from a book in the senior screw's office the addresses of the turnkeys not on duty.

'Then go to their houses and carve them up,' he tapped on the wall.

Some agreed. I had no argument with that in principle, especially if the Bog Trotter was not at work. But, I tapped, it would take too much time and we would risk missing the plane. The idea was dropped.

We would take over the aircraft on the river. The pilot, copilot and a few passengers would be hostages. I would order the pilot to take off and fly down the coast to Sydney. If he refused, he would be shot dead. The copilot would be ordered to take over. With the pilot's corpse beside him, he would not decline.

Nothing would stand in our way. In retrospect, I know this does not relate well with our intention of sparing the life of Lawrence Freebody, but that is the way our desperate and warped minds worked.

By the time we were in the air, the alarm would be out. We knew Sunderlands flew slowly. Air force planes would soon intercept and tail us. We would not be shot down, though, because of the hostages.

Tapping on the walls, we discussed the reception that would await us in Sydney. Armed police and soldiers and gunboats from the Garden Island naval base would be all about at the aircraft's base at Rose Bay, on the harbour.

We decided to land instead on the water off Bondi Beach and, hopefully without too much surf, get the Sunderland to run to the sand. A few shots would discourage interference from any of the surfers. Leaving our hostages on the plane, we would sprint up the beach and commandeer some cars. Then, split in groups of two or more, we would go to our selected hiding places.

Some reckoned they had a good chance of remaining at large and eventually leaving Australia. Art and I did not agree. The lot of us, we felt, would be far too hot for any other crims to hide us. Our families and girlfriends, known mates, would be watched.

Art and I did have a secret plan to elude capture after landing on the beach, but the chances of it succeeding were only fair.

All of us were determined not to be taken alive. If cornered, we would shoot it out to the death. Better dead than back at the Bloodhouse, especially after that bloody break. There would always be volunteers at other jails for a new Football Squad. But, really, any surviving murderous escapee who was caught would be hanged.

Only a few of us realised that the big break would precipitate the nation's biggest ever manhunt. We would be seen as monsters. But we cared little. We had, in fact, been turned into monsters.

All of society's resources would be marshalled against us, but at least the public would come to realise, in the final analysis, something the Department of Prisons and the Grafton turnkeys seemed never to face up to: if you treat men like crazed animals long enough, they will become crazed animals.

Perhaps long after we were dead and buried, a Royal Commission would inquire into what had been going on at Grafton, belatedly responding to that big petition from residents of Grafton.

It was March 1953. We were set to go on the coming Sunday morning, but realised we couldn't. Seven of the ten were not Catholics! We needed at least six. Four to march back to the compound, and at least a couple to stay behind in the chapel.

Three intractables, receiving their inspiration a few weeks apart, began to show an interest in Catholicism. Father Rogers was a fine, frank fellow for whom I had developed a real affection. I felt guilty about fooling him, but we Catholic cons agreed that there was no alternative.

By May, six planned breakers were regularly attending Catholic Sunday services and Father Rogers's occasional midweek Mass. The Protestant minister who visited the jail was not amused by the defections.

One intractable, incidentally, genuinely embraced the teachings he received. He became a Catholic and still goes to Mass every Sunday. A weird conversion, that.

We ten went through the daily routine like zombies, as required. We had to make sure that none of us copped the pound. We would lull even the Football Squad, we hoped, into relative quietude. Still, the sadists invented reasons for hammering us almost daily.

The ten of us decided to stage our mutiny on Sunday, 14 June 1953.

20

Early that morning, Ted Garling feigned severe illness and was allowed to remain in his cell. Fear and weakening from a bashing had overcome him. That did not perturb me. Ted might be chicken-hearted but he was no squealer.

It was a cheerful, sunny morning. Crows cawed in the distance. A regular neighbourhood rooster held forth. The air held the tang of recent rain. Down in the town, church bells rang.

We intractables in blue, plus some local prisoners, were escorted to the chapel. As usual, two screws stood on guard at the chapel's open door. Father Rogers was not there. He was celebrating Mass elsewhere, I guessed. The nuns began the service with several hymns, one of them playing an organ. The other one usually walked among us while the congregation loudly sang.

The strolling nun would chat to us on personal spiritual matters, one at a time, as we sat on the long, low benches. If asked, she would send a prisoner's wife or parents a letter, seeking some innocent family information or assuring them of the prisoner's wellbeing. She also related the essence of letters in reply.

This was humane and harmless, although it would not have done for the turnkeys to know about it. They hated her talking to us under the cover of the hymns.

This day, however, the sister remained singing in front of us. And we sang fewer hymns than usual. The nuns must have limited time today, I assumed. Perhaps some ceremony awaited them at the convent.

Or … or could they have got some divine indication of what was coming?

A sermon always followed the hymns. This day, the sister looked dead ahead, down the aisle at the turnkeys. She spoke of how she realised that people who had to endure all sorts of hardship and brutality would think of rebellion.

But rebellion, she emphasised, rebellion and violence achieved nothing. The best thing to do was to put our trust in God. No matter what we felt, no matter what hatred we had for others, we should contain that hatred. These things should be left in the loving hands of God.

Cons on either side of me nudged my ribs, elevated their eyebrows. Heavens! *Is she alerting us to something?*

The sister paused, stared for a moment at me, and went on to other topics. I warily put her opening advice down to coincidence.

The first four intractables escorted out of the chapel were Max Williams, Robby Moulds, Des Jones and me. Art Martini was pissed off when not called to join us. My nod as I left the chapel had told him he was in charge in there.

And there, standing watching us in the courtyard, as usual, was senior screw Skunky Smith. Great! The front office was empty.

Armoury, here we come! My pulse raced. *Just two more minutes, you bastards.*

We four wheeled into the compound. A cough from me was to signal that the mutiny was on. The others in the chapel would hear the commotion and do their bit.

Standing in the compound was a different screw, who had not been there when we left the exercise yard earlier in the morning. Was something wrong? I had only seconds now. *Do they know? Has someone squealed? No, impossible.*

The other screw, from earlier, must have been called away or taken ill. If they had been told what was planned, we would have been grabbed prior to the chapel and battered into piles of bloody pulp.

I coughed loudly. Max, in front of me, swung a fist and the screw in front dropped. The keys clattered to the ground in front of him. I grabbed them and swung towards the yard I was to open. Des ran for the ladder. Rob Moulds was to block the compound entrance. But, instead, he flashed past me and cowered in a corner.

Suddenly, a whistle blew. Screws descended from all directions. They swung long riot sticks. Three of them dragged Des from the ladder and battered him to the ground.

Others flung themselves at Max. Blows crashed on me.

I glanced at Rob, being ignored as he kneeled on the ground, hands over his head. The bastard had lagged us!

I have no recollection of what happened in the next few minutes. I was told by other cons that I was smashed on the back of the head with a baton by the first turnkey through the entrance Rob Moulds should have been guarding.

They said I was driven to my knees, then sprang to my feet and turned on the screws jostling in through the compound entrance as a living wall.

It seems I went berserk, spurting blood, screaming fury and throwing punches like a thrashing machine. I was finally dragged into a cell and pounded to unconsciousness. The same thing happened to Max and Des.

Back at the chapel, three screws with riot sticks had run from a room behind the altar as soon as the whistle blew. The intractables, realising the plan was blown, did not move. Regardless, they were bashed to the floor in front of the sisters and dragged outside as the nuns and the local prisoners looked on, aghast. They were further pounded before being tossed into their cells.

Every intractable at Grafton, except for Moulds, was batoned. Many of them, of course, had had no inkling of the planned revolt. Yes, even sickness faker Ted Garling copped it.

One prisoner, not involved in the plan, later had ten stitches inserted in a gash in his head. Another had his head split open and an arm broken.

I awoke in my cell, my head in a puddle of blood. Screams from other prisoners echoed around the block. The turnkeys were reopening the cells, one by one, giving the cons another dose.

My door clanged open. Five turnkeys rushed in. I was on my hands and knees, my bloody head hanging. The screws were sweating from the exercise.

Bob the Dog had blood down the front of his shirt. Blood that was not his. These men obviously knew what would have happened to them had my plan succeeded.

'We know you were in charge of all that, Dugan,' said the Dog.

Cursing vilely, they surrounded me and began hacking with their batons like a team chopping a log of wood. I thought to myself, 'If they keep this up, Dugan, you're dead.'

Later that day, I was dragged to the jail surgery, where two doctors sewed up busted heads and set broken bones. The sole injured screw was the one hit by Max.

I was semiconscious, staggering from the surgery to what I thought was my cell. As I entered the door, laughter. It was head screw Smith, looking on as three screws hammered Max with batons. Max was propped against the wall; a turnkey was on each side of him, another in front. It was a shocking sight. His face and clothes were a mass of blood. Raw flesh drooped over one eye, which seemed to be hanging out.

I stumbled into Skunky Smith, still not realising I was in the wrong hole. Smith recoiled in fear. Other screws bundled me to my own cell.

Grafton jail had only two Black Peters. Max went to one; I scored the other. All participants were charged with mutiny, attempted escape, inciting a riot and assaulting prison officers.

In black despair, I condemned myself for not heeding the alerts from the sister in the chapel and delaying the mutiny for a week or three. Thumbs down, head shaking as I left the chapel, not coughing at the gate to the exercise yard, would have called the whole damned thing off.

I learned that Rob Moulds had kept the authorities informed of our plans for months before the mutiny. He would get a big remission from his long sentence. And prompt removal to a softer jail was likely, away from vengeful mutineers.

As an extra precaution that Sunday, a squad of police had waited outside the jail's main gate with two mounted machine guns.

Comptroller-General of Prisons L.C. Nott, whom we still called Elsie, had been alerted a week before the break attempt and cancelled a holiday.

He visited Grafton while we copped 13 days of bashings. Nott said to the media, 'I must congratulate the officer in charge, Mr Smith, and his warders for foiling a most serious and dangerous escape bid.'

It was falsely alleged that four warders — second-in-charge screw J. Morgan, and Messrs J. Comerford, R.A. Fisher and F.R. Collie — were injured. At least Minister of Justice Downing announced that no one had been seriously injured and that no mutineer had a gun.

Mutineers Williams, Golding and Dugan appeared before two magistrates. As with all such hearings, it was closed to the public and the press. We three had no professional defender.

A turnkey alleged that I had hit him in the face, had attempted to strangle him, had kneed him in the testicles and had taken his baton and crowned him with it. Under interrogation, I asked the turnkey if he had any marks to show from such a vicious attack. He claimed he had a small bruise on one knee, but it had gone away.

I pointed out to the magistrate that I had been battered and my head was still about a quarter bigger than its normal size. It was split on top, my eyes were slits, my mouth was cut, and my body was mostly black and blue. I said I believed it was evident who assaulted whom.

I was expeditiously found guilty on all charges. The senior magistrate sentenced me to 14 days' Black Peter on the first charge. The second magistrate sentenced me to 14 more days on the second charge. The senior magistrate gave me an additional 14 days on the third charge. A total of 42 days, almost automatically followed by six months of coercion.

I interrupted and pointed out that they did not have the power to do that. The law, I said, stated that one magistrate could not sentence a man to more than 14 days. Between them, they could give me a maximum of 28 days.

The senior magistrate muttered to his colleague and told me bluntly that I was not going to tell him how to do his job. I got the 42 days on top of the 13 I had already served — plus those six months' coercion, which was just as bad as the Black Peter.

Those magistrates ignored the law they were supposed to uphold.

21

A refreshing change from visits by my usual attackers in the Peter was one by Grafton's sole warder with a conscience, Lawrence Freebody. As he walked in with a dixie of maggoty mush, he said, 'You're all over the newspapers again, Darcy.' He told me the Sydney *Sun*'s headline was 'Darcy Dugan leads 12 in jail mutiny' and the *Mirror*'s was 'Dugan tries again.' The *Sun* described the event as a 'violent clash', while the *Mirror* called it a 'savage melee'.

That stuff was alarming. It would turn public opinion against me and probably fire up more torture from the other screws. 'Thanks for telling me,' I muttered.

Freebody went on to tell me that all four of the papers he'd read claimed that ten were seriously injured and that four of them were warders.

'You'd know that no warder was badly hurt.'

'Propaganda,' I ventured.

'Yeah. Typical.'

Lawrence Freebody was a white knight among barbarians. This moment of sanity was like getting a shot of oxygen.

Finding the courage to converse with a Grafton screw for the first time, I said, 'The tracs really respect you, sir. Do you know that the mutiny plan included putting you in a work cage, unharmed, while a bit of revenge was dished out on the others?'

'Yeah.' Freebody smirked. 'I got a whisper about that. So thank you, Mr Dugan.'

Jeez! Darcy, then Mr Dugan!

'I'm revolted by the brutality you're copping, Darcy,' Freebody said as he was leaving. 'And don't let on that you know about that publicity.'

* * *

In September '53, I heard a screw calling one of the Anglican bishops a 'shit'. I soon learned from a nun that the Bishop of Canberra and Goulburn, E.H. Burgmann, and 200 others had signed a petition to the state governor, Sir John Northcott, seeking an act of pardon for Williams, Golding and me.

Their petition said, 'We are deeply disturbed by the punishment imposed, and are fully convinced that continuation of the separate treatment of these three men is not justified by any of the ethical purposes of punishment, as accepted by modern penologists.'

The petition condemned the intractables system, pointing out that New South Wales was the only place 'within the orbit of western civilisation where isolation of such a duration can be imposed on prisoners'.

Like the Catholic sisters' petition that was signed by 5,000 residents of Grafton, the bishop's plea was ignored.

My gratitude to the Anglican bishop was tempered by private amusement. Glad, I was, that he did not know that the plan for the mutiny included three Anglicans becoming Catholics.

I feel nauseous at the memory of those seven and a half months. Most of the time my hair and beard were caked with congealed blood. My shirt was stiff with it. I do not want further to sicken you with more details.

And informer Robert Moulds? He was appointed jail cook, no longer an intractable. Too many men sought his blood. It was an ugly twist, having to eat the maggoty food he cooked. For all sorts of reasons, including his own protection, Moulds should have been transferred to another jail.

A couple of years later, Moulds was released. The extra time he faced under the Habitual Criminals Act evaporated.

Because of the bar-cutting performance, the homemade-key show and my leading of the near mutiny, a big bulletproof observation gallery was installed along my end of the cell block.

An armed screw, with direct telephone links to senior screw Smith's residence and the local police station, was locked in the gallery every night.

The authorities put about a story that the mutineers planned to rape the Sisters of Mercy. And the nuns' church services were stopped. The claim was poppycock. Every screw at Grafton knew we idolised those sisters. Had a convict ever laid a hand on a nun, we would have slaughtered him.

Did the nuns' petition against the jail, we wondered, generate the ban on them? Or was it because they talked to us during the hymns? Or were they banned because of the apparent warning to us in that sermon?

Eventually, the jail returned to its normal routine. Regular beltings being normal.

22

A little more than three years after the mutiny, the new Comptroller-General of Prisons, my old Long Bay governor, Mr Harold Vagg, interviewed me at Grafton.

'It's about time to move you on, Darcy,' he intoned benignly. 'But first I must have an assurance from you.'

Vagg asked for an undertaking that I would not try to escape again. If I gave my word, he would recommend to the Minister of Justice, Mr Downing, that I be transferred to a 'less rigid' jail.

'But you have to agree to behave,' Vagg repeated.

I readily gave my word. I believed Vagg's attitude to the treatment of hard criminals was more humane than that of his retired predecessor, L.C. Nott, the originator of the intractables system. But Vagg, nonetheless, had to carry out the policies of the state government. He was a part of the vicious system that had turned me into a rabid animal. If he thought they could brutalise me for six years at Grafton, then pat me on the head with the assurance they had forgiven me for being a bad boy, expecting me to behave like a gentleman, a jolt was coming.

They had not broken me.

In December 1956, after six years there, I was escorted out of the gates of the Bloodhouse. No one was there to wave goodbye.

I went to Parramatta jail, also a tight security centre which houses many long-term cons. Few people had escaped from Parramatta, but getting out would be comparatively easy. The relative liberty that prisoners had there was luxurious.

Parramatta's screws had special instructions about me, however. My every act was watched. I was placed in a special security wing with two doors, each of which had two locks.

That amused me, as all four locks were of an elementary type, which I could easily open. Getting material to make keys for them would be a breeze. But the walls at Parramatta were well guarded. Getting over or under them was the principal concern.

The turnkeys' uneasiness had to be lulled, so I went quietly at Parramatta for nearly a year.

In the meantime, Art Martini was also transferred to Parramatta. He would be an ideal confederate in a break. Over many weeks, we formulated a plan that involved opening four locks, holding a gun to the governor's back, and forcing him to order the guards to let us out the front gate. We arranged for friends outside to send in two .45 automatics. That could be done by tossing them over the wall at night to a prearranged location on the jail's garden farm.

By then, Art and I had lost much of our Grafton savagery. We did not want to use the pistols, but if we were cornered, too bad — blood would flow. In case the governor proved difficult and the guards would not open the gate, we had also arranged for our friends outside to send in a stick of explosive with the .45s. We would blast our way out the main gate.

I even had a sweeper, a con engaged in sweeping floors and other maintenance, successfully test a key I made to open the vital lock on the governor's office.

But again I was informed on. A con called the Major saw the sweeper open and close the lock, then return the key to me. He told the governor that he would give details of an imminent escape, so long as he was first transferred to Long Bay and his sentence was reduced. The Major correctly believed conditions would be decidedly unhealthy for him at Parramatta once he informed on us and foiled our plot.

He was sent to the Bay, where he gave a pretty accurate account of how Art and I intended getting to the main gate. But that was the only part of our escape plan that he knew. Then invention took over.

He claimed we would make our move when the Major's wife and baby were visiting him. I was going to grab the babe at the visitors' section near the gate, the Major said, and threaten to kill it unless the screws let us out.

'How do you know this?' he was asked.

'Dugan told me.'

The authorities knew that would never happen. They dismissed the whole story as a fabrication by the Major so he could get away from Parramatta. A couple of Parramatta screws who were 'working hot' laughingly told me about it. 'Working hot' is the jail term for taking bribes, generally from convicts' friends outside, for smuggling messages and assorted items into and out of jail — letters, cigarettes, money, crystal radio sets, food and drugs.

The Major's lagging of us forced Art and me to abandon our plan. The order for pistols and explosives was cancelled for the time being. The Major was marked down for retribution.

Pop, nowadays, was allowed to visit me for 20 minutes once a month. It was wonderful to see the agile and alert 84-year-old looking so much happier now I was out of Grafton. Pop lived for the day I was free again. All through the years of incarceration he had vigorously defended my name.

He was convinced I had not carried a gun at the Ultimo bank and that I had been framed on the charge of robbing that old dear at Edgecliff who Mears and I thought had £2,000 in a hatbox.

He also thought I had not been at the Battle at Mort's Dock. He rightly knew two detectives had threatened to verbal me into jail if I did not turn stool pigeon on my jewel-robbing mates.

I did not have the heart to tell Pop I was guilty of attempted murder at the bank robbery, even though I did not fire a shot. Bank manager Leslie Nalder, I'm glad to report, had fully recovered.

I looked forward to some day caring for Pop, but I was serving the indeterminate sentence of life, compounded by my escape attempts. What chance was there of him living until I was free? The chances of my being with him as an escapee were better.

* * *

A prisoner of about my height, solid build, with longish and prematurely white hair over black eyebrows, strode up to me in the exercise yard. 'Darcy! Darcy Dugan, my boyhood hero. Hell, this is terrific!'

I felt embarrassed in front of the other cons as the man quickly hugged me. 'Hello. Who are you?'

'George Freeman. I spent two bloody terrible years at the Gosford boys' rathouse. Your escapes from there, the way you stood up to the bullies and officers, and even the commandant, are the stuff of legend up there.' He was 15 years my junior and seemed a bright spark. Well spoken.

I said, 'What are you in for?'

'Oh, stealing. I should be released soon.' He looked about at the watching inmates and lowered his voice. 'Darcy, we've got some friends in common and there's something I want to tell you about. Christ, I've been busting to see you.'

Smiling back at Freeman, I led the excited con to an isolated spot. No screw was around. 'Well, George, who do you know?'

'The main one who's talked about you, bragged in fact, is your old associate Lennie McPherson.'

He now had my attention. McPherson, my juvenile fellow shoplifter, former helper and accomplice. He was now at the core of lurking suspicions I had about a swag of betrayals.

'Yeah,' I said, nodding. 'Did a lot of jobs with Len.'

'So have I,' said Freeman, not looking all that proud of it. 'You know Lennie's now a big-time heavy? Has a bunch of corrupt Sydney cops sort of working for him, runs a protection racket at Kings Cross, has a flock of prostitutes?'

'Sort of,' I lied. I had heard nothing about McPherson since he mailed those three hacksaw blades to Grafton. 'Who are his cops?'

'Machine Gun Ray Kelly and that big shit Fred Krahe, a detective sergeant.' Krahe was the one who had taken the credit for finding out that Mears and I were hiding in the house in Lugarno back in 1949. George told me he was known by crims as the Killer Kop. He and Kelly had killed quite a few people and got away with it. And they were only two of a gang of crooked detectives on McPherson's payroll. This setup had given him immunity from prosecution.

'And Kelly and Krahe are looking good in the force from the arrests they make after McPherson tells them who's behind all sorts of crimes and where they are — sometimes ahead of a robbery,' said George. 'In fact, Darcy, he's now known to some of us as Lennie the Squealer, or Lennie the Pig. He fizzed on a mate of yours, Joey Hollebone.'

Joey was the one who staged a ruckus so Mears and I could bust out of Long Bay late in '49. Joey and McPherson used to be partners of a sort. Lennie would find the targets and Joey would do the robbing.

'And some killings, of course,' said George. 'Like the way Lennie does with the slaughterman Chow Hayes.'

Freeman paused, frowning. 'Then, to kick along the career of Krahe, I suppose, Lennie dobbed in Joey and got the poor bastard sent to jail. Joey'll be after Len's blood, but I reckon Lennie or his copper mates will get Joey first.'

That remark turned out to be prophetic. William 'Joey' Hollebone died of a heart attack in 1960, soon after being jailed as a result of being dobbed in to the police by McPherson and then, on McPherson's orders, shot in the chest.

My suspicions about McPherson skyrocketed. White-haired Freeman kicked the ground and stared at me, quizzically.

'So, Darcy,' he continued, 'there's some disgusting stuff I ought to let you know about. Stuff Lennie's bragged to me about. Bragged like a conquering general.'

A screw sauntered over to us. 'Hey, you two. Time to go to the cells.'

That night I lay awake, reliving the two, maybe three, times I reckoned I had been betrayed.

In the morning it was so-called hero Dugan who hurried to talk with his fellow inmate.

* * *

Freeman had prepared his discourse. Over nearly an hour, he delivered a staggering, infuriating narrative.

Soon after pointing Harry Mitchell and me to rob the safe in the dentist's surgery on Christmas Eve 1945, McPherson telephoned Ray Kelly and told him the exact who, what, where and when of the crime. As Verbal Kelly clenched my nuts in the police station, McPherson had sniggered to George, the rotten detective had looked to a promotion. *Merry Christmas.*

George reminded me that it was McPherson who suggested we rob the Mansions House Private Hotel in the city in February '46, when Harry and I were escapees after breaking out of the Black Maria. The Pig reported the plan to Kelly just before the tank bust. The police got there too late, but the dob-in sharpened the hunt for us, leading to our arrest and return to jail.

The very day he took June to see me and Mears at the new hide-out at Lugarno in August '49, our main helper, McPherson, phoned Fred Krahe with the address and description of the house. After the cops swooped on the 29th anniversary of my birth, Krahe was the darling of the force. *Happy birthday.*

After rowing ashore, leaving me and Mears in that cabin cruiser on Sydney Harbour so near to the scene of the shoot-out at Mort's Dock, McPherson anonymously phoned the water police, saying he had seen us take off in a boat. Hence the quick and extensive, but failed, police activity all around us.

Our main helper, McPherson, told Ray Kelly where we were hiding at Collaroy in February '50. It was on the very day he took Billy's sister and girlfriend to see us. Basher Kelly became the force's new hero. McPherson lied when he told me Mears's girlfriend had received the £500 reward. It had gone to McPherson. He knew I would not believe her denials if I ever confronted the girl, which I did not.

Soon after mailing the hacksaw-blade-loaded book to the Bloodhouse in June '51, McPherson told Kelly, who told the prisons' comptroller that he knew reliably that I somehow had the blades. Hence the diligent search of my cell and the guards outside it all night, preventing the so-close first break from the place. Kelly, bathing in more glory, was indebted all the more to L. McPherson.

'So, *six* lots of ratting by Lennie the Squealer. I hate his guts now,' said George. 'Oh, and he also squealed on Pinkie Moran, who he sent the first lot of hacksaw blades to in Grafton.'

We intractables had wondered what prompted the screws' extra-careful search of Pinkie's cell — like the one later in my cell before I tried that first break. I fumed quietly, thinking of revenge.

'But why?' I wondered. 'What did he gain from all that?'

'There are lots of other victims, Darce. He began fizzing long ago. He told me so when he was half pissed in Perce Galea's Victoria Club.' That was a casino at the Cross, later known as the Forbes Club.

'First it was to get payments from the cops, cultivate them,' George continued. 'That was after he collected his take from the crimes he reported. Each-way bets, the bastard called them.

'He roots a lot of women. And that night he bragged, too, about his latest belting of his wife, who'll probably divorce him. Have you met her?'

'Sure, Dawn. A terrific bird! She lined up the house for us at Collaroy.'

'Yeah, I don't think Dawn ever knew about the Pig's ratting on you.'

George explained that McPherson was running a protection racket, extorting big dough every week from scores of businesses in the Cross, threatening that his toughs would smash them up if they didn't pay. McPherson latched on to Kelly, Krahe and others, especially the Kings Cross Vice Squad, as a way to protect his protection racket. Informing to the cops was also insurance against any of his flock of prostitutes being arrested. McPherson now paid between five and eight cops who actually ran some of his operations.

'What did he gain by fizzing on you?' George asked. 'Well, he told me that night in the casino that way back in the '40s, he saw you as the only one with the nous and guts to build a crime empire that could rival his. That's why he saw to it that you spent so long in jail.'

My anger must have been showing. And, yes, shame at not twigging. George tapped my shoulder. 'Sorry, Darce, but I thought you ought to know.'

'I *should* know,' I declared warmly. 'I'm grateful, George. I can repay you by getting you out of Parramatta with me if you like.'

He smirked. 'Nah, thanks mate. Nobody could do it better. But, as I said, I'll be released soon.'

'Fine, I'll use a bit of pull around here to get you some good tucker.'

Freeman looked pleased, and then went on to tell me that since I'd been inside, McPherson had become obsessed with the story of Al Capone. He had gone to America in 1951 on a forged passport and mixed with a mob of crooks in Chicago.

Then, back in Sydney in '53, an honest cop had nabbed him breaking and entering with explosives, and he was convicted and jailed.

'He was paroled last year,' said George. 'Now he's building what he calls a motel — lots of rooms, over a car park in Balmain. A hide-out, mainly for crooks, for God's sake! What chance will *they* have?'

McPherson had told George that he planned to present it as a legitimate business, allocate himself wages and, while he built his crooked empire, use the place as his official only means of income.

'By then, he'll add politicians, security guards, judges to his payroll. And he reckons he'll set up a gang to import and peddle heroin,' said George.

My mind buzzed as I wondered about other deeds by this skunk. 'George, there's a smooth-tongued rogue who often put us onto jobs, prompted by McPherson. Dick Reilly. What's he up to now?'

'Ah, I saw quite a bit of Dick before this time in the slammer. He's now a sort of prince of horse-race fixing and illegal casinos. But he's really McPherson's puppet, doing whatever when Lennie pulls the strings.'

George presented as skilled, suave and trustworthy, but still, it was surprising that McPherson had confided so much to him. I put the loose talk down to grog, which McPherson drank a lot of. He had been pissed when he skited to me about bribing a politician to get him out of Grafton and cut his sentence.

Freeman said he no longer wanted to associate with Lennie the Pig but would probably have to. Freeman planned to operate illegal casinos, be a top illegal bookmaker. Live a life of luxury, free of fear. Heaps of sexpots.

He could not do that without at least tacit support from McPherson and his police and civilian thugs. McPherson would demand a fair slice of Freeman's money.

George no doubt wondered what sort of revenge I would take, but did not ask. I reckoned he had mixed motives for telling me how the Pig had added years and years to my time in jail. It would suit George if McPherson died.

I thanked him again and wandered away for a thoughtful lunch. With limited success, I wiped Mr McPherson from my mind after a few days. I would be in touch with him when I got out.

George Freeman, incidentally, achieved his stated ambitions in a big way. In 1979 he luckily survived a murder attempt, ordered, I understand, by Lennie the Pig.

My old associate Dick Reilly, a bloke I rightly trusted, was shotgunned to death at Double Bay on 27 June 1967 as he was entering his car outside the home of a mistress. The murderer was hired gun Stan 'The Man' Smith, on the orders, I know, of McPherson. He ordered the killing to suppress Dick's diaries, which recorded the rotten activities of McPherson and his politician, judiciary and police confederates.

Terrific blackmail material, it was. Through Police Commissioner Norman Allan, corrupt New South Wales Premier Bob Askin got hold of the diaries, which disappeared.

23

Four of Parramatta's younger prisoners were digging a tunnel to freedom.

It commenced under a small water-pump shed 30 yards from the far wall of the jail's vegetable garden and small farm. They had cut a square hatch in the shed's concrete floor. When the hatch cover was replaced, it was unnoticeable. A screw could examine the floor and walk across it without suspecting anything untoward.

A 22-foot sandstone wall, topped by guard towers on the corners, surrounded much of the garden. Only 'trusty' prisoners were allowed through the gate from the jail proper to the farm. Art Martini and I were not trusties but the boys kept us informed of their digging progress.

They wanted to sneak to the farm, one at a time, in barrows topped with woodchips and garbage. They would take Art and me, and we could leave the jail with them.

I did not share their optimism. The stopper, I figured, would be the depth of that great sandstone wall. The boys had struck water at a depth of only three feet. It was okay to crawl along the tunnel in a few inches of water. But at the wall, they would find that the huge sandstone blocks went down ten feet. No way could they cut through the stone. The tunnel was abandoned.

But the hole remained. It could be the means of a novel escape. With a sense of déjà vu, I began planning.

Also in Parramatta jail was one of the most laughable and endearing, yet most tragic, characters I had met. He was 'Sugar' Jackson, habitual criminal.

Sugar had spent 30 years in the Parramatta slammer, his home. He was never out for long — a few days; weeks at most. Sugar was a petty thief who should never have been sent to a tough prison.

The six-foot two-inch con in his late 40s was built as solidly as a bulldozer. He was the heavyweight boxing champion of the world, he reckoned.

He had won the title from America's Jack Dempsey, whom he'd KO'd in the tenth round. Sugar had also cleaned up Gene Tunney, Jack Sharkey, Joe Louis and Max Schmeling.

A prisoner wrote a letter to Sugar and had a screw with a sense of humour deliver it. The big and illiterate man, who had not received a letter in years, had another prisoner read it to him.

> *Dear Sugar,*
> *I speak as manager and representative of Joe Palooka. I am prepared to put up £20 million stake money if you are prepared to put your heavyweight title on the line over 15 rounds against my boy, Joe Palooka.*
>
> *Nobby Walsh*

A bunch of us crowded around Sugar and asked if he would fight Palooka, who he did not know lived only in comic strips. Sugar quietly assured us he would. Someone asked how he would go. Sugar said, 'I'll knock him out.'

He graciously accepted our good wishes. A week later, Joe Palooka was added to the list of Sugar's triumphs.

Jackson was generous. He gave away millions. Cons soon to be released often told him, tongue-in-cheek, they would rejoin the world practically broke. Could Sugar help?

'How much do you need?' was Sugar's stock question.

'Oh, a million ought to set me up.'

'Get the clerk to give it to you on the way out. He'll have my okay.'

Sugar's generosity, in his sick mind, was genuine. If you inquired, he would say £14 million to £17 million was kept in his credit in the jail's general office. The proceeds, they were, of his boxing victories.

A con wag one day warned that the office clerk, a new man at the jail, was a thief. 'You ought to watch him, Sugar. He'll shoot through with your dough.'

Sugar hurried to the office and demanded of the young clerk behind a desk, 'Where's my money?'

The clerk saw that the big prisoner was fuming. Not daring to order Sugar to clear out, he quickly checked his prison number in the personal-property records book.

'You haven't got any money,' he declared. 'You'd better go.'

Sugar crashed an immense fist on the table. 'Thief!'

Luckily for the clerk, Mr Scott, the jail's governor, heard the commotion from his nearby room and hurried in. Scott was a humane man with wit. He knew of Sugar's aberrations. 'What's up, Sugar?'

Pointing at the white-faced clerk, the world heavyweight champ accused, 'He, he's stolen my money! He says I've got no money.'

Gesturing the clerk to silence, Scott flipped open a ledger and asked, 'How much money have you got, Sugar?'

'Fourteen million pound.'

Governor Scott ran his finger down the column. 'Yep, fourteen million. In the credit of one Sugar Jackson.' He explained that the boggling new clerk had made a mistake.

A satisfied Sugar Jackson returned to the yard. He regularly checked that his fortune was still on the books, developing a wary friendship with the now-wiser clerk.

Sugar, who worked in the garden, decided he wanted some pets. He got a large packing case and some wire netting to make a cage trap for pigeons that nested about the jail. Sugar was allowed to feed his pets, caged in a corner of the farm.

Once, the day after Sugar was released, he bowled up and knocked on the jail gate. 'I want to see my pigeons,' he told the guards. They could not let Sugar in. But he was back 'home' a few days later, after giving himself up for petty theft.

Then Alfie, an unpopular wiseacre and safe-cracker with a lot of jail behind him, stole three of Sugar's pigeons. In the kitchen where he worked, Alfie turned the birds into a broth. He 'treated' Sugar to a cup of it.

That afternoon, Alfie pressed a small paper parcel into Sugar's hand. 'Some tobacco for the night for our boxing champ.'

Sugar soon bellowed obscenities from his cell. He pounded on his door, demanding to be let out. He was going to murder that cannibal bastard Alfie.

Instead of tobacco, the feet and heads of three of his pet pigeons were in the parcel. Alfie wisely avoided the giant for many weeks.

Sick jail humour, I guess. It was typical.

I was not alone in regarding Alfie with contempt. He was one of the jail's 'butch' homosexuals.

One day he asked a young and submissive 'cat' if he would like a large slice of fresh bread, spread with lots of butter and jam. The cat eagerly followed Alfie to his cell. Long-term cons in the yard knew what was on. As did some screws.

The cat emerged from the block looking dejected. Then out came Alfie, eating a large slice of bread with butter and jam.

'The silly bastard wanted the tucker, all right,' he said, grinning at some gathered cons. 'But I told him he couldn't have it until he dropped his strides and I laid him. He wasn't too keen at first, but he came round.

'Then,' Alfie jeered at his victim, 'then the idiot went to pick up the food! I grabbed it and told him to shoot through. You should've seen his face!' Alfie patted his stomach. 'Anyhow, I needed the feed after that.'

Most of us cons despised homosexuals who preyed on weak boys. I had warned off at least 20 butches in jails, bashed three. Many cons took widespread homosexuality for granted. And a lot of screws, notably at Parramatta, jocularly turned a blind eye to it. And some of them regularly raped weak young cons.

I shall never forget the time that butch tried to rape me as a kid at Long Bay. I hoped he never forgot, and learned from, the incident.

* * *

Even to us warped cons, Sugar Jackson was a mental case. Once he was sent to the big asylum that adjoins Parramatta jail.

Screws told me about it. Half the nuts in the place thought they were Jesus Christ, Napoleon or the late King George. A patient would walk up to Sugar and say something like, 'I am God. Who are you?'

Sugar would laugh and say, 'I'm the world heavyweight champion. You're crazy!' Sugar would haul off and thump 'God' on the chin.

After the champ knocked out assorted gods, Napoleons and kings, he was returned to the jail.

24

Late in 1957, I detailed to Art Martini, key player in the Grafton mutiny, my plan to use the excavation under the water-pump shed as an avenue of escape from Parramatta.

It was for only one. We agreed to toss a coin later to decide who it would be. The winner would return to the jail, with accomplices, and free the other.

This intention of storming a big city jail might sound far-fetched but it was feasible to us. It required only enough of the right men, and gear. As well as wanting to get out and see Pop, I wanted to confront McPherson.

Art or I would be hidden in a handcart that regularly took refuse to the big farm garden. Out of the sight of the guard on the nearby wall, the escaper would be carried in a bag into the shed. And into the secret hole he would go.

A snag in the plan was that four cons, the diggers, knew of the hole. And another two, the one loading the escaper on the cart and the other wheeling it to the shed, would know. They seemed to pretty reliable, however.

At 11 a.m. every Monday, a truck left the jail laden with laundry. The word would be put around the jail at 11.15 that whichever one of us was in the hole had escaped in the truck's load of laundry. Getting this news to the jail authorities would be simple. We would tell a couple of the jail's cooperative prisoners in confidence, knowing that they would lag to the screws, sparking a search in the city.

The man in the hole would remain there until the Tuesday night, by which time the alert at the jail should have passed. In advance, the men who dug the hole would run a thin wire to it from the electricity system in the shed. This would give the hidden man electric lighting. The hatch cover had bevelled edges, which would ensure no light showed through.

Getting over the wall on the Tuesday night would present no real problem. The garden wall was not patrolled at night, all prisoners being in their cells.

Art and I procured some civilian clothes, which were smuggled to the hole. I had made myself a crystal radio set the size of a matchbox. It was one of a few unofficial such sets in the jail. I listened to the horse races the next Saturday, as usual, and on the Sunday it was taken to the hole. The man in the hole could use the radio to monitor reports of the manhunt in the city. He could also keep a check on the time. Into the foxhole with the radio went a plastic bag of food for the 36 hours the escapee would be holed up.

The big day was to be Monday, 13 January 1958. After Mass, Art and I strolled to the Sunday exercise yard for the toss and to make the life-or-death pact. The 'winner' would be committed to return to Parramatta, at great personal risk, to free the 'loser'.

Art had procured an old penny. As I joked about it having two heads, he flicked it in the air. I cried, 'Heads.' The brown coin landed on the back of Art's wrist. He clamped a hand over it, slowly drew it away. The king's head shone up at us. I was going in the hole. We wordlessly shook hands on the pact.

At 10.15 the next morning, I went into a tool shed and climbed into a large hessian bag in the back of the handcart. George Freeman placed small planks of wood in the bag around me. Stinking rags and refuse went over the bag to discourage close inspection by the screw always checking traffic in and out of the garden.

I felt the cart stop at the garden gate. The screw checked Freeman's number. I tensed. *If they catch me here, it's back to the Bloodhouse.*

Evidently, the cargo was barely glanced at. George whistled to himself as he wheeled me along the bumpy path to the pump shed. I felt my four pals who had dug the hole lift me, the wood and the bag, in the air.

'This'll be the holiest escape of all time, mate,' George punned, as if to one of the four. They chuckled as he resumed whistling and took the cart on to the garbage tip.

Under the eyes of the armed guards on the walls, they nonchalantly carried me into the shed. I crawled out of the bag, nodded my thanks and scrambled into the foxhole. The boys replaced the concrete cover and disguised it with dust and debris, and I was on my own.

The hole was reasonably comfortable. It was as black as Lennie's sins, but fresh air came in through a slit at the edge of the shed's floor. The hole was about two feet deep, two feet wide and seven feet long. There were three inches of water on the bottom, but my pals had covered it with boards over a few bricks. That kept me dry.

I grimly realised that if I got stuck down here, never to see the world again, I would not die of thirst. Memories came back of my time in the hole under the rock as police hunted for me at the Field of Mars Cemetery.

I felt for the little globe and switched on my electric-light supply, checked the civilian clothes and food in the plastic bag. I fondly handled the radio. No need for that yet. The less noise the better. If some unknowing con working in the garden heard music wafting from the ground, he would talk, or scream, about it. Now to wait until 11 o'clock Tuesday night …

I was missed at the jail's midday muster. All prisoners were locked in their cells and the jail searched. I heard a screw walk into the shed, kick a stone on the hatch cover and leave. I expected that the farm garden would get only a cursory going over, as I was not permitted in there.

Cooperative prisoners were surreptitiously questioned. They related a hot rumour: Dugan had gone out hidden in the laundry truck.

The police were alerted. I heard sirens as they reached the jail. Others pursued the truck and searched it. Dugan, they assumed, had already jumped out of it.

Using the lowest possible volume, I turned on my radio in time to hear the 1 p.m. news. The lead item told how Houdini had done it again. Police were mounting a hunt all over the city. My known associates were being watched. Along with the airport, wharves, bus depots and railway stations.

The bulletin also reported that investigations by the police had found that Dugan had escaped in a delivery truck. I grinned and switched the set off. Was Pop listening to this? June? McPherson?

I was told later that at 2.30 p.m., police and senior men from the Department of Prisons began quizzing Art Martini and my other jail friends. Then every prisoner in my block of cells was questioned, forcefully.

They included the six who knew where I was. And the screws got a dividend. Someone said Dugan was hiding somewhere in the farm.

In the fading afternoon light, a real search of the farm began. I heard many voices and footsteps. They must have got a lead on me, I realised nervously. I heard a screw yell, 'Reckon the smart bugger's really around here?' I did not hear the reply.

Prisons comptroller Vagg and deputy comptroller John Morony participated in the search. They were joined by a big squad of police. I heard thudding sounds in the ground. Crowbars! There seemed to be a line of them, drawing closer.

Would the concrete above me withstand a jab by a crowbar? Probably not. And if the bar burst through? I tried not to think of the hole it might make in me. I was not coming out to them.

The pounding drew closer. Then, footsteps above. One man. His bar bashed into the concrete at the end of the shed, near my feet. The concrete held!

The man above took two more steps. His bar crashed at the edge of the hatch cover. A column of black steel plunged past my left ear into the mud. The cover flew to the side. I looked up into the terrified eyes of a turnkey.

'Quick!' he shrieked. 'Quick, he's *here*.' The screw ran outside the shed; I wished I was a mole.

'Dugan's in a hole in there,' I heard him cry. 'Quick!'

I clambered into the shed, fearing that if certain policemen trapped me in the ground, there would be a fatal 'accident'. But running out of there was risky. There would be a lot of angry, trigger-happy men around. And where, anyway, to run? I reached the shed door as the first few of some 50 policemen, screws and prison officials arrived.

I grinned ruefully as handcuffs clamped my hands together. Pistols were put away. Some of them looked at me grimly.

They hustled me into an office for questioning by new governor Mr Scollan and Vagg, Morony and … and a leering Machine Gun Ray Kelly. I could not help wondering if a certain heavyweight informer, the Pig, had somehow heard of the hole under the shed and told Kelly. *No bloody way!*

Vagg offered me a seat, a glass of water and a smoke. I accepted the seat and the water. *Bloodhouse, here I come.*

'Well, Darcy,' said Vagg slowly, shaking his head at the floor. 'You were given your chance to behave, weren't you?'

I said nothing. What was the point?

'You've let us down again,' the prisons comptroller said.

Kelly glared, clearly wanting to get handcuffed Dugan on his own.

That night, a van, police cars in front and behind, took me to Long Bay. The next day, a magistrate sentenced me to 14 days' Black Peter. A couple of days later, on 11 December 1958, I was back at Grafton, aged 38, facing the reception committee.

25

The Football Squad, the same gloating faces, dull black batons, shiny black boots, waited inside the gate.

That 'welcome home' after 13 months was more exuberant than that received by the average new intractable. I had been back only half an hour before being tossed unconscious in a solitary cell.

Strangely, when I woke, my first thought was of Art Martini. Poor old Art, back at Parramatta! But, as it turned out, *he* had won that toss of the penny. It would be a long time before Darcy went to free him.

Later in the day, I received a second battering. My first couple of weeks at Grafton were spent in 'special confinement', as they euphemistically called it. I was less resentful than before, however. When trying to escape from Parramatta, I knew the consequences of failure.

I returned to shirt sewing. Some of the intractables were new, but all the faces wore the same expressions of anxiety and fear. Depravity. Dugan now was the turnkeys' special property. I was too closely scrutinised to seriously plan an escape. I would have to be patient, put up with two bashings a week.

Except in the work cage, every time my eyes glanced sideways within sight of a screw, I was punched or kicked. They were more determined than ever to break me.

At the realisation of this, I sometimes grinned in the quiet blackness of my cell. Never would I crack. Never. Staring sightlessly at the walls, torment arose from knowing all that was lost. June. Where was she now? With a new man? Did she ever think of me?

A partial panacea was remembering a girl I shall name Joyce, the wife of a con at Parramatta. I had seen Joyce a few times when she visited her husband there. She was a pretty and slim brunette, 25 years old.

I had first known Joyce, purely as a friend, when she was 18 and single. She was an honest, friendly kid who deserved a better hand than the one life had dealt her. Her husband was a spineless character, who, although Joyce stayed loyal to him during his several years in jail for burglary, left her when he was released.

Joyce told me about it in a letter. She wrote regularly, even visited me a couple of times. She was sorry for me, I imagined.

Her necessarily bare, impersonal correspondence — vetted of course by a turnkey — nonetheless was contact with a lovely woman from the outside world. It nourished my mind, and I memorised every word of every letter.

Then, Joyce's letters became more personal, affectionate. Finally, she confessed in her own shy way that she had had a soft spot for me since she was a teenager, when we shared the same friends at dances and parties. Of course, she knew all about June and my deep love in that direction. No one could replace June's beat in my heart, but I was fondly grateful to Joyce.

Living like a robot, with barely any intercourse with other cons, I found my thoughts dominated by June and Joyce, and my simmering determination for revenge and to escape.

As with June's letters to me at Long Bay, a screw would toss in one of Joyce's notes and say, 'Here's more shit from that fucken bitch.'

Some of the turnkeys must have realised I had developed the ability to shut them and their actions from my mind. I seldom cried in agony. They derived little joy from flogging this human sack of sand. Their faces sometimes showed hopes that I would at least snarl defiance.

After some 18 months back at Grafton, though, I developed a hobby. For ages I had wondered about the tricks of that ingenious American Harry Houdini — the character the media had likened me to. How could he have himself handcuffed and padlocked in chains, locked in a box, tossed in a river, and soon after come out smiling?

It had to be self-regurgitation. He had mastered the art of swallowing keys shortly before being trussed, then once he was in the box, spewing them out so he could unlock the shackles. Of course, the keys would have the barest essentials. Long stems and handles would only get in the way. Or perhaps his locks required only one skeleton key.

Sadly, this method was not practical for an intractable in Grafton. A swallowed key surely would have to be regurgitated within half an hour.

During my feigned insanity-cum-hunger strike, I trained my gut muscles to throw up food at will. Why not metal objects? I could not get hold of suitable metal, so I practised with woodchips. At first, they passed right through my system, giving me some anxious and bloody moments. After a few weeks, though, I had mastered the trick.

I knew, too, that sword swallowing was a matter of controlling the throat muscles. After a while, I found it easy to slide dining knives and forks down my throat. I did it when I was out of sight. If screws had seen that, it would have generated big-time bewilderment.

Like other intractables, I missed the Sunday visits by the Catholic nuns, terminated thanks to the attempted mutiny. I seethed about officialdom's assertion to the public that we intended raping them. At least my friend Father Rogers still celebrated Mass. I have never been particularly religious, but Mass at the Bloodhouse was again my social event of the week.

All the time, I watched for a chance to escape, but nothing short of suicide, or the semi-suicide of an unsuccessful escape attempt, presented itself. Being on a life sentence, I had no real goal in the sense of looking to a particular year of release. I had served ten years. I could serve three more years, or six more, or twelve.

Early in 1960, I received a visit from state justice minister Downing. An unprecedented event for an intractable, I think it was. Mr Downing said, in official terms, that I could expect to be released when my jail time totalled fourteen and a half years.

'You've been going quietly, Dugan,' he intoned. 'And I hope you've learned your lesson. If your conduct is satisfactory, you will be out in 1964.'

This elated me. Four years is a long sleep, but now there was a target. All thought of escaping evaporated. I had not been broken, but I would wait it out. Four more years. Then, for this ageing con, freedom!

The letters and 20-minute visits once a month from Joyce or Pop continued, and I was able to share my joy with them. I could have only one visitor each month. Once Joyce was with me when Pop arrived at the jail after a day in the train. I felt bad, as did Joyce, about Pop having to leave and wait another month.

I was transferred to the State Penitentiary at Long Bay in August 1960. The suspicious screws there placed me in the maximum security of the OBS, but I had not the slightest intention of scarpering.

They could have safely left me alone, painting the jail's outer wall.

I managed to get into trouble, though. Many prisoners at Long Bay and other jails had crystal radio receivers like the one I made at Parramatta. They were harmless and tended to keep a prisoner quiet. They were technically illegal, but good jailers unofficially condoned them.

After Grafton, I had craved a radio, so I got one, too. To hear the voices of free people, to listen at night to music, to learn what was happening in the world out there. However, as soon as the jail officials learned that I had a radio, I was hauled before a magistrate. The sentence: seven days' Black Peter, seven weeks' confinement in 'special yards'.

It did not worry me much. The confinement and a reduction in rations of the Bay's awful food were my only punishment.

The Department of Corrective Services years later piped selected radio programs into prisoners' cells. At many jails in New South Wales, it was an outstanding success. Some stations even had special programs of relatives' and friends' goodwill messages and music requested for inmates.

* * *

Shortly after I returned to a normal prison life, however, the Major lobbed back in jail. He was especially unpopular with the prisoners. Most of them knew he was a stool pigeon.

And I knew it was the Major who had told screws that Art Martini and I were planning to burst out through Parramatta's front gate. That I was going to grab the Major's baby from his visiting wife's arms and threaten to kill it if we were not released from jail.

I could not let that score go unsettled. Many prisoners at the Bay knew about it. If a con appeared to be prepared to ignore or forgive such an act, it was near-fatal. The con's all-important standing among other prisoners plummeted.

I spotted the Major when a few other prisoners and I were being marched across the jail yard. The Major stood his ground. Apparently he felt safe. A couple of prisoners looked at me, waiting to see action.

As I drew near, I lunged at him. The enormous Major was tensed and ready. By the time the screws had pulled us apart, the Major had lost a fair amount of skin from his face. He was cringing, blubbering on the ground.

Had he run away, other heavies would later have given him a rough time for being a rat, an informer.

At the subsequent closed-door hearing before a magistrate, cons who saw the brawl swore that the Major had been the initial attacker. He had attacked me, they said, because he incorrectly believed I had once intended using his baby as a shield for escaping from Parramatta jail.

I vehemently told the magistrate that the Major was wrong about that. He had invented the story to get himself out of Parramatta jail and get his sentence reduced.

Both the Major and I received a week's Black Peter and seven weeks' special yards. Never have I enjoyed that sort of punishment so much, knowing the Major was copping similar treatment. Still, we cons were surprised. Stool pigeons were usually treated better than that.

* * *

As at most jails, a few screws at Long Bay were 'running hot', as we called it. And those screws were always keen to get money outside the jail for delivering secret letters from prisoners.

Joyce visited me when possible and wrote to me regularly. And her letters now were distinctly romantic. Though Joyce could never occupy the place June had in my heart, my affection and gratitude towards Joyce had grown deeper. I wanted to write to her in intimate terms.

But I would not have the screws who censored my once-weekly letters chuckle over, then talk about, the things I wanted to tell Joyce.

A con who was a friend of mine, soon to be released, agreed that when outside he would get $20 from Pop. My friend duly took it to a pub near the jail, where a money-hungry screw was a regular. The screw gladly took the money, worth a couple of weeks' pay, to collect letters from me and mail them to Joyce.

They were love letters, full of amorous outpourings from a man sex-starved for years, to the woman who loved him.

The hot screw was bribed a second time, enabling the caper to go on for months.

One day, however, Joyce's estranged husband, now released from Parramatta, burst into her home while she was away. He discovered a bundle of my illegal letters and jealously informed the police. I understand it was Detective R. Kelly who had the 40 or so letters delivered to the Department of Prisons. That meant that L. McPherson would know about them.

I admitted guilt to the charge of clandestine correspondence. The letters being in official hands was highly embarrassing. I wanted the whole matter disposed of quickly. The magistrate was just about to sentence me when a senior screw, despised throughout the jail both by prisoners and many of his colleagues, got to his feet and insisted that the magistrate read the letters.

'They are full of pornographic filth,' he accused.

By the time the screw completed his tirade, I was boiling. The charge was clandestine correspondence. I had pleaded guilty. I had not been charged with pornography. I sprang to my feet.

'As this officer made certain suggestions about the contents of the letters, I feel I should be entitled to make some suggestions of my own.'

The magistrate nodded. Somehow I managed to keep my voice level. 'First, I suggest that the officer examine the meaning of the word "pornography" in a dictionary. He would learn that he is ignorant of the correct use of the word.

'Second, I suggest that the officer learn something of the relationship of man and woman.' I recommended that he read, as I had over recent years, the works of Sigmund Freud, Krafft-Ebing and Havelock Ellis. I told the magistrate that if the officer read Ellis's *Studies in the Psychology of Sex*, he would learn how abysmally ignorant he was.

The officer interjected from his seat, 'If those so-called authorities write the same sort of stuff as you, Dugan, I wouldn't want to learn anything from *them*!'

I suggested to the interested magistrate that the officer would find it difficult to learn anything from anyone. The snapping and counter-snapping continued for a few minutes, until the hearing was called to order.

The magistrate seemed reluctant to read the letters but said that, at the officer's insistence, he would. There was not sufficient time now for the letters to be read, he said. He would have to take them home. The hearing was adjourned for a week.

My official letters to Joyce had always been chatty and fairly impersonal. The illegal ones were sexy at times.

I was returning to my cell on a Sunday when the accusing officer, who had waited in the yard, summoned me to him.

'You arrogant bastard,' he roistered hotly. 'Defiant as ever, aren't you, Dugan?' I shrugged indifferently.

'You'll pay for this,' he continued. 'I'll get your sentence doubled!'

At the hearing, when my antagonist arrived, the magistrate announced, 'At your insistence, I have read Dugan's letters. I have taken note of the sections you referred to.'

The magistrate turned to me. 'Dugan, after reading your letters, the parts referred to are the concern of only you and the person to whom they were addressed.'

He added that the contents of the letters were no threat to the prison's security. They had no bearing on the charge of clandestine correspondence.

The magistrate sentenced me to ten days of Black Peter. There was no mention of punishment to follow, and the arrogant turnkey was nicely pissed off. He did not confront me again.

The joy of 'victory' had a short life. The department had a way of dealing with prisoners who were difficult to manage. On 3 May 1961, not long after the letters affair, I was sent to Grafton for a third term there.

After the 'reception', I felt hollow. Here I was back where I had started from.

Certainly, some of my actions at Long Bay were ill-advised, but I did not consider in my wildest nightmares that they would result in me again being an intractable.

Had I wanted to, I could have escaped from Long Bay many times with ease. For mental exercise, I had worked out in detail 14 different, and safe, ways out. Fair dinkum.

The bashings continued as before. Some of those batons and I had become old acquaintances. Again I managed to exclude the bashings and the daily routine from my mind. The jail library's few hundred books and I were old friends. I read every one of them over and over.

A newspaperman who had shown a particular interest in my case sent me a volume of the *Complete Works of William Shakespeare*. After its covers were examined, the book was added to the library. I borrowed it repeatedly and developed a real appetite for the Bard. Shakespeare is still my favourite writer. Some people look surprised when I quote him in conversation.

Escape from Grafton now was near impossible. They kept too close a watch on me. And besides, the officials still said I would probably be out in 1964.

They were not at all pleased with me, but the department had sent me back to its Bloodhouse, it seemed, just to ginger me along. Maybe they finally knew that Dugan would never be tracted.

I was interviewed politely by the Labor government's new justice minister, Mr Jack Mannix. He even marvelled to me at some of my escapes. I had never heard of the minister in charge of police and prisons visiting a con in jail. The trip from, and back to, Sydney would take him a couple of days. I feared Minister of Justice Mannix was a McPherson bribee.

I also received two visits by the Department of Prisons' new comptroller-general, Mr John Morony, who had been at Parramatta when I was found in the hole.

Both men maintained that providing I went quietly henceforth, I would be released in 1964, as Mr Downing had said. With that assurance, I would not escape.

Mr Mannix came a second time, on 27 July 1962. He said with obvious sincerity that he would like to move me from Grafton right away.

'You've been in this place a long, long time, Darcy,' he said sadly. 'But I can't transfer you until you learn to behave. I see on your record here that only a month ago you spent seven days in the Black Peter. You just have to keep out of trouble.'

'Sir, do you know what that *trouble* was?' I retorted.

'You breached regulations.'

'Sir, many weeks before, I learned from a new intractable that a world-championship fight was coming up. I'm interested in boxing. After I knew the fight would be over, I said to a non-intractable prisoner, who was cutting my hair, "Who won the Dupas–Griffith fight in Las Vegas?"

'A warder was in the room, and for speaking to my barber, sir, I got a bashing and seven days' Black Peter.'

The Minister of Justice frowned. He impressed me as a fair-minded man. He spoke man to man, making it damned clear that he was ashamed of Grafton's intractables system. Hell, he said engagingly, maybe he had the power to end it. At least curb it.

'Are you going to make me stay longer in this place because of that question to the barber?' I asked.

Jack Mannix shuffled awkwardly. 'You have to obey the rules, but no.' He informed me that Griffith won the fight.

I remained at the Bloodhouse for 11 more months.

Advocates of the Bloodhouse system of brutality argued that there must be a place where unmanageable or dangerous prisoners were held and disciplined. Except for the barbaric convict establishments of the early days of Australia's colonisation by Europeans, no such place existed until 1943.

The New South Wales Department of Prisons had got on fairly nicely without a Bloodhouse. So did other Australian states. They still do.

Bloodhouse supporters seemed to ignore, or refused to acknowledge, the fact that since the inception of the intractable system there had been markedly more violence against warders, including murders, by prisoners than previously. This statement stands up, even allowing for the fact that there were more prisoners.

On 12 July 1963, after a record total of 11 years at the Bloodhouse, I was taken back to Parramatta jail.

I went by plane, with two uneasy guards. The sole hostess recognised me. She virtually ignored the guards, lavished magnificent food on me throughout the journey. As the guards looked on darkly, I ate as if food was going out of style. Three rump steaks! Ice cream!

Sydney looked superb from the air. I had not had a decent look at the place in 13 years. That is a big slice from a man's life. I hoped my days of incarceration were nearly over.

26

Parramatta's screws did not relish my return. I did not blame them. The comparative ease of Parramatta, with laxer security, was nearly blissful.

During the week, I sewed on soles in the shoe shop. On Saturday mornings, we cons were allowed to play tennis or golf on a mini course in the garden farm I had made infamous. On Saturday afternoons there was a film. On Sunday mornings, after church, more sport.

At night in our cells, we now could listen to the radio, piped from a commercial station. Music hath charm to soothe the savage beast, all right.

Still, they took few chances with me, not wanting to host my seventh break from custody. My cell in the security wing was fitted with two doors, one of which had two locks. I could have undone all the locks if I wanted to. All I needed was some metal, which was easily available in the jail yards.

But I held firm on my undertaking to Jack Mannix and my decision not to escape. Unless, that was, something happened that looked like lengthening my term. I had been promised release the next year.

Pop visited me nearly every month. During those 20-minute visits, through two sections of steel and wire mesh, and under the eyes of a screw, Pop repeatedly spoke of the happy days ahead. The days we would be together. Me a free man.

The newspapers had learned that I was nearing my release. Sometimes they publicised Pop's visits and carried pictures of him entering and leaving the jail. When newsmen covered his visits, or called on him at his little home at Ultimo, Pop never lost an opportunity to assert my innocence.

Screws showed me and told me of newspaper reports quoting Pop's claims that I had not even carried a gun at the Ultimo bank robbery. And he still believed that I was not involved in the Battle of Mort's Dock. I still did not have the heart to shatter his illusions.

Joyce had reconciled with her jealous husband. Occasionally I got letters from people I had never met — people who had read about me. Supporters, I suppose I can describe them as.

I had received hundreds of such letters in the first months of my sentence. Some were abusive; others offered advice and good wishes. Silly young boys and girls wrote to tell me I was their hero. Religious nuts told me salvation, or the fires of hell, were waiting. A few spinsters unashamedly declared their love!

But I did count among my few real friends the Catholic chaplains and nuns I had got to know in jails. Also the Protestant clergy. The real luxuries in the life of every long-term con were the pieces of fruit and ice cream distributed on Christmas Day by the Salvation Army. Except, of course, at Grafton.

Sugar Jackson was still the millionaire champion of the world. The place had a score of jailbird characters whose stories, to be told properly, demand more space than is available here. There were the preying butches who bullied weak prisoners into submission, sadists who tortured men for kicks, cats who fought with their fingernails for the favours of the queers, stir-crazy wrecks with eyes of blank glass. And the informers, who even most screws despised. It was a crazy society to live in.

One man, a hopeless masochist, pleaded with screws to flog him with their belts until, in final ecstasy, he ejaculated. There were the standover men who ran protection rackets in the jail. Weak prisoners had to give these men their issue of tobacco and cigarette paper or be bashed.

One old prisoner became the prey of three standover men. After he received his tobacco issue, the first thug to face the old chap got the lot. Then others bashed him for not saving 'baccy for them. They turned him into a nervous wreck.

I generally minded my own business and let the other prisoners mind theirs. My reputation ensured that nobody got in my way. I was considered the jail's main heavy but did not flaunt it. Except for a few mates, other cons considered me an introvert to respect. If possible, avoid. That suited me fine.

But I felt sorry for the old chap whom three standover men so regularly robbed and bashed. They had been at it for months. I had to end it. I went to the three of them, one at a time, and warned them off. 'Lay a hand on him again,' I told one, 'and I'll kick your big head in.'

The first two shrugged and stalked off. The old chap would not be bothered again by them. But the third standover man was not one to accept advice. Outside jail, he had a reputation for savagery; he was serving a life term for gunning down a rival thug. And I knew he had murdered at least two others. The police suspected him of one of those murders but could not prove it.

The thug was Rube Morrison. He must have weighed 17 stone. Six feet tall and as solid as a draught horse. Before becoming a full-time gangster, Rube had achieved local fame as a professional heavyweight boxer. He was aged about 38, four years younger than me.

He slouched about Parramatta jail as if he owned it. But he had avoided me and my friend Art Martini. Even Rube's limited intelligence told him that the only way he could beat either of us would be to kill us. As Art and I were small, Rube could certainly give either of us a hiding in a boxing ring. But we were different propositions in an all-in brawl. We would use any weapon necessary to achieve victory. I knew Morrison was also a good street fighter. In and out of jail, he had bashed men to the ground, then kicked them senseless. I hoped I would not have to take him on.

I walked up to Rube in the exercise yard and delivered my warning. Rube clenched his teeth and glared. 'I'll take what I fucking well want off him,' he said, and scowled. 'Him or anyone else. You don't scare *me*, Dugan, you little runt.'

I grinned thinly. 'You rob that old bloke once more and *you'll* have something to be scared of.'

A few other cons had silently gathered around to witness that first time Rube and I spoke to one another. They hoped to see us fight. Rube looked around at them and laughed. 'Dugan thinks he can tell me what to do! I oughta kill the little bastard.'

This was going to be a test. I could not afford to back down now. I glanced at his fists, clenched at his sides like big hams. The thought of them smashing into my face was not good. But he would be slow. In a real brawl, maybe I could take him. But that might require a weapon.

'Just you try me,' I said quietly. 'And I'll kick your thick head in. Don't take tobacco off that old bloke again.'

'You don't scare me, Dugan,' Rube repeated. He walked off, snorting.

I had not wanted other cons to know of my threat to Rube. Now, to maintain his reputation in the jail, he had to again rob the old man. If not, he would demonstrate fear of Dugan. By the next day, every con in Parramatta jail knew of the standoff.

'You're going to have to take him,' said Art. 'What say you and I wait for him and spring him together? Do the job properly. A couple of weeks in hospital will give him something to think about.'

I declined the offer of help. The jail code demanded that I handle it myself.

The old man who was the subject of the dispute did not come near me. He knew about my threat to Rube and the other two. He was more scared than ever. He believed I was moving in on the others' racket. Why else would I stop them?

Sure enough, the following week I was told that Rube had taken the old coot's tobacco. Every other con, and a few screws who knew about it, watched my movements.

Speculation was rife. 'Is Dugan going to let Rube get away with it?' 'Is Dugan really that tough?' 'Rube would slaughter him, wouldn't he?' The betting on the result of Rube and me in combat was even money. Most young cons and short-termers plumped for Rube. Others backed me.

I would have to give Rube the thrashing of his life. The old fellow Rube harassed would suffer no more. But more important was the business of maintaining my upper hand at the jail. If Rube got away with this, others would want to have a go at me. We were a pack of wolves.

My only real worry was that the fight would get out of hand. Most of the screws would be privately happy to see Rube given a lesson, but a fight in which bad injuries were sustained could not be ignored. No way could I risk a return to the Bloodhouse.

There would be an inquiry and, wham, a delay in my release. Still, one way or another, murderer Rube had to be tackled. And beaten. If not, *he* would be Parramatta's top heavy.

I decided to first see how Rube went in a straight-out fight. If I dodged those big, slow hams for the first ten minutes, I could perhaps wear him out enough to cut him up with chops and jabs. Speed and fitness were on my side.

The next morning, I sent a message for Rube to see me in a small, secluded yard near the back of the jail. I waited silently in the middle of the yard as a heap of other cons, spectators, sneaked in.

The big man grimly walked up and raised his fists, John L. Sullivan style. Like mad Dudley, the Aboriginal con at Grafton, when he took me on.

I moved around him, tempting him to charge. No way could I allow myself to get caught inside those bear-like arms. Rube made several wild swings. I ducked, delivered the occasional chop to the side of his head. But Rube hardly felt them. I was like a bird pecking at an elephant. I kept the big man moving, jabbing, ducking and backing away. After some 15 minutes, Rube was breathing heavily. Now to get him angry. Force him into a blind fury of mistakes.

'What's wrong, Rube?' I taunted. 'All that fat slowing you down?'

The standover man lowered his head and charged like a bull. I sidestepped, chopped the back of his neck as he went by. 'You're running round like an old sheila, Rube. I thought you could fight!'

He shook with rage, looking silly in front of the others, who cheered. Screws must be hearing this, I figured, but none came.

Rube charged again. I darted to one side, but this time he caught me in his outstretched arm. He swung his other arm, crashing a huge fist into my chest. I reeled back, taking another blow square on the face. It knocked me against the yard wall.

I saw another fist coming and ducked. His knuckles crashed into the sandstone. I lowered my head and, using both legs as springs, butted the top of my head into his guts.

Rube doubled over. I grabbed the back of his head in both hands and jerked it down. My knee smashed into his face with all my might. His nose was crushed. The edge of my right hand hacked the side of his hairy neck. Rube roared like a wounded lion.

Yes, he was like a bear, an elephant, a bull and a lion. I hammered his forehead into the wall again and again. Cons, the ones who backed me I suppose, urged me on.

'Kill the big bastard! Belt him, Darcy! Smash him to pulp!'

Rube sagged to the ground. But I was far from finished with him. This had to be a lesson he would not forget.

I was about to leap on him when a hand caught my ankle. I toppled backwards. Rube got to his feet. I was still on my knees when his boot crashed into my face. It flipped me onto my back. Blood spurted from my mouth.

His face also bloodied, brow and nose dented, he came at me again. I rolled as another boot crashed into my side. I kept rolling and was again on my knees as he came up to kick.

I ducked to one side. The boot struck my shoulder but I was able to cling to it. Rube fell backwards. I sprang at him, driving an elbow into his face.

At that moment, a screw grabbed me around the neck and pulled me off him. A second screw wrapped his arms around my waist.

'All right, fellas,' said the first screw. 'That's enough for today. I think you're the winner, Darcy.'

Realising I was not resisting them, the screws let me go. It was inevitable that the cheer squad's yelling would eventually attract them.

Rube slowly got to his feet. 'You, thug,' a screw told him. 'Get back to your work. The pair of you!'

By then, the cheer squad had vanished. Rube and I should have been paraded and punished for fighting. But those two screws, I later learned, had known our fight was brewing. They had stood by the yard's entrance for several minutes, unnoticed, as we fought. Many pounds and packets of tobacco that had been waged on the fight changed hands. Art Martini did well out of it.

But the contest with Rube had only just begun. The only satisfactory conclusion would be for me to get his unqualified subjugation. Three days later, I jumped him in the exercise yard. Before he realised what was on, I rammed his skull into the wall. I clouted him repeatedly with a bucket, until he was unconscious, left him face down in a puddle of blood.

A few days later, I waited for him around a corner. As he stepped in front of me, I drove the end of a broom handle into his belly. It winded him. As he lurched to the ground, I swung the business end of the heavy broom at the back of his head. Again, the big brute was left senseless.

After the next tobacco issue, no one asked the old fellow for his ration. Instead, he nervously walked up to me, holding out the weed and cigarette papers. 'Here you are, Mr Dugan,' he said quietly.

'I don't want your stinking tobacco,' I snapped. 'Smoke it yourself.'

I shall never forget the sight of that poor wreck. He could not believe that someone would fight his enemies without having an ulterior motive. He walked away, stunned.

I did not, and do not, smoke, but tobacco is valuable to any man in jail. It is the principal currency. I often played cards and had won quite a lot of 'baccy.

I bashed Rube three more times, after which he was subdued. During the final attack, he pleaded for mercy. He kept well out of my way thereafter.

He was probably convinced I was a homicidal maniac. To stop me, he had to be prepared to lay in wait and kill me. And, he knew, if he did that my friends would promptly slay him.

* * *

I had become the jail's bookmaker. We would all get the fields for the Saturday horse races from the official radio program piped into the cells on Friday nights. The few of us with technically illegal crystal radio sets listened to race broadcasts the next day. Each prisoner was allowed to buy one Sunday newspaper, and from these we got the horses' starting prices.

I paid starting prices, the same as the scores of other illegal bookmakers outside jails. Bookies like freed George Freeman. Much of the currency I won and lost was tobacco and cigarette papers.

As with many other prisoners, though, I got money smuggled into the jail, usually by hot screws. Some Saturdays and Sundays, a hundred pounds passed through my hands. My money was kept in a tin buried under a rock. Other prisoners knew the location of the 'bank', but no one was foolish enough to try a robbery.

A senior screw censored our Sunday newspapers by tearing out stories we should not see, including accounts of activities in jails and crimes on the outside.

Of course, we cons were intrigued when we came upon a torn-out page. A hot screw would be approached, money changed hands, and the following day he would bring in the required page from his own paper. This was done with quite a few reports about me.

27

Perhaps the most memorable inmate at Parramatta was Andy Moss, a bandit, a murderer and a cannibal. Andy was convicted on only one count of murder and cannibalism. But I have been told by prison authorities, and also lately by an honest policeman who was on the case, that Andy had murdered and eaten at least 13 other men.

Those allegations were never made public. In Andy's case, it was pointless to proceed with them, because, as one copper put it, that would only be 'flogging a dead dog'. Moss was the dead dog. With his record, he would never be released.

He was cunning but had little intelligence. When a bushman, his modus operandi was to befriend other bushies, or travellers on the road, slay and rob them, then eat them.

One day Andy killed a traveller and took the dead man's horse and sulky. Before burying the body, he sliced off what he considered the tastiest cuts and took them off in a bag. Andy made camp and, as was his custom, cooked the human flesh into a stew.

Two other bushmen came along. They promptly accepted Andy's offer to share the meal. All three were enjoying the repast — which the guests thought was mutton, I'm told — when one of them bit into something too tough to chew. He pulled it out of his mouth. It was part of a human finger, with a nail. After vomiting profusely, the two men took Andy to a police station.

I first met Moss when I was a young'un at Long Bay. The short, thickset man grew more and more senile. He was given a job in Parramatta jail's farm garden. For years, almost any weekday, Andy sat at the bottom of the garden with a small fire and a billy containing meat and vegetables. It was not easy in prison to get meat. But Moss had his own source.

The farm had a population of cats — the real animals, as apart from 'bitch' homosexuals. I understand cat meat looks and tastes like rabbit. A very few cons, some knowingly, some liking 'rabbit', accepted Andy's generous offers from the stew pot.

Prisoners who knew Andy was a cannibal joshed him about his cat stews. A regular line was 'Can't you get me bit of bum steak, Andy?'

The question of just who and what lived in Parramatta jail, and in other jails, was disputed by people who slept on both sides of the outer walls. As well as maggots in meals, cats, feathered (not stool) pigeons, mice, fleas and ticks — and poultry and pigs on the farm — Parramatta had an enormous community of rats. Real, animal rats.

Some grew as big as small cats. Periodic efforts at extermination never decreased their numbers noticeably. A standing offer in New South Wales prisons was one ounce of tobacco for every dead rat a prisoner presented to the screws. So there was a permanent state of war between cons and rats.

Old Andy Moss was always keen to make an extra buck — or, in the matter of rats, extra tobacco. He made a small rat-trap in the form of a cage with a tripping device at the entrance. Jail rats are abnormally cunning but Andy caught a few. One day he kept a rat alive in the cage until the governor arrived on his 10 a.m. inspection.

Andy proudly held up the cage. 'There's a good one for you,' he said, sticking out his chest. 'Can I get my ounce of 'baccy now?'

The governor directed Andy to the prison store to collect his reward. He turned to walk away, then swung back, saying, 'Just a minute, Andy. You had better kill the rat first.'

Andy hesitated, then plunged the cage and rat into a laundry tub of water. The rat struggled for air, then the water calmed, air bubbles stopped rising. As the governor, some screws and cons looked on, Andy pulled out the cage containing the inert rat. He went to the store and collected the tobacco.

A few minutes later, a prisoner spotted the rat twitching, coming back to life.

As Andy returned, the prisoner told him it was not dead. 'Chuck it back in the tub for a while,' he advised. 'Oh, I'll do the job myself.'

Andy was never slow to see a chance for extra income. Quick as a flash, he grabbed the cage from the prisoner. He yanked the animal out, placed it on its back on the floor and massaged its chest with his thumbs. Water dripped from the rat's mouth. In a few moments, it was struggling to get on its feet.

Andy chuckled gleefully. 'Don't you see? This live rat means more and more 'baccy! He'll be in the cage when the governor's back in the morning.'

Andy fed the rat scraps of bread and repeated his trick in front of the governor at least five times, getting him five lots of tobacco.

But, alas, some dirty dog of a prisoner, perhaps jealous of Andy's prosperity, let it get to the governor's ears that Andy was conning him. The governor, being a sport, took the news of Andy's caper philosophically.

The next morning he casually watched Andy go through his routine of exhibiting the rat, now named Menzies. It was 'drowned', placed in the cage on the floor. Chuckling Andy had the air of a job well done.

With jaundiced eye, the governor informed him, 'This morning I think we'll make sure of him, Andy. Take him out of the cage and hit him on the head.'

I'm told the watching prisoners appreciated the governor calling the rat 'him', not 'it'. For by now the poor critter was a personality. Andy sullenly did as directed. Poor old multi-drowned Menzies ended up in Andy's stew pot. Andy told me, straight faced, that he named the rat in honour of our prime minister. I privately hoped, though, that Sir Robert would never find out about Menzies the jail rat.

Smirking, the governor went on his way. Andy's only reaction was to glare at the laughing prisoners and mutter something about unprincipled informers, and something about a poor old man being deprived of his comforts. From that day, the governor insisted that all rats presented for tobacco were knocked on the head.

Andy Moss died behind bars, aged 70, after serving about 25 years.

28

My latter months at Parramatta were spent working at the piggery on the jail farm. Things were going pretty well, but a couple of screws had a set on me.

'You think you're smart, Dugan,' one said. 'Just you give me half a reason and I'II put in a report that'll land you back in the Bloodhouse.'

He was not kidding. If I returned to Grafton, I could well spend the rest of my days incarcerated. And I was feeling my age. I was a ravaged 44. If the authorities were led to believe I was still uncontrollable on the verge of release, they might decide I could never be trusted in society.

I now obeyed most regulations meticulously. But the risk of accidentally giving those two screws a pretext for sending me up north was scary. Years before, I had resolved that when released I would do my utmost to expose to the public much of the extent of corruption on high in Sydney, especially in the CIB. Also, the rottenness of the state's prison system, particularly the barbarism of the Bloodhouse. And there was the McPherson matter to be attended to. If I returned to Grafton, I would probably never get out to do any of that.

So I decided to write my jail memoir. I asked for, and received, permission to have writing material for what I called English studies.

I spent weeks in my cell each night before the lights went out filling an exercise book with notes about my childhood, my successful and near escapes, and all I could recall of my experiences in and out of jails. I kept the dark truth about multi-murderer Lennie the Pig out of the exercise book. There, he was Les McPhee, a criminal mate as a kid, partner in several robberies and true helper when I was an escapee.

I removed a few pages from the exercise book, and on those I related the real story about McPherson: what I found out and what George Freeman told me about the Pig's numerous betrayals, getting me sent back to jail so often. Detectives Kelly and Krahe and others featured on those pages, too. They would have to remain ultra-secret until one day I found a good young writer I could trust.

The writer I found would have to be skilled and trusty enough to combine it all; relate more about my childhood, the Gosford days, all those robberies; and report a bit about my later life, and probably my death, in a book. *This* book, I hope. Published, importantly, after McPherson and also Kelly and Krahe were dead. If the Pig and co. found out such a publication was on the way, that writer, like diarist Dick Reilly, would be slain.

Despite hot-blooded moments at Mort's Dock and during the Grafton rebellion, I had never killed. Lately, I did not fancy doing in even McPherson. Vengeful detectives and other thugs in the Pig's employ would hunt down and stitch up murderer Dugan.

By day I hid the manuscripts in my cell. Putting such things on paper while in jail was risky but worthwhile. I might die in here. A screw might discover the MS. before I got out of jail and found that writer.

Screws who looked into my cell and saw me scribbling assumed I was studying, as stated when I applied for paper and pen.

I wrote it honestly and, I hope, objectively. When the manuscript was completed, a fellow prisoner I absolutely trusted smuggled it out when he was released. He was good old Harry Mitchell, my fellow robber and escapee from the Black Maria. With the MS. went the instruction that Harry was to keep it hidden, tell no one. I would get it from him when I was a free man. If I died first, he could deliver the MS. to a newspaper, but preferably to a skilled and trustworthy writer, whom Harry could find. It would be my last testament. But dead Dugan's ultra-secret pages could go only to that scribe.

* * *

Mercifully, the antagonistic screws could not make good their threats of getting me back to Grafton. On 24 October 1964, I had a chance to wave a quick goodbye to my mates at Parramatta before being transferred to the Department of Prisons' Brookfield Afforestation Camp, near the small farming settlement of Tumbarumba.

The town nestles behind the massive Snowy Mountains, in southern New South Wales. The prison camp is about 30 miles north of the Victorian border. It exists mainly for prisoners to plant pine forests. But such camps, of which there are several, are also valuable in alleviating that condition often brought about in long-term cons termed 'institutionalisation'.

Conditions at prison camps are much freer than at regular jails. An old con can experience the luxury of fresh air, open space, wide horizons. He can see the sun rise and set. And the moon.

Have you ever wondered what it would be like not to see the moon or the stars for 14 years? Never see a beach, a mountain? A bird in a tree? To have forgotten the feeling of baring your chest to the sun?

Tall, grey walls were no longer my horizons. As I walked across the grounds of the camp to collect the usual jail wear, plus a pair of heavy work boots, I stretched my arms and filled my lungs with the tangy, clean air of the countryside. Somewhere out there, sheep were bleating.

A handful of long-term cons at Tumbarumba were on the final lap of our sentences. The remainder of the camp's complement of about 80 inmates were young men convicted on minor offences and not considered likely to try to escape.

I was placed in one of a row of about ten adjoining timber huts. My room was about eight feet by seven. There were two windows, one in the door, the other in the back wall. No iron bars. I spent most of my first night at Tumbarumba standing at the back window, looking out at the stars. It was exhilarating.

I tended the camp's lawns and extensive flowerbeds. I have never been particularly interested in horticulture but revelled in the open spaces. The food was reasonably good, and prisoners could be sent food parcels. I got a box of chocolates from Pop!

The dozen screws and most of the prisoners treated me warily. They were polite but not anxious to engage me in any more conversation than was necessary. The reputation of Houdini Dugan, the monster, had apparently done the rounds. After a few days, however, I had won their confidence. I joined in tennis matches and began teaching a young, illiterate prisoner the alphabet.

One day I competed in an officially organised 100-yard sprint. Old fella Dugan won the event, too! At least the regular hours and exercise in my cells, the absence of exotic food over the years, had kept me fit.

I thought more and more of release day. The usual transitional term at a camp for a lifer like me was about six months. I still felt some bitterness about officialdom not honouring the promise that I would be freed in 1964, but at least I expected to be out early in '65.

Things went along nicely. Apart from liberty and the wish to be with Pop, I hungered for only one thing — female company. Sex.

I had been bottled up for a long time. Wives and girlfriends of some prisoners visited them at weekends. It was fairly common knowledge that a few of the womenfolk remained in the district overnight. Their men slipped out to spend a few hours with them. The prisoners were back in the camp by dawn. Some bragged about their sexual exploits in the bush beyond the camp fences. One con even kept a stolen car in bushland near the camp. He took it for rides at night. Per the car, a few cons had formed relationships with local girls. Some of them did some stealing, I heard.

'Why don't you go out and win yourself a sheila?' I was asked by a con I will call Pluto. 'You could fix yourself up easy, Darce.'

'No, too much to lose. I'll be getting out pretty soon.'

'A lot of the blokes are doing it,' Pluto persisted. 'You know more about escaping than all of us put together.'

I repeated that I would not jeopardise my future. Pluto's wife visited him at the camp every Saturday. He slipped out on Saturday nights and returned at peace with the world. The Sunday following our conversation, Pluto drew me aside.

'I've told my wife about you and she knows a lot about you from the newspapers,' he said. 'She's talked about you with a girlfriend of hers. The girlfriend's curious to meet you. If I give the missus the nod in a letter before Friday, the girlfriend will be with her next Saturday night.'

Pluto grinned confidingly. 'What do you say?'

I stood there pondering. Said nothing.

'She's a little blonde and a real sexpot,' he tempted. 'She's married to a bloke who goes away working weeks at a time. She'd be a pushover for you!'

Sex-starved Dugan weakened. Getting in and out of the place was pretty easy and common. I asked Pluto to let his wife know I would slip out of the camp on Saturday night.

The upper part of the window at the back of my hut was hinged on central pivoting bolts which went into the framework at each side. Sections swung open to provide narrow ventilation slits top and bottom. That night, I removed the whole window section and set it back on the frame so it could be removed again in less than a minute. It could easily be opened again by one standing outside the hut, getting back in.

That Saturday evening, six weeks after I arrived at Tumbarumba, I was locked in my hut, as usual, at 8.30. By 9.30, I had wriggled through the eighteen-inch by seven-inch window space and was outside the prison-camp grounds with an excited Pluto.

'Blood oath,' he said. 'I'm doing a break with the great *Houdini*!

Pluto's wife was waiting in his car with civilian clothes for us. She drove us to a motel three miles from the camp. Two suites had been booked for the night.

My girl, called here Mary, was waiting. We four had a few drinks together. Mary and ravenous D.D. clicked right away. She was petite and curvaceous, aged about 25. Long, honey hair and smooth skin of gold.

Mary had come mostly out of curiosity about me, and perhaps also about how a man would behave after being kept away from women for so long.

In our room later, she found out. I was very gentle with her. I spent more than an hour caressing her body, before going on to establish what is surely a record, at least for the Tumbarumba district — six times. Many of the frustrations and repressions I had controlled for 14 years surged from my system.

She lived in a town about 70 miles from Tumbarumba. Just before I left her to return to the camp, while it was still dark, she said, 'Do you want to see me again?'

Did I! 'That's probably the most unnecessary question I've ever heard, darling.'

'Tonight?'

'Really?'

'I'll be in my husband's car, parked near the camp's back fence, at nine o'clock.'

Mary had told me her husband used a company vehicle for his work as a commercial traveller. He, she said, was virtually impotent. He had made love to her only once during their three-week honeymoon. He returned home only occasionally.

I made love to Mary that night, the next, and the next. She wanted to return for the fourth night, but I bought off. I had not had enough of her, mind. But I was physically exhausted. She drove me back to the camp just before dawn. I scrambled into my hut in time to prepare for the day's work.

From then on, we met on Wednesday and Saturday nights. Whenever Mary did not arrive to collect me, her husband was at home. Sometimes, I stole into the camp's office at night and telephoned her. We had long conversations, paid for by the prisons department.

After a few months, Mary said she wanted to leave her husband. She knew my release was near. Her husband was no longer sleeping with her, and he did not seem to care. Could she live with me when I got out?

She was a charming companion. I said yes but advised her to remain at her current quarters until I was a free man. This she agreed to do.

On 28 May 1965, after seven months at Tumbarumba, I was transferred to Long Bay, where the governor told me, 'This is it. You have to be examined by two psychiatrists. If they give satisfactory reports to the parole board, you will be released.'

I had not seen Billy Mears for many years. He, too, had spent several months at a prison camp and was now at Long Bay for medical examinations preliminary to release. He had weathered pretty well. We talked together for a few minutes while waiting to be examined separately by the psychiatrists. I still considered Mears a decent enough bloke, but a weakling. I was polite but did not bother feigning delight at seeing him.

Almost as soon as the psychiatrists made their reports, I was able illegally to get copies of them. Mears got one good report, another that expressed minor reservations. Both my reports had favourable recommendations. Now the formality of facing the parole board.

29

Pop was 90 years old. He had been ill for some time and had not been able to journey to Tumbarumba. When a prisoner is transferred to a new jail, he becomes eligible for a visit, and I looked forward to seeing the old man again.

We had regularly exchanged letters, but I had been transferred to the Bay on short notice, which had prevented me letting Pop know I would be back in Sydney.

And the prisons department did not want anyone outside to know I was back at the Bay, on the brink of freedom. They seemed to have an obsession about possible dangers if my impending release became generally known. They wanted no newsmen waiting at the gate when I walked out. A splurge of publicity would give an unhealthy lift to my ego, the authorities reckoned, maybe sending me on a rampage of crime. Perhaps they also feared public opinion would be against ever releasing me.

Or did an official or two fear that Dugan at the jail gate would say too much about Grafton?

My overwhelming desire was simply to be genuinely free. And remain that way. Staying out of jail, I knew, might not be easy. I still had many, many enemies in the CIB. There would be plenty of cops only too anxious to say, 'I got Dugan.' Notable among them was R. Kelly.

Few knew I had changed my surname, way back, to Clare. Perhaps, if the terms of my parole permitted it, I would use that name and move to another state, away from Sydney detectives who again would tell an employer I was the notorious Dugan, then load me again with stolen goods and get me back in a slammer.

I was confident the parole board would be delighted to have me out of the state. At Tumbarumba and now at Long Bay, parole officers had gently suggested that I be spirited out of jail and flown to another state, maybe Queensland.

'You'd be well away when the minister announces your release,' one officer urged. 'I'm pretty sure a job could be fixed up for you.'

There were strong suggestions that if I agreed to that plan, my release would be expedited. The idea of leaving New South Wales appealed to me, but I would have no part of a deal in which I was released only if I immediately fled my state. I wanted first to see Pop, buy myself some clothes, take a ferry ride on Sydney Harbour, walk into a shop and buy an ice cream. And if I left, I wanted to take Pop with me. Tumbarumba Mary could perhaps join us.

I was anxious to see Pop, who I hoped had recovered from his illness. The news that I was now really on the final, short lap would give my dear old man a lift. I entrusted a con, due for release in a couple of days, to go to the old house at Ultimo to let him know I was at the Bay, eligible for a visit.

The con due to deliver the message was still in jail on the afternoon of Friday, 11 June '65, when a screw called me to receive a visitor. I stood waiting curiously behind steel bars and wire mesh on the prisoners' side of the visiting section.

Into the cubicle opposite me came old Pop, grinning like Christmas, his blue eyes sparkling. But he was leaning heavily on a man's shoulder. Lord, I had no idea he was *that* ill! He looked to have lost a lot of weight in the ten months since I had seen him.

'Pop, ask them for a chair!'

'I'm all right, son,' his dour voice crackled. 'It's just that I've taken a fancy to Mike here.' Pop then stood erect to the left of the stranger.

I looked at the stranger questioningly. He wore a fairly well-cut suit, black tie, white shirt. He was in his mid-20s. A bit too short to be a cop! He glanced past Pop at the guard, then grinned confidently at me. I picked him as some sort of welfare officer. By the look of Pop, he needed someone to help him get in here.

I would play it cool until I learned more about this dark-haired, well-built character.

'G'day Darcy, old mate,' Mike said, and nodded. 'Don't let this old actor fool you. In no time he'll be out chasing girls again.'

Old mate?

Pop cut in. 'Mike rang the prisons department yesterday and told them I wanted to see you. He was going to take me down to Tumbarumba, but they told him you were here at the Bay!'

The stranger's brown eyes were fixed on me. Surely, if he was a welfare officer or from the prisons department, he would have said so by now. With that 'old mate' line, he wanted to make the guard think we were buddies. Pop seemed to trust him, but I had to know more.

Who is this Mike? He seemed to read my question. He casually leaned back, glanced again at the guard and, looking at me intently, shook his head. Obviously, he could not state his business in front of the screw. He leaned forward and asked the screw, 'Is it all right to smoke?'

'Sure, go ahead.'

The stranger stepped back so Pop was between him and the screw, standing some ten feet away. As Mike felt in a pocket, Pop began a dull tale about a serial he had heard on the radio. Pop glanced at the screw, who was now looking at the floor, and gently brushed Mike's arm with his right elbow.

Mike pulled out a cigarette packet. He held it to his chest as his other hand fumbled for matches. Against the packet was a white business card.

This had been rehearsed! Pop kept on about the serial as I tried to look casual, eyes straining through the wire mesh to read the block letters on the card. 'MICHAEL TATLOW *SUNDAY TELEGRAPH*'.

I quickly nodded and grinned. I had seen his name on scores of feature articles. Tatlow slipped the card in a pocket as he lit a cigarette. Heck, there'll be a story about this soon. *Exclusive session with Dugan?*

Pop terminated his tale about the serial. 'Mike's been a good friend to me, Darcy. He got a doctor in to see me a few times even though I said no. He's going to help all he can. Trust him.'

Over the years, Pop had developed a distrust of newsmen. On visits to Grafton and Parramatta, he had told me of times reporters and photographers had knocked on his front door at Ultimo wanting to interview him and he had sent them packing. Pop was too cunning to be taken in by a glib-tongued journalist trying to get an inside story on my release. Or exploit Pop's friendship to get the full works from me when I got out.

'Thanks, Mike,' I said, studying him closely. 'It's good to see you again.'

The screw was now preoccupied listening to a con greet his wife. I continued, 'I know you'll do the right thing. Truth is, as you'd already know, I'm getting near my release. I've passed the psycho tests and all that. But, for some reason, the authorities here are concerned about it getting into the newspapers.'

Tatlow shook his head meaningfully. 'That won't happen unless some prison officer, or a released prisoner, tries to make a few quid for himself by going to a paper.'

I replied, truthfully, that only a few cons and screws knew I would probably be out soon. And they were not the type to blab.

'Good,' said Tatlow, checking that the guard was still preoccupied. Looking at his wristwatch, he added, 'There's plenty of time to go. I'm in no hurry.'

I got his meaning. No story for a while. 'Waiting will pay dividends,' I said, grinning again. 'We must have a good yarn some day.'

'I'll write tonight,' Tatlow said. He paused with a smirk at my flash of consternation. 'To *you*, Darcy, giving my home address. Can you write back?'

'Sure. I don't have to tell you *my* address.'

The 20 minutes allowed for visitors soon expired. I could not help smirking as Pop turned nimbly to walk away. Tatlow grabbed his arm, wordlessly reminding the old boy he was suppose to be ailing. Tatlow smiled back over his shoulder. He had come posing as a family friend playing nursemaid.

Tatlow's letter, which I received on the Monday, gave me details of Pop's illness, which Mike had not wanted to state in front of the old chap. For quite a while, Pop had been very weak. It seemed that only his Irish determination to see me a free man kept him alive.

Tatlow mentioned that he had developed a friendship with Pop in the ramshackle Ultimo house in his own, not the newspaper's, time. In the past couple of weeks, the letter said, Pop had rallied. And that Friday evening at home after seeing me and getting confirmation that I would be out soon, he bounded about like a spring lamb.

Tatlow let me know he had used his correct name and home address in the jail's visitors' book. He had not broken any regulation. He had not been required to state his occupation. And, in any case, a man's lawful profession did not exclude him from visiting a jail.

My letter in reply hinted again that I had some worthwhile stories for him when I was released. You can give a reasonable amount of extra information 'between the lines' in a jail letter, providing the scrutinising screw has not been alerted to pay special attention.

One had to hope that the addressee was alert enough to get the message. Tatlow's next letter showed that he had missed nothing.

I was confident that only a week or so remained for me as a guest of the state. I had told my parole officer I would probably leave New South Wales but first wanted to spend some time in Sydney. He seemed to accept this. I was set to go.

Then, out of the blue, a grim warder walked up to me. 'There's trouble at Tumbarumba,' I was told. 'They're on to what you and your mates did down there.'

In answer to my pleas to know what I was supposed to have done, I was informed that a police officer would see me in a day or two. My heart sank. How would Pop take it if he learned of this? What did they know?

On 21 June 1965, I got through the grapevine a dramatic answer. The front page of the Sydney *Sun* newspaper blared the heading: 'Darcy Dugan Probe'. A group of convicts at Tumbarumba were apparently under police investigation into reports that they had been leaving their prison-farm cells at night to carry out robberies and car thefts, and to meet women.

The inquiry had begun when a stolen car was found hidden in a pine forest inside the boundary of the Tumbarumba prison farm on Wednesday, 2 June.

The report, by police roundsman Noel Bailey, said a trap door had been discovered in the floor of the cabin I had occupied.

What bloody trap door?

A local businessman said he had organised a vigilante brigade because of a wave of petty robberies. There were pictures of two push-bikes claimed to have been stolen in the town and found hidden by a creek near the prison camp.

There was no claim that I had escaped from the camp or taken part in any robbery. But the innuendo was applied as thick as a king's mattress. My name was injected throughout the report. In his background on me, Bailey reported that I had shot and critically wounded a Sydney bank manager in 1950. What rot! The gross lie angered me. But my main concern was how the report would influence the men determining the date of my release.

Mike Tatlow later told me that Bailey had been prompted onto the story by my nemesis and torturer, Detective Raymond Kelly. I assumed Kelly was — in part, anyway — acting on behalf of his mate McPherson. Both of them would want me to leave jail only in a coffin.

The story also contained the false claim that at Long Bay I had lately been 'put into a maximum security cell under 24-hour guard'.

(For that report, the Australian Journalists' Association awarded Bailey the Walkley Award for the best newspaper report in Australia in 1965!)

I knew, of course, about the stolen car other prisoners had kept hidden in the trees near the camp. I also knew which two prisoners stole the bikes. That some of them committed robberies. But under no circumstances would I dob them in. How the hell, then, could

I clear my name? I had not stolen a thing — apart, I suppose, from the cost of those phone calls to Mary.

In the next few days, police and prisons department officials fronted me. They accused me of sneaking out at night, of stealing the car and bikes with a confederate, of being the mastermind in several minor robberies. They said that between March and June several cars had been stolen in the Tumbarumba district. I told them I strongly doubted if I still knew how to drive a car.

They said that in some 20 robberies, a quarter of a million cigarettes, hundredweights of tobacco and a great amount of food and clothing had been stolen from retail stores.

My inquisitors further accused me of constructing a trap door in my camp hut and of doctoring the window. They said, too, that I had dispatched clandestine correspondence. I denied the charges. But, sure, I had doctored the window, dammit.

They claimed a former Tumbarumba con, who I knew was a serial stool pigeon, had admitted stealing the car found near the camp. He had named me as his accomplice. I laughed incredulously at that.

I did worry about the effect Bailey's report would have on public opinion. The Liberal government's Minister of Justice Maddison would not let me out if he thought the public was against it. And now, thanks to one newspaper, many people would think it was me, not Billy Mears, who had shot Nalder.

The police sure believed I had carried out the proverbial 'wave of robberies' at Tumbarumba. Even if I was officially cleared, that belief could remain — remain in the mind of Mr Maddison. As I was serving an indeterminate sentence, there was no compulsion to release me by any date.

I felt disillusioned. The Labor Party had recently lost a state election. The Liberals' Minister of Justice Maddison was not bound by the assurances of his Labor predecessor, Jack Mannix, that I would serve a total of 14½ years.

I fondly remembered those visits by Mannix at Grafton. I understood that Maddison was not even aware of the verbal assurance. Had Labor remained in power, I would have been released in December 1964 — six months back.

I record here that I was a stupid ass for jeopardising my future by sneaking out of the Tumbarumba camp to bed Mary. Seeing what so many others were getting away with, I had found the compulsion to be with a woman irresistible.

In my cell at Long Bay, I desperately wanted publicly to clear my name. I managed to get a lot of information transmitted to Michael Tatlow at the *Sunday Telegraph*. I had him told what had really happened at Tumbarumba and what the police and prisons department officials had accused me of.

All copies of the *Sunday Telegraph* delivered to New South Wales jails the following Sunday, 27 June, had a prominent page torn out.

A sympathetic screw risked the sack by showing it to me that night. Tatlow had been busy. In a prominent reported headed 'The truth about Darcy Dugan', the paper revealed that he had been in touch with screws from Tumbarumba and Goulburn, also with a couple of cons just released from Goulburn. He had uncovered that the con who had told police that I was his accomplice in stealing the cars had retracted his claim, but the police were believed to be unaware, because the con had since been transferred to Goulburn jail. The trap door, Tatlow discovered, had been in the hut well before I arrived.

Tatlow, who had visited my bed-mate Mary and confirmed the truth of what I said, had also talked to Mrs Nalder, wife of the shot bank manager. She said she and her husband bore no grudge against me. They felt I had been punished sufficiently.

'After all, it was not Dugan who fired the shot,' she said. 'If Darcy had not abused Mears for shooting Leslie, Mears might have fired again.' Through the report I learned that after recovering from the wound, Leslie Nalder had returned to banking and retired, aged 65.

The author of these reports was described in the *Telegraph* as 'A Special Reporter'. I understand it was not long after this, however, that the warders at Long Bay realised the identity of M.W. Tatlow, signatory in the jail's visitors' book before seeing me with Pop. But, to the department's credit, they did not try to prevent him seeing me again. They apparently respected the fact that he had not written about the first visit.

The papers next morning carried the news that, as a result of the continued police investigation, I would appear before a magistrate in Goulburn jail charged with making night escapes and stealing cars. It would be a preliminary hearing, closed to the public.

Later, on a visit to the prison, Tatlow told me that Minister of Justice Maddison had deferred all consideration of my release until then.

As I pondered, I was informed that a visitor was coming. I was sent to the jail's normal visiting section to wait my 'guest's' arrival. Into the cubicle opposite me walked Mike.

'What? No guard?' he said. 'They must have read in the *Tele* what a trustworthy type you are, Darcy.'

A guard would be here at any moment. 'Quick,' I said, 'what's going on about me?'

A three-stripe screw ran in and stood, glaring, in the aisle between us. He obviously knew about journalist Tatlow.

'Well, as I was saying,' said Tatlow, 'there will be a preliminary hearing at —'

'Stop!' the screw cried. 'It is forbidden to discuss a prisoner's charges. Stick to personal and family matters.'

Tatlow explained that Pop, whom he called Dick, was upset by 'recent crazy stories' and was too ill to see me. But Dick hoped I would be 'cleared of the charges, especially as you would have to go on to an open court —'

'Stop that!' the screw yelled menacingly. 'You can't talk about that.'

'Officer,' Tatlow said quietly, 'this is impossible. What can't we talk about?'

'The charges,' the officer said, glancing back at me. 'You can't say anything about the prisoner's charges.'

Tatlow looked at me questioningly through the mesh. I hoped I saw what he was getting at, and I desperately wanted to know what information he had. The next five years of my life could be at stake. I nodded quickly.

'Officer,' Tatlow continued, 'just what has Mr Dugan been charged with?'

'You know. And you can't talk about it.'

'He hasn't been charged with any offences, to my knowledge, since he arrived at this jail,' Tatlow said, authoritatively.

Such men as the officer were not used to having their authority questioned. 'I'll have to check this,' he said finally. 'You step back from the window, Number Two-nine-two, and I'll check.'

Tatlow and the screw were away for a long ten minutes. When they returned, Michael's face was crinkled with a grin. The screw said not a word.

'As you have not been charged with any offence, Darcy,' said Tatlow, 'we can discuss this matter as much as time permits. And the time I've been away is not counted in the twenty minutes.'

Tatlow said he and some of his friends at the *Telegraph* had arranged for Pop to engage a solicitor, Mr Charles Griffiths, for me. Mr Griffiths would see me soon. He would brief one of Australia's top barristers if the matter was to go to an open court.

'The main allegation against you will come from a Tumbarumba con at the time, Ian Henke,' Mike said. 'He says you escaped from the farm with him twice and stole stuff in the town. They've transferred Henke to Goulburn jail so others at Tumbarumba won't throttle him for being a stool pigeon.'

'Henke's claim is garbage,' I said, grinning thinly. 'He's a regular stoolie, who I barely knew.' I did not spell out any denials. I did not want the tuned-in screw to know any more about how I would respond to the charges.

Tatlow grinned back. 'At Goulburn, Henke admitted to a prisoner that he invented his story to shorten his own sentence. I visited that prisoner, a chap called Joe Wenzlemaier, and had a hand in him writing a declaration that Henke had admitted to his lies.

'But there's a nasty twist, Darcy. Just after submitting his statement, Joe was deported to his home country, Austria. So neither he nor his statement can be used in your defence. I hear that a Detective Raymond Kelly recommended the deportation.'

Looking annoyed, Mike added that Tumbarumba's warder-in-charge, Ling, had made a ridiculous claim to try to nail me. Ling was saying that he had inspected the hut I was housed in and had found a trap door that was not there before I arrived.

'I know for sure that, before he made the claims, Ling had a session at Tumbarumba with a certain Detective Kelly,' Mike added. 'Oh, and there'll be charges against you of having non-prison clothing and of clandestine correspondence.'

The screw listened intently. I later learned that during their absence the screw had, in front of Tatlow, contacted the jail's governor, Mr Cunningham, on the intra-jail telephone. He had outlined the situation, repeated Tatlow's objections and interjections.

After checking his books, Cunningham said No. 292 did not have any formal charge against him.

After that lively visit, I was confident. Surely, on the slim evidence they apparently had, they could not convict me in an *open* court.

Again, Tatlow published nothing about visiting me. To the relief of the governor and that three-stripe screw, I assumed. And they were not likely to be able to prevent the young journalist from seeing me again.

30

A few days later, a special van took me to Goulburn jail. I was charged with having contraband: one pair of socks, one singlet and an old shirt, which I had left in my cabin. On being released from camps, many prisoners who have such items of clothing pass them on to other prisoners. The clothes were already in my hut when I first went there. So, technically, they were in my possession. I could not remember a prisoner ever being charged for that offence. I pleaded guilty. Stipendiary Magistrate Mr R.J. Wingett sentenced me to three days' solitary confinement.

I was also charged with clandestine correspondence. They had found two notes from outside friends and some postage stamps hidden in my cabin. There was nothing important in the notes. Again I pleaded guilty. Sentence: three days' solitary.

A further charge against me was destroying government property, to wit, cutting a trap door in the cabin floor. I pleaded not guilty. The camp's senior warder, Mr Ling, claimed in evidence that the day before I began occupying the hut he had examined it, pulling up the lino, but found no trap door. Mr Ling added that not long after this, he crawled under my hut (18 inches above the ground) with a torch to examine the beams for white ants. He had discovered a new trap door, he said.

Ling admitted that he had had no witness with him when either taking up the lino or crawling in the dirt. Strange chores, they were, for a prison's chief warder, and working alone. I wondered if and why he had done that to only my hut out of the 60 or so he was in charge of. Still, the magistrate said I was guilty. Sentence: seven days' solitary.

I faced two charges of escaping, on 23 and 26 May 1965, with Ian Sidney Henke. I pleaded not guilty and told the magistrate I was not competent to defend myself on such serious charges. I told the court I had been instructed by a solicitor — the one Mike Tatlow and others had arranged — to plead not guilty and to reserve my defence. I said I wanted to be committed for trial to an open court, where I could call my witnesses and be properly defended by my own counsel.

The sole evidence against me for the 26 May charge was the word of Henke. That charge was dismissed.

Another prisoner perjured himself by claiming he saw Henke and me outside our huts on the 23rd. Mr Wingett SM refused committal to an open court and found me guilty of that charge. Sentence: 14 days' solitary.

All sentences were to be concurrent. At least, I reflected, there was no charge of stealing in Tumbarumba.

The obnoxiousness of the evidence against me was that, although I did leave the prison camp at night, I *never* associated with Henke. If my escape charges had been committed to another court, I would have called three witnesses who would have sworn that Henke had several times voluntarily refuted his claim that I had been his confederate. My accomplice, Pluto, incidentally, was not at the hearing to help my defence.

The hearing was not presented with the statutory declaration former prisoner Joseph Wenzlemaier had given prison authorities and that, in the face of the prisons department's opposition, my solicitor had read. In it, Wenzlemaier, whom I did not know, said he would like to testify in court that Henke had told him I had not left camp with Henke. His declaration surely would have been accepted had a hearing taken place in an open court and had he not been deported a few days after making it. He was serving a sentence for attacking a taxi driver and stealing his car in 1961.

I now have letters he subsequently wrote to friends. They reaffirmed his claim. They also said the deportation was recommended by a Detective Ray Kelly.

Henke was serving a term for car stealing. He copped seven days' solitary. I understand he was released, as part of a deal, a short time later.

* * *

I was transferred to the familiar confines of Parramatta jail and served 14 days' special confinement. Three days on bread and water, three days on half normal jail rations, three days bread and water, locked alone in a tiny, dark cell. I was allowed an hour and a half of constant pacing in a small walled yard on the three 'good' days.

No visitors. No letters in or out. With the chance of an open hearing gone, I was in black despair. And how would Pop be taking it?

Normally, a prisoner loses sentence remissions at the rate of four days for every day in special confinement. But the matter was not so clear-cut for a lifer. His fate was at the discretion of the minister of justice and the bureaucrats who advised him.

In the cold isolation of the cell, the stench of my excreta in a bucket reminding me of Grafton, I pondered. Solitary confinement was something to which no sane human being could become accustomed.

Despite the lengthy 'training' at Grafton, I still found it harrowing. Punishment by inflicting physical pain was, at least, not designed to scar a man's mind, but solitary was.

I recalled what Charles Dickens had to say about solitary confinement in *American Notes*. 'I believe it, in its effects, to be cruel and wrong ... There is a depth of terrible endurance in it which none but the sufferers can fathom and which no man has a right to inflict on his fellow creature. I hold this slow and daily tampering with the mysteries of the brain to be immeasurably worse than any torture of the body.'

Solitary is particularly hard going if you are already beset by worries and uncertainties. Your mind dwells like a sick thing on a thousand horrible possibilities. Would I ever be free? Might I go back to the Bloodhouse? Is Pop dead?

Unlike during the days of black solitary at Grafton, I wanted to know the date, what day it was. But the screws would not tell me. I hungered to read a book. Or hear a word of friendship.

If only a guard who retrieved my lavatory tin, who delivered my bread and water … if just one of them would speak! I sank into mental exercises to stop my mind from rotting.

About a week after the confinement, Mike Tatlow brought Pop to visit me. Pop looked frighteningly frail and did not seem to be fully aware of what was going on around him. I was not able to give them any indication of when I might be freed. I wanted terribly to reach through the steel bars and mesh and hold the old fellow. It was agonising.

Tatlow assured me that, providing Pop was well enough, they would visit me again just before my 45th birthday, on 29 August, four weeks distant.

31

On the afternoon of Tuesday, 24 August 1965, I was summoned to the office of Parramatta jail's governor. In there stood the governor, Michael Tatlow and the Catholic chaplain from Long Bay, my friend Father John Taylor. They looked grim. *Pop!*

'It can only be my father,' I said, looking at Tatlow. 'He hasn't gone, has he?'

Tatlow said, 'I'm afraid so, Darce.'

Father Taylor gave the details. Pop had been admitted a couple of days previously to the Sacred Heart Hospice, in the inner-city suburb of Darlinghurst. He was suffering from general depression and chest congestion. My father, Richard, aged 91, had died the previous night, Monday. Peacefully, without pain, a nurse at his side, just before Mike Tatlow arrived there for a visit.

I felt empty, and muttered something about how he had not been well on his last visit.

Mike said arrangements could probably be made for me to attend the funeral. Yes, I said, I wanted to be at that. Moments later, I asked the governor if I could be left alone for a while in my cell. He agreed. I thanked Mike and Father Taylor and left.

I learned later that Tatlow had informed the comptroller-general of prisons, Mr John Morony, by telephone, of Pop's passing. Morony had said he knew how much I had wanted to share many days of freedom with Pop before he died.

Morony said he did not relish the thought of himself or a department officer informing me of the death. I might react violently. Tatlow offered to let me know. Mr Morony arranged for Father Taylor to accompany him.

* * *

Pop was buried, amid the unfortunate whirring and flashing of television and press cameras, at Sydney's Rookwood Cemetery on the afternoon of Thursday, 26 August. Warders in plain clothes drove me to the grave side in a plain sedan car. I was allowed to wear new civilian clothes, including a suit, which friends had brought for me to wear on my expected release.

During the grave-side ceremony, which Father Taylor conducted, I stood between Tatlow and my brother, Tom. Then, to avoid exposure of our mateship to photographers, Mike moved behind me. More than a score of plain-clothes police stood by in case I ran for freedom. Mike told me police patrol cars surrounded the big cemetery.

But they need not have worried. I appreciated being able to attend the funeral, also the fact that during the service the warders and police kept a respectful distance. There were about 50 genuine mourners, 100 strangers, and a similar number of reporters, photographers and TV cameramen. But they, too, kept a respectable distance.

I was able to lay on the coffin a wreath, in the shape of a cross, I had made in jail. Other wreaths were stacked deep around the coffin. After the ceremony, which included the reciting of the rosary, the warders and police let me quietly mingle for several minutes with relatives and friends I had not seen for many years.

Tom was married, had a young family. I reflected that had I not been such a darn fool all those years ago, I, too, would now have a wife and kids. And Pop would not have died in such loneliness. Tom had repeatedly asked Pop to live with him in an outer-suburban home. But Pop, staunchly independent to the end, had refused.

I was looking back for the last time, as earth was being shovelled gently on the coffin, when a woman from the crowd tugged my arm. 'Remember me?' she said. 'I've been singing your praises ever since that day twenty years ago when you came along and chased off those two men who were trying to assault me. This is the first chance I've had to thank you.'

I remembered something about what she spoke of, but this was not the time for such matters. One of her attackers was Lennie

McPherson. She was Mrs Rene Suleau, of the suburb of Abbotsford. I nodded my thanks to Mrs Suleau and, after glancing at a few detectives I recognised, walked to the waiting car. None of the bad ones was there. No McPherson or Kelly.

That bittersweet taste of freedom preceded a lonely night inside the sandstone walls at Parramatta.

My attendance at the funeral attracted an extraordinary amount of publicity. All Sydney newspapers had it on their front pages. The next day, they speculated on when I would be released. Minister of Justice Maddison was quoted saying the matter was 'weighing heavily' on his mind. Then came a remarkable statement. It was not likely, Maddison announced, that there would be any review of Dugan's case 'until publicity over his father's death comes to an end'. Was my fate in the hands of the media?

The publicity continued. Radio and television stations ran debates on whether I should be let out now. Magazines ran features on Houdini Dugan's 'career'.

Jail officials told me bluntly that the publicity would have to stop well before my release was considered. I was also told several people were clamouring to visit me. They included a few criminals I had met in jails, such as now big-time George Freeman. Those associations, I was told, would go against me.

They seemed to think I had control over the mass media and over whoever wanted to see me! And who had I had an opportunity to make friends with in the past 15½ years other than jailbirds?

But still, well-intentioned but misguided do-gooders, and the crackpots, kept turning up at the jail's gate wanting to see me. Like in the old days, I received scores of letters, many of which were from nuts.

My hopes lifted in mid-September when Bill Mears was released. He had lost fewer remissions than I had, but, the way I calculated it, I could not be far from release in view of him being freed. After all, he was the shooter at the bank. Before the Tumbarumba business blew up, Mears and I had been due for release at the same time. My 14 days' solitary had cost me a remission loss totalling 56 days. So

I expected to be out in a couple of months. Christmas Day should see me a free man!

But, alas, the news of Bill's release attracted more public speculation about my future. Speculation that irked the Department of Prisons.

Out of the proverbial blue, I was told I was going from Parramatta to the old jail on a hill on the outskirts of Bathurst, west beyond the Blue Mountains and 135 miles from Sydney. It would be more difficult for people to visit me there.

I protested in vain.

Bathurst was a bleak tight-security jail, which, in terms of its unpopularity rating with prisoners, came second only to Grafton. I spent two years at Bathurst. I kept largely to myself and generally obeyed regulations.

By then, the Department of Prisons had developed a respect for Michael Tatlow's integrity. He would be important, they rightly reckoned, in helping my rehabilitation once I was released. He and Father Taylor, and a lawyer or two, were the sole people outside the criminal belt in whom I placed complete trust.

A few times when Tatlow visited, he was accompanied by the head of the Department of Prisons' parole section, Mr Frank Hayes, who personally took on the job as my parole officer. That involved having many talks with me before my release, gaining my confidence. Hayes and Mike clearly had become buddies, and told me they stopped off for meals together going to and from Bathurst. I came to know Hayes as an outstanding and enlightened man.

I had given Tatlow strong hints of the existence of my secret, partly completed, autobiography. I had, incidentally, arranged for the exercise book and other pages to be delivered to Tatlow if I died. Covering notes detailed the material about McPherson and other matters that Mike was not to report in the *Telegraph*.

Those revelations would break in this book. Which was not to be published until the Pig had gone to the sty in the sky — or underground. And not before certain crooked cops were also dead. Tatlow already had a notion of why.

Sydney's two afternoon tabloids continued running pieces quoting 'prison sources' saying I would soon be free. The prisons department was infuriated.

Mr Maddison interviewed me twice at Bathurst. He apologetically said I would not be released amid such publicity and 'emotionalism'.

They were frustrating days. I behaved myself, but on one occasion I could not resist a bit of malarkey. I worked at the time in the jail's tailor shop, making clothes for prisoners and tailoring uniforms for turnkeys. One day, a prisoner called me over to see an item of second-hand clothing that seethed with lice. The seams were packed with them.

'You'd better burn it,' I said. 'I'll call a screw.'

I turned to summon the screw, then paused. A few moments earlier I had been watching a con make a uniform for a particularly vicious turnkey. Grinning, I gingerly relieved the con of the infested cloth.

'Forget you ever saw those lice,' I said.

Using scissors, I carefully scraped hundreds of the lice and lice eggs into a matchbox. When the box was full of the vermin, I took it to near the prisoner making the turnkey's uniform. The coat was almost complete.

Soon afterwards, the prisoner went to the toilet. I quickly emptied the lice and eggs between the inside and outside layers of the blue serge where the sleeves were not fully sewn on. I was back at my normal work when the prisoner returned.

I was told that the vicious young screw was happy with his new coat. He wore it home that night. When he reads this, he will know how his house became lousy. It was my payment to him for beating up an old con who, in the grip of debility, had called the turnkey a 'bloody mongrel'.

* * *

Just before midnight on Wednesday, 13 September 1967, I woke to see the jail's governor, Mr Wallace Thoroughgood, standing outside the cell door. I jolted upright.

He put an index finger to his lips. 'Shoosh,' he said. 'This is it.'

My heart leapt to my throat. '*What?*'

'You're going out — release!'

He quietly opened the door of the cell, smiling. 'Come to my office.'

Adrenaline gushed through my system as I followed him along the darkened corridor. Was this really it? Really? *Or is it a trick? God, make it true.*

The unheralded midnight announcement seemed to be in keeping with the department's odd attitude to the manner in which I would be freed. They wanted no one but the jail's two senior officers to know I was going out. Loose talk by screws was blamed for the media getting hold of the information the previous two times I was on the brink of liberty.

I had been led to understand that, when the time finally came, I would go in the back of a police security van, as if it was a normal transfer. The word would be put around the jail that I was off to Long Bay for tests of some sort and would be back.

'Well, Darcy,' Mr Thoroughgood said triumphantly, sitting down behind his desk. 'You're nearly a free man. How does it feel?'

'Good. If it's true!'

I tried to bury my exultation. Hope had been dashed too often. I was given a brief lecture on the department's hopes that I had reformed, and on the responsibilities of being a member of the community.

Still in prison garb, I was driven out through the immense gates in a department car. As it headed down towards the township, I looked back at those tall, black walls that had surrounded me for two years. In front were the lights of Bathurst. It was the first time I had seen them.

'Where are you taking me?' I asked my driver, Mr Thoroughgood.

'To see a couple of friends at a motel,' he said enigmatically. 'You can change into your civilian clothes there and they'll take you to Sydney.'

Waiting in a motel room in the town were Frank Hayes and Miss Elaine Barnett, the department's parole officer assigned to Parramatta and Bathurst jails. As with Frank Hayes, I had come to know her well. The pair of them, who I knew genuinely had faith in my intention to go straight, were elated to see me free.

After a while, they left me alone in the motel room to change my clothes, which had been delivered from the jail. I had worn them only once, at Pop's funeral. I wondered how it would be, mixing freely with people, able to make my own decisions after a decade and a half of regimentation.

Soon, I could even decide what to eat! When and where to sleep. And with whom. I peered into the room's big mirror. It was the first time in more than 17 years that I had looked into one any more than a few inches square.

It was two weeks after my 48th birthday. I looked thin; the skin on my face was wrinkled. My brown hair was thinner, and peppered with grey. But, being free, I smiled at my ravaged countenance.

I thought of June. No, I would never see June again. She was married, had a couple of kids.

Later, Frank Hayes detailed the terms of my parole. They were very fair, perhaps better than I deserved. I was to be on parole for five years, he said. A breach of that parole would land me straight back in jail, perhaps never to be released.

First, there could be no crime. I was free to move anywhere in New South Wales, but the department would want to know my whereabouts. I was to contact Hayes once a week, but there would be no strict timetable. The department was placing a reasonable degree of trust in me, he said.

Soon after dawn, Mr Hayes, Miss Barnett and I set off for Sydney in Frank's car. It was a warm and cheerful day. We stopped beside the road, by a forest, and had a picnic breakfast on the cool, clean grass. I revelled in a brief stroll among the trees.

I was not these people's prisoner. They treated me as an equal. During the latter stages of the journey, as I looked out over sprawling Sydney from the Blue Mountains, I silently wondered how other people would regard me.

I still felt I had deserved a long prison term for my crimes, but the debt was paid. I could never expect to be accepted, trusted entirely by everyone. All I wanted was to be given a fair go, a reasonable opportunity to become a normal and useful citizen. I would definitely attract close attention from the police. Especially the crooked ones, confederates of McPherson. Kelly, Krahe — I was determined to let the public know of their corruption.

As if tuned to my thoughts, Frank Hayes remarked, as we passed the familiar Nepean River, that should I be harassed by policemen, I was to inform him immediately.

Mike Tatlow had told him about the two detectives who got me sacked, planted stolen jewellery on me and concocted a confession to a robbery, trying to get me to become a stool pigeon. 'That's disgusting,' Hayes said, as Elaine frowned.

'And, Darcy, Mike knows you're on the way,' he added. 'You'll be with him soon.'

I knew where that would be. I was surprised, but said nothing, when the parole officers dropped me, with a small bag of belongings, at the outer suburban home of my brother, Tom. I had my 17-year jail earnings of $170 in cash, a Department of Prisons' hand-out of $20, and $150 friends had left for me at Bathurst.

No Tatlow. No Tom. Tom's wife got a shock when I walked in. She did not know I had been released. Tom was in the city, she said, with a journalist. Had kindly Frank Hayes delivered me to the wrong place? Or had he brought me here because he didn't want to be seen to know the location of the arranged rendezvous, at the home of a convicted criminal?

I took a taxi to 768 Darling Street, Rozelle, the comfortable little home of my old mate Harry Mitchell, who had smuggled out my exercise book and other pages when he was released from Parramatta. I knew Harry was now going straight.

Mike and Tom were there. Within minutes, Mike deposited a long-promised double-headed ice cream in my hands. A *Daily Telegraph* photographer called in to take a photo of me with that delicious treat. The photo was on the front page of the paper the next morning.

We three and Harry's wife, Josephine, talked and talked. I was relieved to learn from Mike that Machine Gun Ray Kelly had retired from the police force about a year back. The man, officially on only a detective's wages, had bought a big block of lavish apartments.

That evening, I negotiated to tell the *Telegraph*, through Michael, my life story for $12,000 in the nation's new decimal currency. Next morning, the rest of the media knew I was out. Reporters galore pestered the department to tell them where I was.

Harry, with me at his shoulder, answered a knock on the front door. Before us stood two uniformed police officers. Between them was a middle-aged man in a suit — a detective, I figured nervously.

'Hello, Darcy,' the suit said, extending his hand and shaking mine. 'I've been wanting to meet you for a long time. I'm Noel Bailey, from the *Sun*.'

My immediate thought was to give a verbal blast to this police roundsman who had repeatedly branded me as the shooter in the Ultimo bank, and won Australia's top journalism award for it. Harry courteously invited the three of them inside.

As he walked into the dining room, Bailey looked alarmed to see Mike Tatlow there. Tatlow had savaged Bailey in a pub for defaming me, and looked ready for another go at him. Pretty obviously, the sight of the cops also had Mike curious.

'What are these officers here for, Noel?' he asked.

'Oh, they told me where Darcy is.'

Bailey paused, then turned to me, smiled and said, 'Darcy, I'm a longtime admirer of your exploits and I want the public to get the facts from you — *your* side of the story.

'My newspaper group, Fairfax and Sons, is very keen to get the story of your amazing life,' he continued amicably. 'I would write it and make sure you approve of every word. The offer for that exclusive is sensational, Darcy. We want to pay you $34,000!'

That was big, big money then. I reckoned it would buy a mansion beside Sydney Harbour. I had not yet signed the deal with the *Telegraph* — for less than half of Bailey's offer. I glanced at a stilled Tatlow, then back at Bailey, who I knew had been in league with Machine Gun Ray Kelly over the Tumbarumba affair.

'I'm not interested, Noel,' I said quietly. 'Please leave.'

Mike stood there smirking as Bailey angrily left the premises with the policemen, who had not said a word. Harry followed them to the front door.

Mike said, 'That wasn't police business. I suppose Bailey hoped that the cops being here would intimidate you into signing up with him. It implied that you either give him the story or get arrested.'

I simply shrugged. 'No way would I deal with Noel Bailey.'

Even if the *Telegraph* did not pay me a penny, only Tatlow was getting my story.

Harry Mitchell returned to the room several minutes later, looking tense. He said, 'I followed them for about 50 yards up the street to make sure they were leaving our neighbourhood.

'They went to an unmarked police car. And who do you reckon was in there waiting for them?'

'Len McPherson?' I said, getting a good laugh from Mike.

Harry's face stayed serious. 'Worse, Darce,' my old mate said. 'Sitting in there, and hiding under a hat, was Raymond bloody Kelly!'

'He's retired!' I exclaimed.

'Yeah,' said Harry. 'But the bastard must still pull a bit of weight in the force.'

Mike said, 'He does. And I wouldn't be surprised if he's also a commission agent for the Fairfax empire.'

Harry nodded his agreement with that. 'Hell, Mike, you'd better keep Darce well away from Kelly. And Darce, with no story for

Bailey now, Kelly might try to fit you with a crime and put you back in the slammer.'

Mike said, 'Well, we'll be sneaking out of town tomorrow.'

Harry's wife, Jo, came in to say a caller was waiting for Mike on the telephone. The journo came back grinning. 'That was Frank Hayes. He wanted to be sure I'd caught up with you, Darce. I told him about the visit from Bailey and the cops, with bloody Ray Kelly lurking outside in the car. Parole master Frank was furious.'

32

Later that day I signed the *Telegraph* deal with the corporation's urbane Editor-in-Chief, David McNicoll, and met the paper's big and beaming owner, Sir Frank Packer.

Standing in his enormous office, which had its own drinks bar and overlooked Hyde Park, Sir Frank wished me well. He said that, through Mike, his papers and television station TCN9 would continue reporting Dugan matters accurately, unlike some other media. Mike obviously was the rosy apple in the millionaire's eye.

Mike drove me to a plush suite in a hotel in Canberra, where, a hat low over my brow, I signed in as D. Clare. The rest of the media, and Kelly and co., were not likely to find us there. Other newspapers, television and radio stations were soon blaring that Dugan was in hiding.

Working 15 hours a day, Mike studied the smuggled exercise book and quizzed me, and then two women he had hired took turns shorthanding and typing his dictated material.

As this was before the coming of e-mail and home computers, Mike's stories were teleprinted daily to the *Telegraph* through its Canberra bureau at Parliament House.

I revelled in good company, marvellous food, a soft double bed. No one, but no one, was ordering me about. My sole duty to officialdom was making a phone call each week to parole chief Frank Hayes, who promised Mike that he would keep our location a secret.

Hiding my face as much as possible, we dined at night at a few small restaurants, where I gradually became accustomed to fine cuisine. The biggest shock to my system was my first-ever meal of Chinese food.

Mike soon knew why his airing of Lennie the Pig's role in my life, and other things revealed in this book, would have to await my death. And McPherson's, Kelly's, Krahe's ...

We spent three busy weeks in Canberra, where I even resisted making a play for one or both of those lovely, friendly stenographers. Mike churned out two to four newspaper pages a day, featured prominently for more than two weeks in the *Daily* and *Sunday Telegraph*. Oddly to me, they ran it as 'By a Special Reporter'.

'Oh, Sir Frank Packer doesn't want to big-note me,' Mike explained with a smirk. 'Packer and McNicoll don't want to heighten my reputation, maybe tempting a good salary offer from elsewhere, or giving grounds for a pay rise. No bonus, either.'

Mike, who I knew rented a house in Manly with his wife and young son and daughter, refused a few thousand pounds I offered for his longtime help of Pop and me.

We returned to Sydney, where I spent $9,000 of the money from the *Tele* to buy from my mate Harry Mitchell and his wife, Josephine, their comfortable little home in Rozelle. Harry had kept my secret writings there for four years. I finally owned a residence.

As I settled in there, the subject I had brooded on for years in prison resurfaced. Now, dammit, it was time to expose some corruption, notably the CIB detectives' rampant fabrications and perjury in courts of law — and not just at my expense.

Of course, many guilty prisoners claim innocence. And the vast majority of prisoners deserve their incarceration. But scores of cons whom I trusted had told me about having guns and allegedly stolen goods planted on them by cops. Of being verballed. Of detectives lying about them on oath to judges.

And here my memoir ends. Mike will, I hope, write about the rest of the days of Dugan.

33

By Michael Tatlow

I confess that, as a young investigative reporter, I initially courted Dick Dugan to get Darcy's life story when he was freed. However, a genuine friendship developed with Dick and, of course, Darcy.

Darcy and I socialised regularly. We went sailing and fishing on my old timber motor sailer. He took me to the horse races at Warwick Farm and Randwick. At my Manly home, he was soon good friends with my wife, Frances. And Uncle Darcy to our children. I understood when Darcy smirked as I introduced him to our five-year-old daughter, Kelly. Handing out lollies, Uncle Darcy immediately won over our toddler son, Nicholas.

Darcy anxiously told me he had learned through George Freeman that McPherson and his police associates had conferred about whether I was aware of the betrayals and their corruption he had suffered from, and if I would write about it.

There was a big chance, Darcy said, of his home and mine being searched for evidence of that. I locked the exercise book of memoirs and the pages about McPherson and co. in a bank safety-deposit box.

In 1968, Darcy was hired as a social counsellor at the Wayside Chapel, an arm then of the Methodist Church that helped needy, addicted kids at Kings Cross. Darcy was popular there and helped scores of addicts and lost souls find productive lives. The Rev. Ted Noffs, who ran the organisation, told me how thrilled he was to have Darcy on his team.

From the chapel, he began his public campaign against graft and corruption in the Criminal Investigation Bureau of the New South

Wales Police Force. He carefully distinguished between responsible police officers, whom he respected, and the others.

Darcy took extended leave from the chapel in 1969 and spoke at Apex, Rotary, Lions and RSL clubs and other gatherings, calling for reform of the CIB and the replacement of Police Commissioner Norman Allan, and for accused prisoners to be allowed to have their own legal counsel at those closed-door hearings in front of magistrates.

One of his regular charges was that certain police used false, unsigned records of interview to get convictions. He also cited specific cases of CIB detectives running protection, gambling, prostitution and abortion rackets. His charges also included the widespread raping of prisoners by warders, particularly at Parramatta jail.

I travelled with him to one of his speaking engagements, at the Wollongong Rotary club. Ron Chrisfield, president of the Kings Cross Rotary club, who was driving, said, 'Don't start your speech in an inane way like "Ladies and gentlemen, thank you for having me here." Make it dramatic.'

Darcy said, 'Okay, Ron, I'll do that.'

At Wollongong, he winked at me and began, 'At this moment there are seven thousand men in this state's jails. A third of them are cold, a third are hungry, a third are being fucked, mostly by warders. That might be why they're called screws.'

On the ride back, he grinned and asked Ron, 'Was that start dramatic enough for you?'

His campaign was reported in all the media; he was regularly interviewed on television and radio programs. My newspapers, the *Sunday Telegraph* and the *Daily Telegraph*, were his chief public advocates. They ran many reports of Darcy's allegations of graft, the alleged threats by police, plus government and police denials of them.

He was a hit, with a leading role, for weeks, in the play *Fortune and Men's Eyes* at the Ensemble Theatre, Kirribilli. On stage after the play each night he furthered his condemnation of corruption. I was impressed that this man, so isolated from the community for so long, was such an engaging and eloquent actor and speaker.

My buddy's social life was enhanced by meeting lovely Margaret Elder at a dance. They went out together often and looked likely soon to marry.

In August 1969, he was interviewed for more than two hours about Sydney corruption and prison life on Adelaide's radio 5AD. Afterwards, there were rumblings against him in the government, led by Premier Bob (later, on his own recommendation, Sir Robert) Askin.

Police harassed Darcy regularly. Detective Sergeant Herbert Talarico told him, 'Shut up or you'll *be* shut up. We'll find a gun on you and get you back to Grafton.'

Darcy reported the threats to parole officer Frank Hayes and Minister of Justice Maddison. Hayes was alarmed. Maddison did not respond.

On 14 October, Darcy related his concerns to Sydney's splendid anti-corruption solicitor, brown-eyed and dark-haired Noel F. Bracks. Bracks wrote forcefully about the threats to Premier Askin, the Attorney General, the Minister of Justice, the leader of the Opposition, Police Commissioner Allan, the Anglican Archbishop of Sydney, Catholic Cardinal Gilroy, firebrand cleric Allan Walker and the Chief Superintendent of the CIB.

Meantime, I was made News Editor, sometimes acting editor, of the *Sunday Telegraph*. I had been promoted to Chief of Staff of the *Daily Telegraph*, in charge of 55 journos, deciding what stories we covered and briefing assigned reporters, when one day the senior police roundsman, Ced Culbert, told me he would need to go soon, at short notice, to report a major robbery.

'Good,' I said. 'How will you know the where and when?'

'A contact at the CIB will ring me.'

'They're not acting to prevent it?'

Ced did not know. An hour later, a junior crime reporter slinked into my room. 'Ced lied to you, Mike. It's a police setup, to get

Dugan. They'll be waiting at the scene with planted movie cameras.'

Like many crime reporters, our Cedric was close to the police; he got tips for stories in return for presenting their side of events and writing raps about police he drank with.

Darcy and I expected that his home phone was bugged. I called him with the agreed code: 'P – I – G'. He called back to my direct line moments later from a public phone box. I told him what I knew.

'Yeah,' he laughed. 'An experienced old robber wants me to knock off a jewellery store with him. He's coming back tomorrow. I think he now works for McPherson. Even if you hadn't called, no way would I be in that, Mike. No robberies, ever.'

A week later, after work, about one o'clock in the morning, I went to the Latin Quarter nightclub to join talented colleague Ron Saw and St George and international rugby league star Johnny Raper. The popular club was in Pitt Street, near the *Tele* offices, and run by my colourful American friend Sammy Lee.

Musos were performing in front of many tables of drinkers as Ron handed me a glass of wine at the small bar. He nodded towards a table near the stage. 'See that bastard over there?'

It was McPherson, with three other known criminals.

After hearing Johnny Raper's version of a rugby match, I crossed the club to the men's toilet. I was facing the urinal when a man walked in. 'I've been wanting to see you, Tatlow,' he said.

It was Leonard McPherson, red tie, dark suit, thickset, short and curly brown hair over a broad and stern face. At 48, he was 18 years my senior; taller than me.

I turned and shook his hand. 'It's about time we met, Lennie,' I said engagingly, zipping up my pants.

McPherson's eyes narrowed. He said, 'I'm here because I know you come to the Quarter sometimes. And I know you wrote that shit about Dugan.'

I said nothing.

'Tatlow,' he continued, 'what's Dugan told you about me and my business?'

'Not much, Lennie,' I lied. 'I've not written anything about you.'

'You planning a book? A film?'

'No, Len.'

'That's what *you* say.' He stepped closer and put his right hand inside the top of his jacket. He withdrew it, showing the black handle of a pistol. It went back into its holster.

I tensed, ready to kick the psychopath in the crutch. I felt I could beat the rat in a brawl. There was, though, no beating of a bullet. That would make me the third one McPherson had killed in the Latin Quarter. If I flattened him, he or his brutes would soon eliminate me. Perhaps also Fran, Kelly and Nick if the killers struck at my home.

'Is this a threat?' I asked, staring back at his grimace.

'Tatlow, I've got good contacts. I'll know if you're writing anything from your mate Dugan about me or my business. Or my friends in the bloody police force. If you're doing that, Tatlow, big-shot journalist or not, *look out*! Fact is, I was Dugan's main offsider as a kid and when he was on the run. But don't you even write about that. Got it?'

'Okay.' I found a smile. 'You must be the Les McPhee he's named from those days. You got some hacksaw blades to him at Grafton and he damned nearly got out. Well done!'

'Yes. But, Tatlow, you write anything from Dugan about me, *anything*, and my associates and I'll get ya.'

He walked out. He had not wanted to urinate.

In rushed Johnny Raper. 'Hell, mate, are you okay? Ron's too pissed but I ran over here when we saw that bugger McPherson go in after you. I feared I'd hear a gunshot. I'd have taken on that bastard.'

I feigned surprise. I did not want Johnny or Ron talking around town about what had happened, or Ron reporting it for the *Telegraph*, even though I could spike his story.

'Gee, thanks Johnny,' I said to the rugby whiz, 'but I've just come out of a locked cubicle. I heard someone come in and leave. Didn't know it was Lennie the Pig!'

Back at the bar, big Ron Saw looked fearful. 'Christ, McPherson'd hate what you've written about Dugan and corruption. He and his hoods have just left.'

I picked up my glass of claret and smirked. There was nothing I could do about that encounter. My wife, Fran, would be terrified if she knew. Hell, if I told Darcy, he might go gunning for Mister Big. And me telling the police, my word against McPherson's, would not be productive.

I warily realised that it was not McPherson's style to threaten an adversary in advance of killing him.

I was the *Telegraph*'s pictorial editor about a month later, writing occasional feature articles, when summoned to the office of my boss, David McNicoll, with whom I sometimes dined. The drinker of French champagne liked to call me Tatters.

Silver-haired David was uncommonly tense. 'Michael,' he declared from behind his desk, 'I'm afraid your employment has been terminated.'

I slumped in a chair. Was he joking? Not long before, he had called me the bright young spark of Australian Consolidated Press. I was their youngest-ever News Editor or Chief of Staff.

'What?'

'Terminated. Sir Frank has directed me to dismiss you as part of a restructure. Nothing personal. You're to go to the reporters' room for a week, then leave. No termination pay, either, I'm afraid.'

I had never seen him look so awkward. My eyes watered as I left the room, stunned. I felt that the 'restructure' talk was nonsense. No one else was fired. One day I would get the truth of it from David.

Could it have anything to do with Darcy? I knew from Noel Bracks that the solicitor had rung Sir Frank to chat about my series on Darcy and his client's future. Sir Frank had said to Bracks, 'Don't hesitate to contact me if I can be of any help.'

I went to tell Darcy at Rozelle two days later, on Thursday, 13 November 1969. He echoed my suspicions.

'Bloody McPherson or his crooked cops have gotta be behind this, mate,' he declared, banging a fist on his kitchen table. 'They want to silence the *Tele* as my main mouthpiece and defender. To do that, the bastards'd have to get *you* out of the way.'

'Yeah, but how the blazes would they influence Sir Frank Packer? He's tough, and I got on well with him.'

Angry Darcy shared my wonderment. 'Your sacking,' he said. 'It's interesting timing. I was about to go and see you with my *own* bloody bad news.'

An honest cop he knew had taken the risk of alerting him to a plan by detective sergeants Fred Krahe and Herbert Talarico to arrest him over the weekend. The Rozelle house would be raided. Stolen goods and guns would be planted and 'found' there. The whole CIB, Darcy was told, wanted to stop his public revelations of corruption. They wanted to put him back in jail.

'Your public attacking of police corruption is hardly the conduct of an active robber, cobber,' I remarked.

Darcy reported the foreshadowing of his arrest to Noel Bracks and, in Frank Hayes's absence, parole officer Mrs Helen Boyle.

Back despondently at the *Telegraph*, I wrote a report quoting Darcy about a plan to raid his home, but not naming Krahe or Talarico. It was not published.

Packer was in an elevator when I entered it and went to the ground floor. The big previously engaging newspaper baron silently glared at me.

A few newspaper editors I knew and asked for a job awkwardly declined to take me on. It was implied that Sir Frank had told their publisher bosses not to employ me.

My suspicions festered.

On 17 November 1969, I was recovering from a farewell drinkathon with colleagues from the *Telegraph*, who were mystified about my sacking, when the radio news reported that Darcy had been arrested at his home for being one of three men who robbed Kleemo's jewellery store in Pitt Street, near the *Telegraph* office.

The police alleged that he had a pistol in a tissue box. Six small but suspicious diamonds and a bracelet were in a glass phial hidden in a carpet sweeper. The gun had been wiped of fingerprints, said the leader of the raid, Detective Sergeant (later Superintendent) Herbert Talarico.

Acting on Darcy's request in the event of an arrest, Noel Bracks fronted at the police headquarters as soon as he heard about it on the radio. As he recounted to me later, the place teemed with reporters, photographers and armed police.

While Dugan was allegedly confessing to a multitude of crimes, the reception clerk, Sergeant Coleman, told Bracks he did not know if Dugan had been arrested or if he was in the building. On Bracks's insistence that his client must be there, Coleman left the desk to 'check that'. The sergeant returned to announce that he could not confirm if Dugan was there or at any other police station. Darcy thus was denied the presence of his lawyer. It was later revealed that Darcy had in fact been at the headquarters.

I was wryly amused at home to hear that Darcy had confessed to various crimes. That he had refused to sign their 'record of interview'.

A reporter, tipped off to the raid, wrote that the ceiling of Dugan's home was searched by experienced officers of the police rescue squad. Nothing incriminating was found up there.

Noel Bracks has confirmed to me that, while Darcy was at Long Bay, Detective Sergeant Krahe told two young constables, 'Go back to Dugan's place and search it again. Look for guns in the ceiling. Here's the key.' Within minutes, a constable found two more guns, in a cavity in the ceiling already searched by the police rescue squad.

Now unemployed, I went to Long Bay but was refused permission to see prisoner Dugan or fellow arrestee and alleged associate Bobby McKinnon. The prisons department's trust in me had, it seemed, vanished.

The city office of Darcy's solicitor, Noel Bracks, was broken into every week between Dugan's arrest and the end of his trial. The only items stolen were dictation machines, which held information to be used by the defence.

My home at Manly and a business office I had just rented at North Sydney were also robbed. Grooves showed that the latch on the back door at home was forced open at night when my family and I were away. Taken from there were some 20 letters Darcy sent me from jails, my notes from our working sessions in Canberra and a stack of clippings of my stories in the *Tele*.

The lock on the door of the office was smashed, the room ransacked. Gone were my 1969 and 1970 diaries of appointments and reminders. Plus two pages I had typed about my belief that Darcy was framed on the charges of having stolen jewellery and guns at his home and of robbing the Kleemo's jewellery store.

I was so pleased that all Darcy's notes about McPherson and co. were locked away at a bank.

Nearing Darcy's date in court, Bracks learned that the glass phial of medication allegedly found at Rozelle, allegedly containing stolen jewellery, was never fingerprinted. Because, the police custodian explained, it had been smashed in the door of the exhibit safe.

When examining the smashed phial, Bracks saw that the medication was from a chemist named Cruikshank, whose pharmacy was close to the Darlinghurst police station. Bracks visited the chemist, said he was acting for Darcy Dugan.

Cruikshank said, 'You'll get my full cooperation. I was a friend of Leslie Nalder, the bank manager Mears shot at Ultimo. Les always said how unfair it was that Dugan was sentenced to life in prison, because Dugan in fact *saved* his life. He stopped Mears from shooting again.'

Cruikshank said he would have recognised Darcy Dugan if it was him who had bought the phial. The buyer, he felt, was a plain-clothes policeman. His later testimony, however, bore no fruit for the defence.

Bracks gave evidence in court of his denial of access to his client at the police station. That, Noel reflects, did not appear to concern the jury, nor cause them to doubt the 'confessions', the unsigned record of interview. Their veracity was sworn to by detectives Fred Krahe, Herbert Talarico, Frederick Smith, Robert John McNamara and Keith Aitkins.

Judge Harvey Prior asked the jury, 'Who do you believe? These men of impeccable character, with scores of years of service to the community, or this defendant, with a string of convictions, who is trying to save himself?'

Judge Prior, especially among lawyers, was nicknamed Fletcher Jones, after the famous clothier chain, which advertised that they could 'fit any man'.

Darcy vehemently swore that the crime was committed not by him but a criminal named Francis Patrick Foley. Crown witness Foley gave evidence implicating Dugan. The defence strongly suggested that Foley attributed his own robbing to Darcy Dugan at the behest of certain police.

Foley confessed to being an accomplice but was not charged. However, he faced charges for three prior armed hold-ups.

Dugan made a statement from the dock and subjected himself to cross-examination.

As the trial proceeded, away from the court, Bracks approached the two co-accused, Donald McKenzie and Darrell Burke, and asked if Dugan participated in the robbery. When they told him that Dugan was not involved, he asked them to name the third man.

They refused to name the third man or give evidence, because, they said, they feared recrimination from the police for telling the truth.

'Was it Foley?' Bracks asked. The two defendants simply grinned.

Anticipating a bad result, Darcy sold his Rozelle home back to his friend Harry Mitchell on 5 December 1969. Tearfully, he told Margaret Elder that their plan to marry was suspended.

34

On 6 May 1970, Dugan was found guilty of robbing Kleemo's. He was sentenced to 14 years' jail. His licence for release on the Ultimo bank attempted-murder conviction of 1949 was revoked. So, added to the 14 years was an indeterminate life sentence.

Affidavits from McKenzie and Burke exonerating Dugan, though still not naming the third robber, were presented at the hearing of an appeal against the conviction and severity of the sentence. The truth of the evidence from the 'honourable' detectives was not questioned. The appeal was summarily dismissed.

This was well before Justice Wood's Royal Commission into the New South Wales Police Service, plus the Moffitt Royal Commission in 1973–74 into organised crime, showed there were as many criminals in the police force as elsewhere. As Noel Bracks says today, Darcy's trial was corrupted. The verdict might have been different if Judge Prior and the jury had known about the corruption then rampant in the state CIB.

By an order from the Attorney General, the three prior charges of robbery by Crown witness Foley were dropped.

Noel Bracks and I were among many who were cynical about that reward for perjury. Foley had 46 convictions in three states over a 17-year period. His testimony was the key to putting Dugan back in the slammer.

Dugan's public charges about police corruption had ended. I heard that there was a big-time celebration party by many detectives the night of the guilty verdict.

To this day, dedicated and perceptive Noel Bracks is certain that Darcy was framed, that police directed by Krahe planted the guns and jewellery at his home. Even chief parole officer Frank Hayes told me over a quiet drink that he was disgusted by the conviction.

The media, which I was no longer a part of, had a field day.

I was alone at home at Manly when my wife, Fran, returned from shopping with our son and daughter. 'I had an awful moment at the newsagency,' she said, grinning. 'It was crowded. I was getting a magazine when Nick saw a front-page photo and yelled out, "Mummy, there's Uncle Darcy!"

'The whole place was stilled, apart from some muttering. We got a lot of stares as I grabbed Kelly and Nick.

'A woman cried out, "Are you Dugan's tart?"

'I fled.'

As Noel Bracks confirms, several newspaper pieces, fuelled by police statements, grossly defamed D.E. Dugan. One paper carried a police allegation that they had found an exercise book. I gripped that paper damned hard until I read, laughing with relief, that said book of Dugan's allegedly laid out plans to kidnap children of a couple of wealthy families.

The police had reported the plans to the families, they said, before Dugan's trial. Despite repeated requests from Bracks and others, the exercise book was never produced.

Darcy vehemently said the book and the plan were police inventions. Never would he consider a kidnapping.

Relying on free work by Noel Bracks, Clive Evatt QC and some junior barristers, Darcy in May '67 began 18 prosecutions for defamation.

Mirror Newspapers Ltd raised the defence that a person of tainted blood, one convicted of a felony or serving a life sentence, had lost his right to sue. The Supreme Court and the Court of Appeal accepted that defence. All Dugan's prosecutions, including appeals to the High Court of Australia, failed.

The Council for Civil Liberties, the Prisoners' Action Group and prominent citizens called on the Attorney General to legislate to remove restrictions on a prisoner's right to sue. The entire law allowing prisoners to be fair game for defamers was repealed, but not retrospectively. So Dugan did not benefit from that. Nor did he benefit from a later prohibition of police verbals. An amendment of the law said all interviews with prisoners had to be recorded electronically. There is no doubt that Darcy's public claims of him and others being verballed stirred politicians to make that amendment.

I organised a two-month national concert tour by that splendid American singer Sarah Vaughan. The tour began wonderfully, but it got me bankrupted when Sarah contracted a throat infection at Surfers Paradise and flew back to the United States.

A Kings Cross hotelier, owed money for accommodating the Sarah Vaughan party of six, got a dodgy detective to arrest me in the street. I was put in a cell at Darlinghurst.

The detective peered at me through the bars and said, 'I know you're the reporter who stuck up for that turd Darcy Dugan. Make a written statement that you know Dugan robbed Kleemo's, that his stupid claims of police corruption are inventions, and I'll let you out.'

I declined the officer. He would be on a slice of anything paid to the hotel, I figured. There was no formal charge, no show in front of a magistrate.

That first and last time in custody gave me a glimpse of what Darcy had endured. After an hour, I managed to get — for $2 — a junior constable to take me to a telephone. I told Noel Bracks where I was, and why. Noel, infuriated, got me out of there in an hour.

On reflection, I should have agreed with Noel and prosecuted that detective and the publican.

Darcy and I kept in touch by letters and I saw him a few times at Parramatta. He wrote, perhaps for the benefit of vetting warders, that his treatment was more humane than before. 'But don't you write it yet,' the letter added.

Then, Darcy told me, warders planted and 'found' a $10 note in his cell. Their action was payback for his media charges that Parramatta screws regularly raped prisoners. Found guilty of having the $10, he was consigned back to Grafton — where he was the prime target for the Football Squad for 16 months.

In December '71, they sent him to the jail at Maitland, then Long Bay, Maitland again, Long Bay, and Maitland a third time. He was given no reason for copping two months of solitary confinement at Long Bay early in 1972.

He was delighted to hear on the grapevine in '74 that Detective Sergeant Krahe's superiors had evidence that he ran a gang of crooks; he was discharged from the police force as 'medically unfit'.

It seemed odd to Darcy that the unfit ex-CIB heavy was innocently hired as a 'consultant on organised crime' by John Fairfax & Sons Pty Ltd, publisher of the *Sydney Morning Herald* and the Sydney *Sun*.

My family and I moved to live in Hobart, the city of my birth. Darcy wrote to me there from Maitland jail early in '75 and said that he was leading the prisoners' debating team. It engaged with non-prison teams and won several competitions. Darcy took up painting and sold some oils at art shows in Sydney and Newcastle. He wrote and sent to a television station a play about prisoners, which might have later inspired a popular TV series on the subject.

As he was serving a life sentence concurrent with 14 years for armed robbery, Darcy again had no release date to look forward to. He petitioned the jail's governor, the Minister of Justice and the Nagle Royal Commission into New South Wales Prisons. His sole verdict was from the minister. It said, 'The Life Sentence will be considered at the expiration of the 14 years sentence.'

Darcy wrote in 1978 to tell me he was the jail librarian, his debating team had won the coveted Rostrum Cup and he had been visited in jail by pretty Jan Simmonds.

She was the sister of Kevin Simmonds, who had murdered a warder at the Emu Plains prison farm. He had died very suspiciously at the Bloodhouse. It was a self-hanging, the warders claimed. Many were sure it was murder.

Jan was aware that Darcy had known her brother. She wanted to interview Houdini for a book about Kevin. The relationship, fuelled by letters to and from, continued during the rest of Darcy's term in prison.

Darcy's low moment in '78 was the High Court's majority dismissal of his appeal against the defamation verdict. It was run by Clive Evatt QC, who was instructed by the loyal Noel Bracks.

Darcy was released on Thursday, 29 May 1980. He had spent a little over 30 years, more than half his life, in jail since the bank hold-up at Ultimo.

Jan Simmonds and the media were waiting at the gates of the prison. Dugan's brief address made it clear that his campaign against corrupt detectives was not over. For interviews on ABC-TV and Channel 10 he was paid $4,500 — four times his pay during 11 years' jail.

Jan had a business in Canberra. He lived there with her, and they were married by Ted Noffs at the Wayside Chapel on 12 July. They accepted a honeymoon trip to Perth, Western Australia, sponsored by radio 6PR, to continue his campaign against graft and corruption. The Sydney police were again rankled.

The couple returned to Sydney to live, and Darcy tried to earn a living from his paintings. He produced excellent artworks, but his now-slow artistry and low prices made it unrewarding. With the approval of parole officer Hayes, he gained employment on building maintenance with two old mates from prison.

But the parole board refused him permission to work with ex-criminals. As he protested to Noel Bracks, who else did he know after more than a decade in prison? Who else would employ notorious Dugan?

Frustration about not working morphed into frustrations in his marriage. At every opportunity, he railed at police graft. Jan became sick and fearful of it.

Ageing Darcy resumed ballroom dancing, which did not interest his wife. With no income, Darcy grew distressed. It was a husband's duty, he swore to me in a letter, to be the provider. Jan returned to Canberra.

In May '81, Ted Noffs found Darcy, aged 61, accommodation at a halfway house known as Glebe House. But still, no job.

Jan sold her business and bought a home unit in Sydney. Noffs arranged a happy reconciliation, which lasted only a week. Jan went back to Canberra.

Darcy found low-level work at Glebe House, being paid less than unemployment benefits. Taking that sort of public money would make him a leech on society, he declared to Bracks. Too bad, he added, about the cost to taxpayers of his latest, police-engineered, time in the clink.

He continued to publicly criticise the police at many forums.

Darcy rang me in Tasmania to report that he had had a few drinks at the Forbes Club at Kings Cross with George Freeman — and Leonard McPherson.

'It was a pretty tense time,' he said. 'McPherson at first was damned wary, and had a shooter thug nearby. And George was waiting for me to throttle the Pig any moment.'

With forced joviality, the three reminisced about the Battle at Mort's Dock, the Ultimo bank job and the hacksaw blades McPherson sent to the Bloodhouse.

'Lennie the Squealer looked a bit testy when I mentioned that his involvement in those jobs was never leaked. That he was never charged,' Darcy told me.

McPherson had betrayed Darcy six times or more and had added at least 17 years to his jail time. 'I lusted for the blood of that bastard,' said Darcy, 'but I decided not to fix him, not even talk about it.'

McPherson had asked if Darcy was doing a book with my help, and he'd replied that it was possible — but that he would be called Les McPhee, just a larrikin kid Darcy knocked about with who later put him onto some jobs.

Darcy chuckled down the line as he told me about Freeman's anxiety. 'Once, when I glared at McPherson for a moment, George nearly cleared out,' he said. 'If McPherson knew I knew about his fizzing to cops, and that George first told me about it, George'd be in a death scene.'

But protecting Freeman was not why Darcy kept the peace. The Pig's gunman standing there wasn't, either.

'Knowing the truth, if he survived my attack, McPherson would go to any length to stop the book. And that, Mike, would mean stopping *you*.

'Do I have to ask again? Don't do the book until we're all dead.'

In June '81, through ex-convict Noel Frith, Darcy met criminal John Andrews, whose bakery Frith was painting. Darcy did not know that Andrews's landlord was a detective. That Andrews did the detective favours, dobbed in active crims, in return for immunity from being arrested for crimes himself.

The laws of defamation prevent me from identifying the (still living) detective Darcy named, who had engineered the meeting and promised cash to Andrews if he delivered a prize that many police craved. It was well known that police critic Dugan was frail, broke and depressed about his failed marriage.

Andrews persevered in fostering a friendship with Darcy. An easy job at a service station would get some money, Andrews tempted. An employee at the station had promised that if fronted by a gun, he would hand over a pile of money.

To make it convincing, though, the gun had to be pointed at the employee. Andrews said he had a gun ready for Darcy. The job would be a piece of cake. The employee, on a small slice of the action, would never identify the robber. The station owner was insured against robberies.

I know Darcy at first abhorred the thought of returning to crime, especially with a gun. I did not know, though, how desperately he needed cash.

Andrews good-heartedly persisted. And ageing, bespectacled Darcy succumbed. The robbery would be on the night of Sunday, 12 July 1981.

That day, Jan arrived to see Darcy, hoping for a reconciliatory dinner. She had remembered it was their first wedding anniversary. Darcy had not.

He was committed to the easy, foolproof robbery, which of course he could not tell Jan about. No, he announced sadly, he could not go out to dinner with her. He had to keep a vital appointment that night. Humiliated, Jan left the unit as Darcy sat, dejected.

The station wagon Andrews drove to the crime scene had been wired up to record the handover of the gun, a doctored job from the police that would not fire.

A squad of armed police hid nearby in the quiet of that Sunday night. A police helicopter waited nearby.

Grey-haired Dugan tottered past petrol bowsers and entered the building, his wrinkled face covered by a handkerchief. Hidden cameras whirred as he pulled the pistol from a pocket and shouted at the sole employee there, 'Hands up!'

Police swooped from all directions, from inside and out of the building. They jubilantly drove the old bloke to the floor and handcuffed him. Driver Andrews left the scene unhindered.

A few hours later, Jan was advised of her husband's arrest. She could not believe that a planned robbery had prevented that make-up dinner. She rang Noel Bracks and asked him to act again for Darcy.

Bracks was astonished, and angry. Could Darcy be so stupid? he wondered. Pride must have prevented the old jailbird from admitting to his parlous state and seeking help from Bracks and a score of others who had stood by him for years. It seems that depression and desperation for money had warped Darcy's determination never to engage in another criminal act.

Bracks refused to act for Darcy. He offered to help, and did — but he could not bring himself to represent Darcy again.

I arrived in Sydney on an ABC-TV assignment two days after the arrest, conferred with Noel, but was again refused permission to visit the accused.

Veteran state Commissioner for corrective services, Ron Woodham, later revealed that the main plotter with the police to get Dugan arrested at the service station was one Leonard McPherson.

Darcy was convicted of one of the charges laid against him for the robbery and was sentenced to three and a half years' jail. Jan Dugan watched and wept throughout the old man's trial.

He sent me a brief note from prison. Part of it said, 'When you write you know what, tell the truth about what a silly ass I've been.'

Darcy served longer than the imposed sentence because his previous licence had been revoked. He suffered a stroke that irreparably damaged his health. A legacy, no doubt, from years of vicious torture.

Jan was waiting outside the gate when he was released on 7 November 1985. She was alarmed at his faltering voice, unsteady gait.

His full-time care was beyond Jan, but distressed Ted Noffs arranged medical help, after which Jan took Darcy to recuperate in Queensland. During about two months there, his health and speech improved.

But Jan could not continue caring for him, and Darcy detested being a burden. He returned to Sydney and resided at Glebe House, the halfway house where he formerly lived and worked.

Meantime, in Hobart in June 1990, while I was out fishing, my home was broken into and robbed of some cash in an old wallet and a folder containing photographs and notes about and from Darcy, preliminary to finalising this book. Despite an obviously extensive search, the robber did not find my key Dugan file, hidden in a compartment behind a painting.

About a week after the robbery, a Melbourne detective rang me to advise that Darren Charles Grainger, aged 26, had been arrested at Dubbo airport, New South Wales, with my wallet in his bag.

Grainger had been charged with bashing a 75-year-old man to death in Melbourne three days after the robbing of my home. He was convicted of murder.

I sorely wanted to know who had assigned him to steal my documents. But, despite my repeated requests, neither the Tasmanian nor Victorian police, it seems, even questioned Grainger about the robbery. I became pretty certain that the robber was acting for Sydney crooks who wanted to prevent this book's publication. Lennie McPherson, for instance, was still alive. I was tormented a bit at the thought that Grainger might have been on orders, if he found me at home, to make sure the book was never written. By terminating me.

It was the third robbery of my Dugan papers, after break-ins at my home and office in Sydney. And solicitor Noel Bracks's chambers were robbed several times while the police were setting up Dugan on the Kleemo's jewel-robbery charge.

Forlorn criminal celebrity D. Dugan remained at Glebe House as his condition worsened, from Parkinson's disease. He was moved to a nursing home at Cabramatta, not far from Parramatta jail.

Darcy Ezekiel Dugan died there peacefully a week before his 71st birthday, on Thursday, 22 August 1991. Counting two years at Gosford, he had spent 44 years in custody.

EPILOGUE

Back from Hobart a year later, I visited Darcy and Dick Dugan's graves at Rookwood.

Why I was fired from the *Telegraph* still rankled me. It was time to find out about it.

The Packers had sold the *Tele* to Rupert Murdoch's News Limited. They still published the news magazine *The Bulletin*, which I had edited for a while. A senior on the staff was my old boss and friend David McNicoll. He greeted me warmly in his Park Street office.

After exchanging pleasantries, I congratulated David on being made a Commander of the Order of the British Empire and, by the French government, a Chevalier of the Légion d'honneur. After a pause, I said, 'David, why did you *really* fire me?'

He looked embarrassed. 'Mike, for ages I've been wanting to tell you the truth about that awful business.'

I sat and waited. He scratched the silver fuzz on his head and poured me a glass of Bollinger.

'You'll know that in those days Lennie McPherson and his police confederates were hellbent on shutting up Darcy Dugan. They wanted him back in jail, or dead.' But, David explained, they knew that if they set up Dugan with a phony conviction or got rid of him, I would reveal the truth in the *Telegraph*.

'I now have it on absolute authority that McPherson had a conference about it with a few cops and ex-cops. Ray Kelly, Fred Krahe, Talarico.' McNicoll took a gulp of bubbling Bollinger. 'Before nailing Dugan, they had to turn the *Tele* against him and get you sacked.'

'The bastards,' I exclaimed.

'When you find out who else was there, it'll shock you.'

'Who?'

'A real heavy, Mike. The Premier, *Sir* Bob Askin.'

I studied him for a moment to see if he was serious. I knew Askin; had lived opposite his place at Manly. He gave me a lift a few times in his chauffeured car when I was going to work. I didn't know then how rotten he was.

'How do you know that, David?'

'Years later, Askin quietly confessed it to his former deputy, Jack Maddison. And disgusted Jack told *me*. I couldn't really write about it in my memoir and felt too damned guilty to tell you. I'm sorry.'

I nodded my appreciation now, champagne nearly curdling in my gullet.

McNicoll went on to explain that, as they had planned, Fred Krahe telephoned Sir Frank Packer and said the police had quietly raided Dugan's home when he was not there. They found, Krahe said, notes Darcy had made in an exercise book that revealed a plan to kidnap Sir Frank's two grandchildren — Kerry Packer's children, James and Gretel, then aged three and four.

He smiled thinly at my stilled countenance. 'Packer was livid. And scared! Krahe said you, Dugan's mate, surely knew about it. He claimed your name was in the book. You, Mike, would know the layout of the Packer home at Bellevue Hill.

'Mike, I refused to believe it, but Sir Frank was positive he'd been told the truth. He insisted that I act on it.'

I said, 'It's amazing that he believed that garbage. The exercise book was never produced, I suppose?'

The debonair former columnist and Editor-in-Chief looked guilty. 'No, of course not.

'I was instructed to sack you, straightaway. But not tell you why. As you know damned well, Mike, one didn't refuse a directive from that old bugger. I hated, bloody *hated*, having to do that.'

David shook my hand and apologised. 'Sir Frank said he'd urged Krahe to slam Dugan in jail, if not kill him. And Krahe assured him that Dugan would soon be arrested — which, of course, he was. For that suspect Kleemo's robbery.'

'The police didn't even question Darcy about their kidnap swindle,' I told him.

The newspaper and television baron realised he had been conned, David continued, after judicial investigations revealed the horrifying extent of corruption in the CIB. And after Krahe was rightly blamed for six murders, and Raymond Kelly for five, Sir Frank had phoned Krahe and abused him. Packer died soon after, in May 1974.

'Pity he didn't ring me, too,' I said. 'Does Kerry or James or Gretel know about that now?'

'They probably don't. Otherwise, surely you'd be compensated for your grief, the termination of your career.'

David McNicoll died eight years later. His explanation was confirmed when I rang Noel Bracks.

When Bracks had called Packer for help to pay barristers' fees after Darcy was charged with the Kleemo's robbery, Packer just about roared. 'I wouldn't help that bastard, come what may,' he said to Bracks.

Bracks replied, 'But you told me to ring you —'

Packer cut in and said, 'Dugan was going to kidnap my grandchildren.'

When Bracks asked where that crazy notion came from, Packer said the police had Darcy's exercise book. 'And, Packer growled, the kidnap plan was set out in it,' Bracks told me. He recommended that Packer sight the book before accepting the word of the police, and asked who had told him about the alleged plot.

'He said it was Fred Krahe. I repeated that he definitely should see the exercise book before believing that demon Krahe,' Bracks told me. 'Packer said he'd think about it, and hung up. Obviously, he didn't get the book.'

Back in Tasmania, I checked over a letter Darcy had sent me months before he died. I thought when getting it that the letter related a joke to confirm our suspicions about why I was sacked. The letter said the Wayside Chapel's Rev. Ted Noffs had told Darcy months after my sacking that he had been with Kerry Packer when the police rang Kerry and told him that Darcy planned to kidnap his children. I did not have a phone number for Darcy then for confirmation, and my friend Ted Noffs was ill in hospital. Nor could I contact Kerry, who was overseas

Many jurists, criminologists, investigators and civil libertarians brand Darcy Dugan's arrest and conviction for robbing Kleemo's jewellery store as major travesties of justice, a triumph of evil over good. Had the jury then known how rife corruption was in the state police force, they may not have found him guilty.

If that conviction had not occurred, Darcy would have had a chance to shine. He might have curbed the corruption later proven by judicial inquiries. Astute lawyer Noel Bracks, objective social worker the Reverend Ted Noffs, parole officer Frank Hayes and I all knew that Darcy was serious then about ending his days of crime.

Without that extra jail time, his health deteriorating from decades of mental and physical torment, destitute Darcy may have been less susceptible to inveiglement into the stupid crime of trying to rob a service station, with police organisers of the crime ready to swoop.

George Freeman, whistle-blower to Dugan about McPherson's betrayals, said in 1988 of Mr Big's henchman Krahe, 'He had his own pricing scheme. You'd pay him to get bail. You'd pay for remands. You'd pay to prevent him giving evidence against you.'

When Krahe died, late in 1981, six murders — nearly as many as McPherson's likely toll — were attributed to him in assorted media. However, the detective was never accused in court of being a murderer.

There was Griffith anti-drugs campaigner and federal Liberal Party candidate Donald Mackay, shot dead in July 1977. Krahe was found to be working for Mackay's political rival, corrupt federal minister Al Grassby, and drugs tsar Robert Trimbole.

Juanita Nielsen, the publisher of Kings Cross newspaper *NOW*, had campaigned against the building of a $140 million high-rise complex near her home in Victoria Street, Kings Cross. Nielsen was harassed by Krahe, who worked for the developer, before she disappeared in July 1975. An inquest determined that Nielsen had been murdered.

Police Superintendent Donald Fergusson was shot dead at the CIB headquarters in February 1970, on the eve of exposing Krahe's involvement in an abortion racket. Fergusson's body was found in the station's toilet. It looked like suicide.

Krahe's rival, criminal Ronnie Williams, and Kevin Gore, a criminal who carried out hold-ups Krahe allegedly arranged, were slain in suspicious circumstances.

And Shirley Brifman, brothel madam and prostitute, was found dead in her flat in March 1972, soon before she was due to testify in court to Krahe's corruptness. A year later, a teenage prostitute, thought to know that Krahe had slain Brifman, was also found dead. Krahe's number seven?

On 8 December 1971, the *Sydney Morning Herald* reported that 111 police officers had been dismissed in the previous 12 months.

Gunner Raymond Kelly died a wealthy man at his home at Fairlight, in Sydney, aged 71, on 11 August 1977. At a dinner to mark his retirement from the police force in '66, then Premier Askin said, 'No fictional detective could hold a candle to Ray Kelly.'

Retiree Kelly, who bought a block of home units allegedly from his police pay, was a regular golfer, dabbled in real estate ventures, and was a consultant about crime prevention for several business enterprises. He was glorified in 1975 by becoming, on Askin's advice to the Queen, a Member of the Order of the British Empire.

Alleged multi-murderer Leonard Arthur McPherson brought American Mafia hoods to Australia to peddle drugs and boost his protection racket. Mr Big was worth more than $10 million. A few murder charges he faced were quietly dropped.

Dawn divorced McPherson in 1960 after he arrived home drunk, pistol-whipped her and shot up the oven his dinner was cooking in, because the meal was not ready. She charged him with assault, but after a conciliation session, the charge was dropped. The conciliator was Raymond Kelly.

McPherson was aged 76 on 28 August 1996, doing time at Cessnock jail for bashing a 'business rival', when he died of a heart attack.

George Freeman, aged 55, died in hospital from an asthma attack in March 1990.

William Cecil Mears was an invalid pensioner when he died at Waterloo, aged 82, in October 2002.

Houdini Dugan — compulsive robber as a youngster; victim of decades of viciousness in jails, and lies and betrayals by police and their criminal confederates — was an engaging companion who showered my children with generosity.

Seeing crime as a natural way of life, and law enforcers as the enemy, were entrenched in him as a child.

The six-time escaper from custody, five-time near escaper, and an escapologist many more times had he wanted to be, told me he acted on a credo that warders were employed to keep him behind bars. His job was to get away. His overriding regret was that he carried guns during some robberies.

Darcy deserved, and told me he deserved, his early days in reformatories and jails. Not, though, the barbarity dealt him. The torture during his record 11 years at Grafton jail surely would shatter the health and spirit of most of us.

Crimes by McPherson, Krahe, Kelly and others made the real and invented robberies by Darcy, who was never a murderer, look like chicken feed.

REFERENCES

Chapter 7

p. 92 'Australia's Houdini', *Daily Mirror*, 5 March 1946.

p. 92 'Dugan, India-rubber man', *Daily Telegraph*, 5 March 1946.

p. 92 'The greatest manhunt in Sydney's history ...' *Daily Telegraph*, August 1949.

Chapter 11

p. 135 'Hunt for desperate criminals after break from gaol. Underworld combed; city search', Sydney *Sunday Herald*, 21 August 1949, page 1.

p. 135 'High walls did not a prison make', Sydney *Truth*, 21 August 1949, page 1.

p. 137 'If cornered I will give in ...' Darcy's letter in the *Daily Mirror*, 28 August 1949.

Chapter 20

p. 231 Comptroller-General of Prisons, L.C. Nott after the prisoner mass mutiny, *Sydney Morning Herald*, 16 June 1953, page 3.

Chapter 21

p. 233 'Darcy Dugan leads 12 in gaol mutiny', *The Sun*, 15 June 1953, page 1.

p. 234 Petition from Anglican Bishop E.H. Burgmann, pleading for less severe punishment of prisoners after the Grafton jail mutiny, *Sydney Morning Herald*, 7 October 1953, page 5.

Chapter 29

p. 287–88 'Darcy Dugan Probe', Noel Bailey, *The Sun*, 21 June 1965, page 1.

p. 290 'The truth about Darcy Dugan' by a Special Reporter (Michael Tatlow), *Sunday Telegraph* 27 June 1965, page 3.

Chapter 30

p. 296 'I believe it, in its effects, to be cruel and wrong ...' Charles Dickens, *American Notes*, Chapman & Hall, London, 19 October 1842.

Epilogue

p. 334 '[Detective Fred Krahe] had his own pricing scheme ...' *Sin City*, www.hht.net.au/sincity/players/fred_krahe

PICTURE CREDITS

Page 1: Police mug shots of Darcy Dugan — all images courtesy of the State Library of New South Wales.

Page 2: The tram from which Dugan and Robert Porter escaped — both images courtesy of Victor C. Solomons, Sydney Tramway Museum.

Page 3: August 1949: the escape route taken by Darcy along the roof of the reception section of Long Bay jail © Newspix / News Ltd / 3rd Party Managed Reproduction & Supply Rights.

Darcy's and William Mears' escape route into the city after Darcy cut a steel bar of a window of their cell at Sydney's Central Court, 15 December 1949. © Newspix / News Ltd / 3rd Party Managed Reproduction & Supply Rights.

Page 4: Tilly Devine — image courtesy of Michael Tatlow.

Page 5: Len McPherson — image courtesy of Michael Tatlow.

Page 6: December 1949: reward poster Darcy Dugan and William Cecil Mears © Newspix / News Ltd / 3rd Party Managed Reproduction & Supply Rights.

Page 7: Front page of the *Daily Mirror*, 14 February 1950, covering the arrest of Darcy Dugan and William Mears, written by Bill Jenkins © Newspix / News Ltd / 3rd Party Managed Reproduction & Supply Rights.

Page 8: Front page of the *Sun*, 15 June 1953 — image courtesy of the State Library of New South Wales.

Page 9: Grafton Jail, the Bloodhouse — image courtesy of the State Records of the New South Wales Government. Detective Sergeant Ray 'Gunner' Kelly — image courtesy of Michael Tatlow.

Page 10: Darcy Dugan talking to visitor Alan Potter outside the Wayside Chapel in Kings Cross, Sydney, 9 April 1968 © Newspix / News Ltd / 3rd Party Managed Reproduction & Supply Rights.

Page 11: Front page of the *Daily Mirror*, 18 November 1969 — image courtesy of the State Library of New South Wales © Newspix / News Ltd / 3rd Party Managed Reproduction & Supply Rights.

Page 12: Darcy inside Maitland jail, New South Wales, 5 October 1979 © Newspix / News Ltd / 3rd Party Managed Reproduction & Supply Rights.

Page 13: Front page of the *Sun*, 28 May 1980 © Fairfax Syndication.

Page 14: Darcy Dugan and his wife, Jan Simmonds, on their wedding day in July 1980. © Newspix / News Ltd / 3rd Party Managed Reproduction & Supply Rights.

Page 15: Darcy Dugan (centre) with Lennie McPherson and George Freeman in Sydney, 4 May 1988 © Newspix / News Ltd / 3rd Party Managed Reproduction & Supply Rights. Author George Freeman shows his autobiography to Darcy in Sydney, 4 May 1988 © Newspix / News Ltd / 3rd Party Managed Reproduction & Supply Rights.

Page 16: Darcy at a halfway house in Glebe, Sydney, 11 August 1986 © Newspix / News Ltd / 3rd Party Managed Reproduction & Supply Rights. Letter from Darcy Dugan to Michael Tatlow — courtesy of Michael Tatlow.

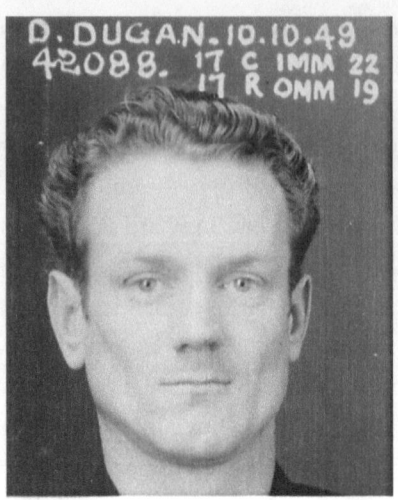

Darcy Ezekial Dugan (1920–91) was a career robber and Australia's most brilliant prison escape artist. He committed numerous armed hold-ups but was never a killer, and became more famous for his daring escapes than for the crimes that landed him in prison. He masterminded six escapes from custody – one after only 25 minutes in Long Bay jail, others from a prison tram and a van transferring him from jail to courthouses – earning him the monicker of 'Houdini of the prison system'. He planned and attempted three dramatic escapes from Grafton jail, the infamous 'Bloodhouse'.

Dugan spent 44 years in prison, more than half his life. He knew better than most of the brutality and corruption within the system, and in later life he became a passionate and outspoken campaigner for reform. In the process the former criminal became the archenemy of Sydney's criminal underworld, corrupt police and prison guards, and was marked for life.

While in prison Dugan wrote in secret most of this brutally honest account of his life in and out of jail. He had the exercise book in which he wrote it smuggled out and kept safe from his enemies. He had good reason to fear execution by crime boss Lennie McPherson and police on his payroll if revelations in the book became public.

He asked his friend, journalist **Mike Tatlow**, to keep the manuscript safe and suppress it until both he and his enemies had turned to dust. Tatlow kept his promise and went on to write the concluding chapters of what would become ***Bloodhouse***.

Darcy was a creative painter, a ballroom dancing champion, a popular public speaker and starred in the play *A Fortune in Men's Eyes* at Sydney's Ensemble Theatre. He worked as a rehabilitation officer until his health deteriorated and he died from Parkinson's disease in 1991.

After working as a rabbit trapper and fisher for shark and crayfish, aged 15, author, journalist and historian **Mike Tatlow** started his journalism career as a reporter in Tasmania. He went on to become a cadet reporter for Sydney's *Daily Telegraph*, graduating to feature writer and book reviewer for the *Sunday Telegraph*.

In 1967 he became the paper's News Editor. In 1968 he stepped in as Acting Editor of the paper and also the news magazine, *The Bulletin*. He was Chief-of-Staff of the *Daily Telegraph* for two years and the paper's Pictorial Editor.

Mike later became Producer and Chief-of-Staff for ABC-TV News in Tasmania.

A longtime friend of Dugan's, Tatlow was entrusted with the exercise books containing his amazing life story, which had been smuggled out of prison. He kept his promise to suppress it until both Dugan and his enemies had 'turned to dust', and wrote the concluding chapters of this extraordinary story.

Tatlow is the author of *A Walk in Old Sydney, A Walk in Old Hobart, A Walk in Old Launceston* and *A Tour of Old Tasmania*.

He lives in Hobart.

www.ingramcontent.com/pod-product-compliance
Lightning Source LLC
Chambersburg PA
CBHW022028290426
44109CB00014B/786